Text Message

Text Message

The Centrality of Scripture in Preaching

Edited by
Ian Stackhouse
and
Oliver D. Crisp

PICKWICK *Publications* · Eugene, Oregon

TEXT MESSAGE
The Centrality of Scripture in Preaching

Pickwick Publications
An Imprint of Wipf and Stock Publishers
199 W. 8th Ave., Suite 3
Eugene, OR 97401

www.wipfandstock.com

ISBN 13: 978-1-61097-673-2

Cataloguing-in-Publication data:

Text message : the centrality of Scripture in preaching / edited by Ian Stackhouse and Oliver D. Crisp, with a foreword by Thomas Long.

xxvi + 238 pp. ; 23 cm. Includes bibliographical references.

ISBN 13: 978-1-61097-673-2

1. Preaching. I. Stackhouse, Ian. II. Crisp, Oliver D. III. Long, Thomas G., 1946–. IV. Title.

BV4211.3 S811 2014

Manufactured in the U.S.A.

To Stuart Reid, a herald of the gospel,
and in memory of
Revd. William Still,
Minister of Gilcomston South Church,
Aberdeen 1945–97

Contents

Foreword

Thomas G. Long

THIS REMARKABLE COLLECTION OF essays on preaching by an international group of scholars and pastors shares more than a common subject matter. Running like a river through these chapters is the vision of preaching as a faithful *craft*; that is, as a skilled and complex practice possessing standards of excellence, embedded in a rich tradition, and performed out of deep theological conviction.

In a self-absorbed, self-referential culture, it is sometimes easy to lose sight of the idea of preaching as a disciplined craft that can be studied, learned, practiced, and, to some extent at least, mastered. Twenty-five years ago, a team of North American professors of preaching, in the thrall of various upbeat, student-centered approaches to education then in vogue, chirped optimistically, "Each of us has within us the effective preacher God wants us to become. We teachers of preaching know that when we guide wisely in the process of learning preaching, we help students cultivate and harvest what God has planted in them. . . . We aim to help each person in class start on the road to becoming with God's help the best preacher each has it in them to be."[1]

However much this statement gained in pedagogical compassion it quickly lost in utter naiveté. It is one thing to recognize that people do bring instincts and inner gifts to the ministry of preaching, but the notion that students waltz into preaching class with a tiny "effective preacher" somehow tucked away inside them, like a caterpillar in a cocoon, waiting to emerge and take wing manages to reinforce some of our culture's (and the pulpit's) worst tendencies toward narcissism. As W. H. Auden once

---

1. Wardlaw, ed. *Learning Preaching*, 1.

ix

reportedly said, "Poetry is not self-expression. If art is self-expression, keep it to yourself."

The main problem, however, in believing that students are homiletical buds waiting to come to full flower is that it overlooks just how much about good preaching lies outside of one's natural impulses. Christian preaching is not the result of naturally gifted orators who somehow stumbled on a really good message. It is rather the reverberation in frail human speech of Easter's thunderclap. It is not finding voice for that which wells up from within. It is instead rooted in the astonished cry uttered in the discovery of what God has done in the world.

The church has, through fire and trial, learned slowly over the centuries many lessons of the Spirit about how to preach faithfully, how human words can be obediently shaped as vessels of proclamation. Preaching is not a science, but it is surrounded by a deep vein of accumulated wisdom, which constitutes a homiletical tradition that can be passed on and learned. To say, "Each of us has within us the effective preacher God wants us to become" ignores this tradition and is like saying each of us has within us the effective thoracic surgeon, nuclear engineer, symphony conductor, or Boeing 777 pilot God wants us to become. Yes, preaching depends upon an inner call and a set of personal gifts, but there is also a body of knowledge to be acquired as well as a lore about good practice given to the company of preachers over the centuries.

The authors of this volume, who stand firmly in this stream of wisdom, underscore that good sermons spring from acts of biblical interpretation. At the risk of sounding flip, nothing invigorates preaching more than having something to say. In the Christian homiletical tradition, having something meaningful to say is a product of an encounter with Scripture. These preachers who have produced this book are convinced that good preaching results from faithful exegesis, which involves critical inquiry, textual analysis, and genre exploration, but which can by no means be confined to mere method. Procedural and rule-bound exegesis can so often be an autopsy on a now-deceased text, and some preachers, as Karen Case-Green reminds us in these pages, "dissect the text, forgetting Balthasar's warning that 'Anatomy can be practiced only on a dead body.'" By contrast, faithful preaching requires waiting and prayerful expectation for the living Word to be born anew in these ancient texts. The God who became flesh in the incarnation continues to advent in Scripture, becoming living Word again and again.

The authors also recognize that each generation of preachers brings a new context to the homiletical and exegetical task, which creates a living and growing preaching tradition. This allows them to glean insights about preaching not only from biblical exemplars but also from the luminous figures from church history, such as Jonathan Edwards, Dietrich Bonheoffer, and Charles Haddon Spurgeon, and from contemporary preachers and theologians, such as Jana Childers, Richard Lischer, and Walter Brueggemann. The company of preachers and the gathered wisdom about the ministry of preaching spans the whole history of the faith.

But what bubbles up most from these pages is a great passion for the ministry of preaching itself. Emma Ineson notes that, in Matthew's account of the first Easter, the women left the tomb "with fear and great joy." She adds, "That is a good description of what it's like to preach. There is the sense of great joy that I have a message to deliver, coupled with that ever-present fear that I may not do justice to what God has given me, fear of how the message (or I) may be received, fear that I may have gotten it wrong."

The theologian Karl Barth once observed that the only fitting attitude for a preacher to have in the pulpit is embarrassment—embarrassment because we do not have what we are there to give: the Word of God. We stand there, then, as beggars, utterly dependent upon God to supply both the gospel and the strength needed to proclaim it. But, even in our embarrassment, we stand there also joyful that we are the ones given the great privilege of trumpeting the good news.

The authors of this book are persuaded that God's grace is made perfect in our weakness, and they are, therefore, emboldened to take up ever anew the task of proclamation. The blend of courage and humility that permeates the chapters of this book reminds me of an essay written years ago by James A. Wharton, a fine pastor, a creative Old Testament scholar, and an innovative teacher of preaching. In the essay, Wharton remembered his junior high French teacher. The students called her "Fifi," not out of affection but out of mockery over her large and awkward body, for her clumsy social manner, and mainly for the way she would purse her lips and pronounce French phrases with an exaggerated accent. "We snickered behind our hands," he wrote, "and traded malicious glances, and dismissed Fifi as an inherently ridiculous person."[2]

---

2. Wharton, "Protagonist Corner," 28.

One fall, Fifi related to her students that she had taken a wonderful summer trip to France and that she had seen the most beautiful sight in the world, the famous Mont Blanc, which, of course, she pronounced "Moan Blawnnnnnnk." Wharton writes, "For the better part of a term it was 'Moan Blawnnnnnnk' this and 'Moan Blawnnnnnnk' that until we all went into a frenzy of heartless hilarity every time Fifi honked the name." Every time she mentioned the place, the class would break up, but Fifi would just stand there undeterred, seemingly confident that, if the class could have been there, could have stood where she stood and seen what she saw, every student would have been equally overwhelmed by the sight of "Moan Blawnnnnnnk."

Late in the term, Fifi proudly announced to the class that she had brought color slides of her trip to show the class. Now the students could see for themselves the magnificence of "Moan Blawnnnnnnk." But things did not go as Fifi had planned. When she projected the blurry image from the Kodak slide onto the screen, "the imps of hell could not have matched the screech of laughter that greeted Fifi's ears from her hysterical students." The screen was filled with an image of Fifi herself, in profile and in all her awkwardness. In the left upper corner of the screen, was Mont Blanc, "a tiny, snowy triangle perched saucily on Fifi's voluminous bosom." The students howled with scornful glee.

Writing now as a grown man and remembering that eruption of derisive and callow laughter, Wharton says, "It is only recently that I have gained the maturity to wonder how Fifi managed to cry herself to sleep that night." And then Wharton asks Fifi for forgiveness—forgiveness because he is now an adult and a preacher, and he knows how it feels to have seen something so beautiful that he wants everyone else to see it, too, only to find his ridiculous self getting in the way:

> It is now my turn to try to express to other people what I take to be a transcendent wonder. In my heart of hearts, when the clarity of faith is on me, I cannot imagine any wonder remotely comparable to the victory of God's self-giving love for the world in Jesus Christ our Lord. . . . Yet every time I stand to proclaim the wonder, I am painfully aware that it is my comic figure, and my ridiculous words, that confront people in the foreground. I have to hope that people can somehow concentrate on the snowy triangle of the gospel, perched somewhere indecorously on my person, and perceive the wonder in spite of me. . . . God grant that my next slide-show will let the mountain fill the screen.[3]

3. Ibid., 29.

The authors of this volume are aware of their limitations and the fragility of any human being trying to preach the gospel. But they keep clear focus, and they keep underlining in manifold ways the call to "preach not ourselves but Christ Jesus." Because of what is written in these pages, those of us who preach have a prayer that, in our next sermonic slide show, the mountain of the gospel will fill the screen.

Acknowledgments

A NUMBER OF PEOPLE helped with the production of this volume. We would like to thank Brian Lee and Daniel Salyers, whose assistance in copyediting was invaluable. Special thanks also go to our families for their patience and support. In addition to the dedication Ian gives to Stuart Reid (in the Introduction, below) Oliver would like to dedicate this volume to the memory of the Revd. William Still, minister of Gilcomston South Kirk in Aberdeen, Scotland, under whose expositional ministry he had the privilege of sitting as an undergraduate in the early 1990s. We thank God for such faithful preachers.

Contributors

Karen Case-Green teaches in the School of English and Languages, University of Surrey, England. She has an MA in Theology and Art from King's College London/the National Gallery, and has spoken at various conferences, as well as written articles, on the subjects of preaching and spirituality. She and her husband spent a number of years as missionaries in Peru, working with Navigators.

Oliver D. Crisp is Professor of Systematic Theology, Fuller Theological Seminary, Pasadena, USA. Among his recent publications are *Jonathan Edwards on God and Creation* (Oxford University Press, 2012), *Revisioning Christology: Theology in The Reformed Tradition* (Ashgate, 2011), and *Retrieving Doctrine: Essays in Reformed Theology* (Paternoster/IVP Academic, 2011).

Philip Greenslade has over forty years' experience in Christian ministry having originally trained for the Baptist ministry at Spurgeon's College, London, England. He is currently Senior Tutor at CWR a Christian Resource Center based at Waverley Abbey in Surrey, England, and is Consulting Editor for CWR's *Cover to Cover Every Day*. Philip is a highly respected theologian and his books include *Voice from the Hills* (CWR); *Leadership and Ministering Angles* (CWR); *A Passion for God's Story* (Paternoster); *Worship in the Best of Both Worlds: An Exploration of the Polarities of Truthful Worship* (Paternoster, 2009).

David Hansen is the Pastor of Heritage Church, Cincinnati, USA, and has been engaged in pastoral ministry for thirty-four years. He is the author of four books including the highly praised *The Art of Pastoring: Ministry Without all the Answers* (InterVarsity Press, 1994).

David Howard, Jnr. is Professor of Old Testament, Bethel Seminary, St Paul, USA, having previously taught at New Orleans Baptist Seminary and Trinity Evangelical Divinity School. He was President of the Evangelical Theological Society in 2003. His most recent publications include *"My Words Are Lovely": Studies in the Rhetoric of the Psalms*. Library of Hebrew Bible/Old Testament Studies 467, co-edited with Robert L. Foster (New York: T & T Clark, 2008), and *The Psalms: Language for All Seasons of the Soul*, co-edited with Andrew J. Schmutzer (Chicago: Moody Publishers, 2013).

Emma Ineson is Principal of Trinity College, Bristol, UK and is ordained as a minister in the Church of England. She is the author of *Busy Living: Blessing not Burden* (Continuum, 2007), and with Chris Edmondson has co-authored *Celebrating Community: God's Gift for Today's World* (Darton, Longman and Todd, 2006).

Steven D. Mathewson is Senior Pastor of CrossLife Evangelical Free Church in Libertyville, Illinois, USA. He also teaches preaching as an adjunct professor at Trinity Evangelical Divinity School in Deerfield, Illinois. His DMin degree is from Gordon-Conwell Theological Seminary. He is the author of *The Art of Preaching Old Testament Narrative* (Baker Academic, 2002).

Robert May is the Associate Minister/Pastor at Guildford Baptist Church and has been in pastoral ministry for fourteen years. He trained at Spurgeon's College and continues to serve there as an Associate Lecturer and Online Learning Tutor. He is presently engaged in a part-time MPhil degree: "The Homiletics of Stanley Grenz: Towards a Post-Foundational Theology of Preaching."

Peter J. Morden is Vice Principal of Spurgeon's College, London, England, where he also teaches church history and spirituality. His PhD was on C. H. Spurgeon's spirituality, and this has been published as *"Communion with Christ and his People:" The Spirituality of C. H. Spurgeon* (Regent's Park College, 2010/Pickwick, 2014). He has also written the more "popular," *C. H. Spurgeon: The People's Preacher* (CWR, 2009). Peter is a Fellow of the Royal Historical Society and a Fellow of the Centre for Baptist History and Heritage, Regent's Park College, Oxford. He was formerly Senior Pastor of Shirley Baptist Church, Solihull and preaches regularly in London and further afield.

David Ridder is Senior Pastor of Bayside Chapel in New Jersey, USA. Previously, he was Dean of Bethel Seminary in St Paul, Minnesota, USA from 2007–11, and prior to that served as Senior Pastor of Grace Point Church in Newtown, Pennsylvania for twenty-three years. He holds the DMin degree from Trinity Evangelical Divinity School in Deerfield, Illinois, USA.

Ian Stackhouse is Senior Minister of Guildford Baptist Church, UK, and the author of several books including *The Gospel Driven Church: Retrieving Classical Ministries for Contemporary Revivalism* (Paternoster, 2005), which was his PhD thesis, *The Day is Yours: Slow Spirituality in a Fast-Moving World* (Paternoster, 2008), and *Primitive Piety: A Journey from Suburban Mediocrity to Passionate Christianity* (Paternoster, 2011). He also teaches in seminaries in the UK and overseas.

Andrew Walker is Emeritus Professor of Theology, Culture and Education and the founder of the Centre for Theology, Religion and Culture in the School of Social Science and Public Policy in 1995 at King's College, London. He is an ecumenical canon of St Paul's Cathedral, and a lay missioner in the Eastern Orthodox Tradition. He is the author of numerous articles and chapters in collected works. His books include *Telling the Story: Gospel, Mission and Culture* (SPCK, 1996), *Remembering Our Future: Explorations in Deep Church*, (Paternoster, 2007), and, with Robin Parry, *Deep Church Rising: The Third Schism and the Recovery of Christian Orthodoxy* (Cascade, 2014).

John Woods is the Minister of Lancing Tabernacle and a tutor in the College of Preachers. He also teaches at Latvian Biblical Centre in Latvia. He holds a DMin on preaching from the University of Wales and has authored *Fly on the Fence* (OM Publishing/Paternoster, 1998) and written articles on homosexuality, church unity, and contemporary culture for a number of UK publications.

Introduction

> A typical Protestant sermon is a verbal essay on a contemporary theme, sometimes employing biblical illustrations in support of the essayists' point of view. The preacher who is bound to the text, confined to what he or she perceives as the biblical point of view, is a curiosity. Most often, the congregation is constrained to hear the Gospel according to the Reader's Digest, the National Review or the New Republic, depending on the preacher's orientation.[1]

To USE A TERM that is used a lot these days, preaching is not very sexy. Preaching, in the classical sense, as exposition of Scripture, has fallen on hard times. Antipathy towards the idea of one person standing over a crowd of people from the vantage of a pulpit, preaching from the Bible in an authoritative manner, is well-nigh ubiquitous. Indeed, the caricature of the preacher as "standing six feet above contradiction" or, to use another well-known jibe, "six days invisible one day incomprehensible," is so deeply ingrained in the popular psyche on both sides of the Atlantic that anyone who feels called to this ministry must overcome a great deal of negativity in order to get a hearing. This has been the context in which I have been preaching now for well on twenty-five years, and the disdain is showing no signs of abating. If anything it is getting worse.

The reasons for the demise of preaching (has it ever been popular?) are many and varied, foremost among them being what French Reformed theologian Jacques Ellul termed "the humiliation of the word." Writing in the sixties, Ellul prophesied the ascendency of image over and against the word, echoing to some degree the age old conflict between the pulpit and the altar.[2] But for all his iconoclasm (which is

1. Lee, *Protestant Gnostics*, 214–15.
2. Ellul, *Humiliation of the Word*, 1985.

extreme to say the least), I don't think even Ellul could have predicted how pervasive the screen was going to be over the next few decades, and therefore how thorough-going the decline of preaching was going to prove. Such is the preponderance of image in our day that the audio event, which at the very least is what preaching can be described as, looks very odd indeed. And the fact that preachers are now taking up visual media such as PowerPoint in order to buttress their preaching is not so much an answer but an admission of defeat.[3]

Another factor in the demise of preaching, strangely enough, is charismatic renewal. Emphasis on the gifts of the Spirit over the last few decades, arising from a renewed appreciation of the Pentecostal life of the church, has, with some notable exceptions, meant the relativization of preaching in favor of the prophetic, so-called: the disparagement of the weekly exposition of Scripture in favor of something more immediate. It is tragic that it should be this way, for preaching, as I have argued elsewhere, ought in many ways to be *the* charismatic event.[4] Pentecost begins with tongues but ends with a sermon. The unction of the Spirit that issues forth in praise in other languages at the beginning of the narrative is the exact same unction that we discern in the preaching of the apostle Peter—indeed, it is the exact same word that is used.

By this observation, I do not mean to imply the conflation of preaching and prophecy. Quite clearly there is a difference between the routinised exposition of Scripture and the immediate word of prophecy. But to suggest, as many charismatics do, that sermonising is dead speech in contrast to the lively word of prophecy is nothing short of woeful. It may well be trendy to invoke the Puritan preacher Jonathan Edwards in order to support the kind of religious phenomena that charismatics prize, but what the same people conveniently fail to acknowledge (apart from the obvious point that for Edwards affections are most definitely not the same thing as mere feelings or experience), is that Edwards was also thoroughly committed to the preaching exposition of Scripture. Indeed, it was through the power of preaching Scripture, as Oliver Crisp points out in his chapter, that the religious affections were aroused. Sadly, much of this is incidental to contemporary evangelicals because such commitment to the text, as far as many are concerned, plays right back into the hands of

3. See Lischer, *The End of Words*, 24–27 for a discussion on the demerits of PowerPoint in the context of preaching.

4. See Stackhouse, "Charismatic Utterance" in G. Stevenson, ed., *The Future of Preaching*, 42–46.

a supposed dead orthodoxy. As far as I am aware, this false dichotomy not only persists within certain strands of charismatic Christianity, but in some instances seems to be getting worse.

And then, a final attack against preaching comes from those who deride it as ecclesiastical authoritarianism —"a piece of cultural baggage" that needs to be jettisoned if the church is to be taken seriously in the post-modern world.[5] David Norrington posits a now somewhat familiar argument that preaching, by which he means sermonising, was something that arose as Christianity detached from its Hebrew moorings and entered the world of Greek oratory. In other words, sermonizing finds its direct antecedents not in the New Testament but in the Greek lecture hall. Go to the New Testament, he argues, and you will be hard pressed to find sermons at all, in the way we understand sermons, but rather the democratic speech of the charismatic community, where all are given to prophecy, or the dialogical speech of the small group.[6]

Passing Norrington's book back to me a number of years ago, one of my colleagues remarked that his thesis proves only one thing: "the man can't preach." But be that as it may (and I have no idea if he can or he can't preach), what is so dismal about Norrington's thesis is not simply his hostility to gospel preaching in an ecclesial context but also his short-sightedness concerning the biblical data. Like the infamous story about the girl who went out one day to spot the hippo in the river, standing all day on a large grey rock in order to see better but returning home disappointed, the reason Norrington can't spot a sermon in the New Testament is because he is standing on one. As Philip Greenslade points out in his chapter, not only do we discern traces of sermons throughout the New Testament, we also have one actual sermon preserved for us in its entirety, namely the letter to the Hebrews. For sure, it may not conform exactly to what we now experience as a sermon. In that sense, our sermons are most definitely culture bound. But what we see in the letter to the Hebrews is precisely that homiletical trinity of preacher, text, and congregation that is played out in pulpits every Sunday. What preachers do by reading a text, and then seeking to expound its meaning and application to the congregation they serve, is no different, in essence, to what was happening in the synagogue in Acts 13:15. Whether synagogue worship can be recontextualized for our own day is a moot point, of course, and, to be

5. Pearse and Matthews, *We Must Stop Meeting*.

6. Norrington, *To Preach or Not to Preach?*

fair, one of the main points people like Norrington want to make. But to suggest, in the process, that preaching just cannot be discerned in the New Testament just flies in the face of the data.

The Retrieval of Preaching

In seeking to redress this situation, I am aware of a number of dangers, not least the danger of confusing a commitment to preaching with a particular style of preaching, be it the classical three point sermon, or even the popular interpretation-application model. Indeed, I am aware that as soon as one mentions the term expository preaching it is very hard not to associate it with a particular style of homiletics which, for all its attraction to a certain generation of preachers, will ensure that others will not even advance beyond the first chapter of this book.

The truth is I have hardly ever preached a three-point sermon in my life, nor do I intend to begin now. Trying to squeeze a biblical text into three points all beginning with the letter "p" is rather like trying to put the proverbial quart into a pint pot. In its own way this kind of alliterative trickery abuses the text every bit as much as the most liberal of sermons, for it fails to take the text seriously as text. And what this book is about is taking the text seriously. Whether from a theological, historical, biblical, or homiletical perspective, what each contributor is seeking to convey is the importance of the biblical text for the task of preaching. Above and beyond rhetorical skill, charismatic personality, and pastoral sensitivity is the sheer energy that emanates from the Scripture. This is not to deny the kerygmatic element of preaching, nor to suggest that all gospel speech must have a text attached to it. There is a great deal that goes under the name of preaching that is simply, to use the old adage, one beggar telling another beggar where to find bread. But it is to say that congregational life is best formed over the long-term by the routinized exposition of Scripture. As Bonhoeffer said to his students at Finkenwalde: "The torment of waiting for fresh ideas disappears under serious textual work. The text has more than enough thoughts. One really only needs to say what is in it."[7] It is enough to be handed a text and say what is in it.

Again, this does not mean we have to look like a Puritan in the pulpit in order to pull this off, nor that we can afford to be neglectful of what

---

7. Fant, *Worldly Preaching*, 130.

is going on in the world. Barth's dictum that we carry a Bible in one hand and a newspaper in the other is as true today as it has always been. But whether we are talking about Spurgeon, Edwards, or even Chrysostom; whether we preach with notes or without notes; whether we preach from narrative, psalms, or epistles; or whether we are preaching four weddings and a funeral; what is central, as each contributor points out, is an immersion in the biblical text. In fact, precisely because Scripture itself is not simply applied ethics but the testimony of salvation history culminating in the death and resurrection of Jesus, my argument (echoing something that Steve Mathewson brings out in his chapter) is that by staying faithful to the text it is likely that not only will we preachers expose our congregations to the whole counsel of God, but also deliver to them the basic core kerygma. In other words, the congregation will receive a fresh rendering each week of why we call it gospel in the first place. After all, kerygma and didache are not two distinct, mutually exclusive categories, as C. H. Dodd supposed, with the one pertaining to unbelievers and the other to believers.[8] Rather, all kerygma must eventually lead to didactic; and all didactic must arise from kerygma. The one assumes the other. To say one is an expository preacher is not to say one is simply teaching the Bible, nor simply offering moral imperatives (which, sadly, is what preaching often amounts to), but rather that one is preaching the gospel.

One only discovers this of course by preaching. Left to ourselves we might simply and erroneously conclude that the Bible is a simply a repository of truth, something to be referred to for matters of salvation. And in one sense this is true. "All Scripture," Paul says to Timothy, "is God breathed, and useful for teaching, rebuking, correcting, and training in instruction."[9] But precisely because Scripture is God breathed, it means that as soon as we begin to exposit Scripture, whether it be narrative, proverb, psalms, we will likely move very quickly from mere learning into actual encounter, from didactic into kerygma, because right at the heart of Scripture—indeed, the thing that carries it along, as Dave Hansen's concluding chapter celebrates—is the core message of the gospel.

The person from whom I first heard this gospel speech, under whose ministry I got converted and then formed, embodies this truth more than anyone I know. To say Stuart Reid was a Bible preacher was to say he was a gospel preacher. He still is. And it was my great privilege to not only sit

8. Dodd, *Apostolic Preaching*, 7–8.

9. 2 Tim 3:16.

under his ministry for many years, but also to learn from him as I took my first faltering steps in the call to preach about twenty-five years ago. "Whatever you preach," he would say, "whether it is the law, the prophets, a psalm, or an epistle, make sure you leave them with the gospel." It is to Stuart that I would like to dedicate this collection of essays.

PART ONE

BIBLICAL AND THEOLOGICAL

1

Hebrews as a Model
for Expository Pastoral Preaching

Philip Greenslade

THE SCHOLARLY CONSENSUS IS that the *Letter to the Hebrews* might be re-titled the *Sermon to the Hebrews*.[1] When we hear Hebrews we are exposing ourselves to early Christian preaching.[2] Hebrews is the nearest we get to an example of first-century preaching.[3] Of particular interest here is the author's own description of what he has been attempting to do: "I appeal to you, brothers, bear with my word of exhortation, for I have written to you briefly" (Heb 13:22).

We might demur over "briefly," but what attracts serious attention is the phrase *tou logou tēs paraklēseōs*—"the word (or message) of exhortation (or comfort)." This phrase appears to be a technical name for *a sermon preached in a synagogue*.[4] The phrase occurs at Acts 13:14–15 where Paul and Barnabas are invited to give *logos tēs paraklēseōs* to the congregation in Pisidian Antioch:

> But they went on from Perga and came to Antioch in Pisidia.
> And on the Sabbath day they went into the synagogue and sat

1. Witherington, *Letter and Homilies for Jewish Christians*, Part 1.

2. Lane, Hebrews, *A Call to Commitment*, lxix–lxxv.

3. Walker "A Place for Hebrews," 237. See also Guthrie, *Hebrews*, while Lindars attaches the word "*expository*" to the mix.

4. Especially significant here is France's *The Writer of Hebrews as a Biblical Expositor*, 245–76. France, as others do, references the study of synagogue homilies by Wills, "The Form of the Sermon in Hellenistic Judaism and Early Christianity," 277–99.

> down. After the reading from the Law and the Prophets, the rulers of the synagogue sent a message to them, saying, "Brothers, if you have any *word of encouragement* for the people, say it."

In this synagogue context there is an expectation of hearing the word of the Lord derived apparently from an exposition of the lectionary readings drawn from the law and the prophets (Acts 13:15a; see Luke 4:16–21). This is precisely what Paul goes on to offer, in his presentation of Christ as the fulfillment of law and the prophets, and as the climactic chapter of the story. The "word of encouragement" is nothing less than the "message of salvation" (Acts 13:26). The sequel is instructive in suggesting that the language of gospel preaching can easily morph into "word of God" (Acts 13:34; 13:46) and "word of the Lord" terminology (Acts 13:48–49). This is in line with earlier incidents of "word of God" (Acts 13:5–7) and "teaching about the Lord" (Acts 13:12)—a conflation that is typical of Hebrews.

Our working hypothesis then is that Hebrews is a situation-specific sermon, or series of sermons, of an expository kind, sent as a letter to address the traumas of certain Jewish Christians, probably in Rome at or after the Neronic persecution, who were feeling under pressure to draw back from full commitment to Jesus and needed a bracing challenge and strong reassurance.

We may draw attention to some features of *oral* performance in Hebrews by *noticing first the signs of speech rather than writing.*

Take, for example, the phrases "of which we are speaking" and "it has been testified somewhere" (Heb 2:5–6). These suggest that at this point the preacher can assume knowledge on the part of his audience or, perhaps, does not want to get side-tracked into a discussion of psalm authorship.

And what of his comment, "About this we have much to say, and it is hard to explain?" (Heb 5:11). Here he seems to be getting his retaliation in first while in the same breath highlighting the seriousness of what he is teaching.

When he says, "Since you have become hard of hearing" (Heb 5:11), we suspect the preacher is needing to wake his audience up by shouting louder or banging on the pulpit! His words, "though we speak in this way" (Heb 6:9) or "now the point of what we are saying is this" (8:1) sound like a classic mid-sermon summary of the main burden of the message.

As for remarks such as "of these things we cannot now speak in detail" (Heb 9:5) or "what more shall I say?" (Heb 11:32), they seem to invite the response, "Tell it preacher, tell it all." Though "time would fail me to tell . . ." sounds too much like a typical preacher's complaint!

All the way through, we can hear the pastoral voice making its appeal to those who are "brothers" and "beloved" (e.g., Heb 3:12; 6:9).

"Hebrews," says Tom Long, "like all good sermons, is a dialogical event in a monological format."[5] It may be worth recalling, at this juncture, Aristotle's threefold rhetorical analysis which measured oratory in three ways: by *logos* (word), by *pathos* (emotion), and by *ethos* (character).

As far as Hebrews is concerned, the *logos* of his exhortation is the entire storyline of salvation, climaxing in God's final word and perfected work in his Son, Jesus Christ.

As for *pathos*, the preacher to the Hebrews exploits every emotional approach to elicit a response. He appeals, provokes, cajoles, invites, warns, celebrates, and reassures. He seeks to arouse both confidence (Heb 4:18; 10:19), and fear (Heb 4:1), urging his listeners/ readers, as it were, to "fear God rather than men," not in craven terror (Heb 12:21) but, nonetheless, with healthy reverence and awe" (Heb 12:28). Paradoxically, he invokes the specter of shame—the possible disgrace of *not* disregarding the dishonor heaped upon them (Heb 10:36–39)—seeking, as it were, to shame them into being *un*ashamed!

As to *ethos* the author commends himself by his pastoral warmth and empathy. By his frequent use of "we" and "us" he shows his solidarity with them in the fight of faith. This serves to enhance rather than diminish his authority as one who practices what he preaches. As for the character of God, he is trustworthy in promise-keeping (Heb 6:18; 10:23); as for Christ, he is the faithful one par excellence (Heb 2:17; 3:6; 12:1–2).[6] In all these ways, the integrity of word and speaker is brought home to the hearers.

Paying closer attention to the various literary genres of Scripture would give our preaching a sharper edge and deeper color.

Hebrews segues from style to style and mood to mood. If we view Hebrews—or any part of Scripture—as a contourless landscape of flat propositions, then we may well end up trying to liven it up by imposing our personality on it.

---

5. Long, himself a professor of homiletics, in *Hebrews, Interpretation Commentary*, 6; 124.

6. See on this Koester, *Hebrews*, 87–92.

Richard Lischer has wise words on this:

> The preacher who is only concerned with self-expression may be neglecting the rich array of styles available in the Bible. The text will tell you when to be angry, ironic, funny, or sad. It will tell you when to reason with your hearers and when to tease them with parabolic utterance, when to teach your parishioners and when to soar with them to the third heaven.[7]

Lischer adds: "The preacher makes adjustment in matters of diction (word choice, figures of speech, and manner of speech (tone of voice)) not on the basis of his or her personality or mood but in deference to the nature of the text and the demands of the occasion."[8]

What might Lischer's phrase "in deference to the nature of the text" mean as far as Hebrews is concerned?

It might mean recognizing that the opening catena of texts in Hebrews is less a list of proof texts but more a litany of praise which cries out to be preached as proclamation. It might also mean that the sobering typological comparison of Israel and the church in chapters 3 and 4 calls for a tone of warning and a solemn, urgent pleading. It might surely imply that to be confronted by hearers who are "dull of hearing" and needing immersion in deeper truth is not the cue for a few jokes or light-hearted stories to sugar the pill, but a cue to swallow hard and embark on a patient, careful exposition of truth, that takes the time and trouble to spell out in detail the wonders of the gospel. Finally it might suggest a recognition that chapter 11 is not the cue for an over-idealized panegyric to the spiritual giants of faith but a chance to fire the imagination of the hearers with the sweeping narrative of faith and to get them to see themselves (and all unsung, home-grown heroes of faith) as a part of this adventure. All these are signs of a spoken address which is now being sent in letter form to a wider audience with a suitable postscript in Hebrews 13:22–25.

In attending to features of *oral* performance in Hebrews, we might notice *the homiletical interweaving in Hebrews of exposition and exhortation.*

The sustained exposition of the superiority of Christ is regularly dovetailed with urgent warnings (Heb 2:1–4; 3:7—4:11; 5:11—16:20; 10:19–39; 12:14–29). So subtle is this interweaving that it is hard to know which is prior. Recent commentators privilege exhortation over

---

7. Lischer, *The End of Words*, 79–80.

8. Ibid., 79.

exposition, the latter funding the former. In truth, the preacher both warns and encourages: he makes them afraid they might miss out on the ultimate prize and positively urges them to emulate the faithful who have gone before, especially Jesus. So exposition and application alternate: a "pattern, which . . . is characteristic of a sermon."[9]

We might note, reflecting on Hebrews 13:22, the definite article "*the* word." Is this significant? Perhaps not. It may simply signify *the* message—that is, the one I have just presented to you. The absence of the definite article in Acts 13:15 may simply mean "bring us *a* word" which, when it is over, becomes "*the* word" just spoken. But I wonder if there is not more here. I am inclined to think that *paraklēsis* in this context, given the magnitude of what the preacher has said, carries some of its full value as shorthand for the comfort of new covenant salvation (see Isa 40:1ff; Luke 2:25).

The Dutch pastoral theologian Jacob Firet suggests that we give *paraklēsis* its full prophetic weight as a synonym for the consolation of messianic salvation (e.g., Luke 2:25).[10] On this basis, pastoral preaching must continually link people to the larger salvation which all enjoy. True exhortation or *paraklēsis* presupposes the gospel and consistently draws upon its energy to motivate people to faith; hence perhaps the conflation in Paul's address at Antioch of "message of encouragement" and "message of salvation" in Acts 13:15–26. This Hebrews pattern must be followed if preaching is not to lapse into legalism or succumb to that moralistic nagging of the congregation that is so self-defeating.

Firet comments:

> What *paraklēsis* calls for exceeds human possibilities: it is not a moral appeal, but a reminder of what God has done, an exposition of the saving deed already accomplished. It does not call for brand new initiatives and achievements; it calls for fruit-bearing and an answer. (It) is an appeal to change but the appeal takes place within the context of the gospel.[11]

So it is with the preacher of Hebrews. He combines pastoral sensitivity and studied craftsmanship in order to appeal to his hearers' deepest convictions and emotions and bring home to them the urgency of his message. "Seen in this way," comments Andrew Lincoln,

9. Lane, *Call to Commitment*, 20.

10. Firet, *Dynamic Pastoring*, 133.

11. Ibid., 71, 74.

it can be said to contain features that make it an excellent model for any preacher. What is more, it reflects a confidence about the efficacy of preaching. Faced with a community that is in danger of drifting and finding other options more attractive than its confession of faith, this pastor does not suggest superficial remedies. Instead he preaches, and he preaches scripturally, theologically, and Christologically in a sermon which is directly targeted at the most pressing needs of the hearers and which does not shrink from confronting them boldly.[12]

In seeking clues to the *oral* performance of Hebrews, we may notice *the selective use of Scripture passages which form the material for exposition.* As R. T. France convincingly shows, the Sermon to the Hebrews "after the raft of Scriptural citations in chapter one, and while not excluding many other scriptural allusions and echoes, revolves primarily around an exposition of *seven* Old Testament passages."

Psalm 8:4–6 in Hebrews 2:5–18

The saving story of Jesus, the Truly Human One, redeems our Adamic humanness and with it the reason for Israel's covenantal existence.

Psalm 95:7–11 in Hebrews 3:7—4:13

I will reflect on this passage further below.

Psalm 110 in Hebrews 5:5—7:28 (see 1:3; 1:13)

Just as the Chronicler appears to re-route the whole human story from Adam through the children of Israel till it reaches its intended climax in the establishment of the Davidic kingship in Zion,[13] so Hebrews traces the redemption of the Adamic story through Abraham (and one greater than Melchizedek), to Moses (and beyond Sinai; Heb 3:1ff), through Joshua (and beyond the "rest" found in the land; Heb 4:8) until it is entrusted to "great David's greater Son" (Heb 1:5; 2 Sam 7:14) and finally "comes home" to Mount Zion and to the sacrificial priest-king who rules there (Heb 12:22).

12. Lincoln, *Hebrews,* 21–22.
13. See Hahn, "Liturgy and Empire," 13–50.

Jeremiah 31:31–34 in Hebrews 8:1—10:18

Here is posed the sharpest contrast with the previous dispensation and its institutions. The references in Hebrews to Jeremiah's "new covenant" form an *inclusio* so that "all that goes between these two quotations contributes to the reader's understanding of why the old covenant needed to be replaced."[14]

Habbakuk 2:3–4 in Hebrews 10:32—12:3

The faith and faithfulness typified in the prophet's stance stimulates an extended challenge to the preacher's hearers to do likewise.

Proverbs 3:11–12 in Hebrews 12:4–13

The proverbial wisdom serves as a catalyst for the Preacher's urgent concern to help his beleaguered readers sustain their faith while living lives "against the grain" as disciplined sons.

Exodus 19 in Hebrews 12:18–29

France concedes the obvious, that there is no explicit citation, but contends that Exodus 19–20 is clearly in the preacher's mind as he recalls the smoking mountain motif of the Sinai narrative whose convulsions he connects with the eschatological shaking of the cosmos in Haggai 2:6.

Hebrews represents expository preaching. To say this implies no cramping of a preacher's style. Nothing here forces upon us *one* style of exposition, certainly not the rigid, stereotypical, and usually uninspiring verse-by-verse running commentary on the Bible text that at one time passed itself off as expository preaching.

To the objection that we live in a biblically illiterate age inimical to Scriptural preaching, we might counter that this is a reason *for* not *against* such preaching. Paul's approach to the largely Gentile Corinthians is a case in point (e.g., 1 Cor 10:1ff). Since the human story, and Israel's story, and the Jesus story are inextricably bound together, a biblical education

---

14. France, *The Writer of Hebrews as a Biblical Expositor*, 264. Witherington affirms that these are not random selections; *Letter and Homilies for Jewish Christians*, 50–51.

is unavoidable, even though it may require a patient and creative "conversion of the imagination."[15]

Elizabeth Achtemeier's challenge is sharp: "Because much of the church . . . no longer believes or expects to hear God speaking through the Scriptures, it therefore is not very Christian anymore."[16] The Bible is the *text* of preaching. "The Bible is the *test* of preaching."[17]

This presupposes, as Paul Scherer puts it, "God kept on speaking after his book went to press."[18] This is not to advocate extra-biblical revelation but to ask: "Do we really believe that Scripture is the voice of the Living God?" Hebrews says "yes" and we may briefly explore why. If we are to maintain confidence in the efficacy of preaching, not least expository preaching, we need to share the outlook of the preacher of Hebrews in a number of obvious ways:

1. Hebrews "reflects confidence that God is a speaking God" (Heb 1:1).

As the business pundits say "the main thing is to make the main thing the main thing." Revelation is the preacher's main thing. Without this, preaching is pulpiteering, mere religious hot-air, a hollow echo of our self-expression. But for biblical faith and preaching, the base line is that God exists and he is not silent. And, as William Willimon says, "We are the only listeners God has got!"[19]

2. We need to share the confidence of Hebrews that God has spoken in Scripture (Heb 1:5–7).

However undeveloped our doctrine of inspiration, however tentative our notion of inerrancy, Warfield's dictum, albeit suitably nuanced, remains our default position: "What Scripture says, God says." As James Denney said of his friend J P Struthers, "He never reads scripture as if he had written it. He always reads as if listening for a voice."[20]

3. Hebrews is confident that God has spoken in his Son, Jesus (Heb 1:2ff).

15. Hays is especially helpful on this in *The Conversion of the Imagination*, 1–24.

16. Achtemeier, "The Canon as the Voice of the Living God," 120.

17. Lischer, *The Theology of Preaching*, 57.

18. Scherer, *The Word God Sent*, 26.

19. Willimon, *Shaped by the Bible*, 81.

20. Cited by John Randolf Taylor in *God Loves Like That!* 133.

Hebrews may not have a fully-developed *logos* doctrine but the Preacher is rightly fixated on the embodied Word. All preaching of Scripture is in the deepest sense a preaching of the Word who is Jesus.[21] All scripturally sourced preaching should gravitate to Jesus and be an unfolding of the gospel. Bernard Lord Manning was not far off the mark when he defined preaching as "the manifestation of the Incarnate Word from the written word by the spoken word."[22] Hebrews even hears the psalms as if spoken *by* Jesus (Heb 2:12; 10:5f). This prompts us to note a fascinating feature of Hebrews that may tell more about how preaching works.

4. Hebrews hears in Scripture an intra-Trinitarian dialogue!

In Scripture, the Father speaks to the Son (Heb 1:5, 8, 13; 5:5–6; 7:21); the Son speaks to the Father (2:12, 13; 10:5–7); the Spirit bears witness to what God says (3:7; 10:15). Harold Attridge, who draws attention to what he terms this curious "conceit," shows that this "dialogic oratory" serves two vital pastoral purposes.[23] Firstly, it enables the preacher to reassure his readers/ hearers about the deepest intentions of God: "They can walk with assurance in the way of the covenant because in the words of Scripture they have overheard God talking to his Son and to them. They have heard words of encouragement as well as words of warning."[24] Secondly, it enables him to hold forth the Son's response to the Father as a model for his hearers to emulate (cf. 12:2). "They have heard in the person of God's Son a model for their own dialogue with God, a paradigm for words of faith lived out in action."[25] As our baptism told us, the Trinity is not so much a doctrine to be confessed as a drama in which to be immersed. Hebrews invites us into the loving divine embrace and generous hospitality by drawing us into the very dialogue going on within the Trinity. We are *ear*witnesses rather than eyewitnesses and through preaching we are made party to the affirming, approving, and responsive trust within the Godhead.

All this raises interest in the *hermeneutical stances* the preacher adopts. If, as I would contend, homiletics (how we preach) is 90 percent hermeneutics (how we interpret the Scriptural text), the approach of

---

21. See Fant, *Bonhoeffer*, 126–30.

22. Manning, *A Layman in the Ministry*, 138.

23. Attridge, "God in Hebrews," 103–8. See also Katherine Greib, "Time Would Fail Me to Tell . . . : The Identity of Jesus Christ in Hebrews," 207–8.

24. Attridge, "God in Hebrews," 110.

25. Ibid.

Hebrews proves instructive in this regard. Hebrews 3:1—4:13 acts as a sounding board for this:

a. 3:1–4 Hebrews encourages an unabashed *Christological* reading of the text.

The Preacher of Hebrews connects us to the over-arching covenantal story of redemption past and future as made good in Jesus Christ. The Christological focus of 1:1–13 is developed in terms of Christ's climactic person and work. As to his person, his status as God's unique Son outranks God's finest servants (3:5–6; cf. 1:1–2): he is superior to Moses, to Joshua, and to the Levitical priesthood.

As to his achievement, it fulfils and eclipses all that has gone before; offering a "better" sacrifice, with blood that speaks "better things" than Abel's, based on "better" promises, and establishing a "better" covenant. All roads lead to Jesus; all eyes are to be fixed on Jesus (Heb 12:2). As Barth said: "There is a river in the Bible that carries us away, once we have entrusted our destiny to it, away from ourselves to the sea."[26] That river of redemptive grace flows via Bethlehem and Calvary through the very gates of hell to reach us and to sweep us up in its new creation energies as it surges on towards the New Jerusalem.

So Hebrews 1:1—2:9 is a vital preface to the seemingly exclusive Jewish narrative that follows. It functions much as Genesis does to Exodus to remind us that Israel was called to be the sample new humanity for the sake of the world. Preaching like this, therefore, aims to set before its hearers the goal of salvation which is to become *fully human again.* To do this means to take as seriously as Hebrews does the enfleshed humanness of Jesus (Heb 2:9; 2:14–15; 5:7–8).

Hebrews 2:1–4 connects the Christ of faith with the historical Jesus and with the original apostolic testimony and endorses the view that the true apostolic succession is the succession of the gospel handed down to us and received by us.

And this thrust does not falter when we get to the preacher's distinctive presentation of the *High Priesthood of Christ* (Heb 6:20—29:28). We are deterred from preaching this, I suspect, because it threatens to immerse us in the *un*user-friendly small-print of the Old Testament—indeed of Levitical small-print. But we sell people short when we do. It is vital to preach the gospel of the ascension and exaltation as the ongoing ministry of Jesus. Not least, this is because the incarnation is completed

26. Barth, *The Word of God and The Word of Man*, 34.

only by the ascension which both guarantees the final redemption of our humanness and a Savior who retains his own humanity now glorified and therefore perfectly attuned to sympathize with our human condition.[27]

This in itself steer us away from the gnosticization to which a super-spiritual charismatic spirituality is prone and back to a full flesh-and-blood view of how holiness is worked into a growing humanness—one which is consummated not by out-of-body experiences or even near-death experiences but by the full and final redemption of our bodily wholeness which the New Testament calls resurrection.

b. 3:7–19 Hebrews endorses an *ecclesiocentric* reading of Scripture.[28]

The repeated "let us . . ." in Hebrews is a sharp rebuke to our perennial tendency to over-individualize the impact of the gospel and a strong reminder that God has intended, from the outset, to call out a people for his name. Moreover, despite the discontinuity affected by the Christ event, Hebrews affirms the essential oneness of God's covenant family across the generations.

Typology is at work here, a real correspondence between real events, and it is to be relished as an interpretive key. But typology is more than analogy. Hebrews assumes a real connection between us and the people of God in an earlier stage of the story so that their experiences whether for good or ill become a parable of ours. The challenges and opportunities they faced—albeit in different guise—are mirrored in the testing of our faith and patience. Faithful exposition of the psalms (here Psalm 95) in the light of the gospel, draws us, the current hearers of the word, into the urgent dialogue between God and his people Israel, and challenges us to keep faith where the wilderness generation did not (Heb. 3:16–19). We are urged to emulate those who did keep faith as in the so-called portrait gallery of saints (Heb. 11:1–41). Even here, the gallery metaphor is too static an image; as though there were an identikit picture of the ideal saint or a one-size-fits-all model of the faithful believer.

These are the stories not of perfect exemplars of faith or spirituality but of witnesses caught up in the covenantal activity of God. They are meant to motivate us to engage in the same redemptive story they were involved in and to play a part, albeit this side of Easter, with a

---

27. For help in refocusing on the Ascension ministry of Jesus and its implications, see Farrow's work, most recently, *Ascension Theology*; and more accessibly for preachers, Dawson, *Jesus Ascended*.

28. The phrase belongs to Hays, *Echoes of Scripture in the Letters of Paul*, chapter 3.

boldness and zest encouraged by their faith. "Believers can now be addressed in their situations with an appeal to the fact that they are in the story, in God's new beginning, in Christ."[29] That this is the story of the ongoing fight of faith, and not a march-past of former heroes, is clear from the preacher's punch line in verses 39–40—that without *our* story theirs is incomplete.

Here the discontinuity in the continuity serves the preacher well, so that he never loses sight of his Christological focus. Only one person has been utterly faithful, or has ever fully accomplished what God gave him to do; only Jesus is the finisher of faith (12:1–2) and the one who brings the story to its final resolution by returning (9:28).

Homiletically, our task is to take our hearers back into the strange new world of the Bible so that they may learn to indwell the text as their story. Homiletically, we may employ all our creative skill imaginatively to fuse the two horizons, perhaps by the use of "deliberate anachronisms"— as with Moses who *"considered the reproach of Christ greater wealth than the treasures of Egypt"* (11:26; cf. 4:2).[30]

    c. Hebrews invites an *eschatological* reading of the text.

For Hebrews, God's *"rest"* remains to be enjoyed (4:1, 6); God's future beckons. Sabbath rest was the climax of creation, a sign that God's first creation work was done and was fit for purpose. Its restoration was symbolized by the Land promised to Abraham and his descendants. In turn, the *"rest"* of the Promised Land which the Israelites aspired to enter served as a token of that final, "unscathed world"[31] which will be the *"rest"* of the accomplished new creation.

In recognition of the fact that in Christ the final word has been spoken and the ends of the ages have come upon us, we live in the awareness of being in the *"last days"* (1:1). To that end, preaching summons us to trust and travel with God as his pilgrim people facing our own wilderness testing and marching on in faith to the *"city that is to come"*

29. Firet, *Dynamic Pastoring*, 71.

30. On "deliberate anachronism," see Campbell's introduction to a collection of sermons by Brueggemann who employs the technique brilliantly in *The Threat of Life*, vii–xii. See also Mosser's contribution to the symposium, *The Epistle to the Hebrews and Christian Theology*, 391.

31. Moltmann, *The Way of Jesus Christ*, 107. Of Jesus' miracles, Moltmann comments, "In the context of the new creation, these 'miracles' are not miracles at all. They are merely the fore-tokens of the all-comprehensive salvation, the unscathed world, the glory of God."

(13:14). Preaching like this echoes the voice that shakes all things and passionately advocates the kingdom that cannot be shaken, comforting the disturbed and disturbing the comfortable as it does so (12:25–27). God's rest remains: strive to enter it; it's too good to miss. These are the notes struck by preaching.

d. 4:11–13 Hebrews operates with a *dynamic* reading of God's word.

> Let us therefore strive to enter that rest, so that no one may fall
> by the same sort of disobedience. 12 For the word of God is liv-
> ing and active, sharper than any two-edged sword, piercing to
> the division of soul and of spirit, of joints and of marrow, and
> discerning the thoughts and intentions of the heart. 13 And no
> creature is hidden from his sight, but all are naked and exposed
> to the eyes of him to whom we must give account.

Firstly, Hebrews models preaching the word from Scripture and the gospel as the "*living*" word of God.

If what Scripture says is what God said by original inspiration of the Holy Spirit then he speaks it afresh as the now word ("*the Holy Spirit says*" as in 3:7). The "*word of God*" here (4:12) is not Scripture *per se* but God speaking through Scripture in the gospel about his Son by the Spirit and brought home to us as a preached word. Connecting up the Scrip-ture, the gospel, and the Spirit in this way makes for an encounter with the "today" voice of God (3:7). By this means, God's "today" word spoken to Joshua and re-iterated in Psalm 95 is made powerfully applicable to God's contemporary hearers (so 3:7—4:10).

Our task as always therefore is to *let the text speak*. We let the text speak, confident that God will speak again to the Son and to his siblings in Christ through the Holy Spirit.

I have elsewhere tentatively suggested how this perspective on the *living* word of God may help us with the vexed passage in Hebrews 6:4–8 about "falling away." How do we approach the "once-saved-always-saved" conundrum? If the Bible is a textbook of theological propositions then we must stand back from it and as neutral observers seek to subsume all its seemingly contradictory directives under one consistent schema. But if the Bible is actually the story of God which is *still ongoing* and we are *here and now participating in it*, then we are *not* in a position to stand aloof from it with lofty detachment and at-tempt to reconcile perseverance, eternal security, conditional faith and the risk of apostasy in one remit. We are not *outside* the Bible looking in on God's story from a vantage point of supposed objectivity so that we can one weigh one item against an other and balance them out. Rather we *indwell* the Bible; we are *in* the story the Bible tells. And right in the thick of the story as it unfolds, we hear both voices as God says different things at different stages of the journey. We only see the need to reconcile what seem conflicting voices, or indeed to opt for one over the other, if we think of ourselves as standing apart from the unfolding drama and able to offer detached comment on it. Rather, on the journey round the mountain we hear God reassuringly say, "Do not be afraid; the road is safe; I am with you all the way; you will make it to the end," *and* at some stage, of necessity, we need to hear God warn: "don't go near the edge, if you disobey me, you will fall to your death."[32]

Isn't this precisely what Hebrews is doing (6:9–12)?

If Hebrews is anything to go by, today's word will always be an expression of God speaking through Scripture about and in his Son by the Spirit. Spoken by the living God, God's living word is life-imparting. The Bible translator, J. B. Phillips, whose *The New Testament in Modern English* was *The Message* of its day, once said that working on the Greek text of the New Testament was like rewiring an old house with the current still on. The word we preach is a living word and, incidentally, it helps to use the *present* tense when declaring it.[33]

Secondly, Hebrews models preaching of the word from Scripture and the gospel as the living and "*active*" word of God.

Hebrews surely reminds us that the word of God not only *says* things but *does* things.

Currently preaching is under fire from those post-moderns who accuse it of being locked into an outdated Greek rhetorical mode of discourse. This criticism, I would argue, is misguided.

Preaching, as Hebrews demonstrates, is not indebted to the Greek philosophers but is rooted in the tradition of the Hebrew prophets. For the prophets, God's word was fire and hammer and sword (as here 4:12)—implements of truth in action, weapons of a word to be enacted as well as said, an active force that was set to achieve what it declared to be God's will. This is the view summed up by Isaiah (Isa 55:10–11): "For as

---

32. Greenslade, *Ministering Angles,* 230–31; see also Schreiner, "Warning and Assurance," 89–106.

33. Much more could be said on this, but, akin to the "deliberate anachronism" mentioned earlier, it is a device which by vividly contemporizing old texts helps to prevent us hearing them merely as ancient history.

the rain and the snow come down from heaven and do not return there but water the earth, making it bring forth and sprout, giving seed to the sower and bread to the eater, so shall my word be that goes out from my mouth; it shall not return to me empty, but it shall accomplish that which I purpose, and shall succeed in the thing for which I sent it."

Our modern understanding of the word's ability to accomplish what God purposes with it may be enriched by a fleeting glance at rhetorical, speech-act, and sacramental theories.

For all the criticism of rhetorical influence on preaching, recent scholars show how helpful to the preacher *rhetorical analysis* of New Testament texts can be. Whether the use of language is forensic as in a law court, or deliberative so as to argue and persuade, or epideictic (as largely in Hebrews) so as to encourage and celebrate[34]—such analysis is beneficial. At the very least, it forces the exegete and preacher to ask not only "what does this text *mean*?" but "what does this text intend to *do*?"

Modern *speech-act theory*, too, is useful in highlighting this dynamic potential of language.[35] Preaching in this mode is "performative speech." Empowered by the Holy Spirit, it has the capacity to effect what it describes.

A *sacramental understanding*, unfamiliar as such thinking is to Evangelicals, can also enrich our view of preaching at this point. Preaching is not so much a means of communication but a means of grace. P. T. Forsyth long ago warned that Catholic worship centered on the Mass would always have the advantage over Protestant worship "so long as people come away from its central act with the sense of something *done* in the spirit-world, while they leave ours with the sense only of something *said* to this present world."[36] As Gerhard Forde has it: "The preacher must see the proclamation itself as a sacrament, the moment when what the text authorizes is actually to be done once again in the living present not just explained or talked about."[37] The cynical view is that when all is said

34. See especially Witherington's work, not least on *Hebrews in Letters and Homilies for Jewish Christians*, 45.

35. Speech-act theory is best accessed through the work of Austin, and is helpfully employed by evangelical scholars. See Vanhoozer, *First Theology, God, Scripture and Hermeneutics*, especially part 2; Horton, *Covenant and Salvation: Union with Christ*, 220–30.

36. Forsyth, *Positive Preaching and the Modern Mind*, 81.

37. Forde, *The Preached God*.

and done, more is said than done. On the contrary, Forsyth contends, "In true preaching, as in a true sacrament, more is done than said."

Darrell Johnson helpfully suggests that we stop asking how to "*apply*" the word to our lives and replace the word "apply" with the word "*imply*." This is not mere semantics. "Applying" the word tends to a mechanical "elastoplast" approach to texts and furthermore puts us firmly in control of the hearing event. "Imply," on the other hand, allows the text to control the response and to determine the outcome—an outcome which cannot be foreclosed.[38] The implications of the text implicate us, so to speak. Preaching like this turns directives into directions. Preaching like this moves us not only emotionally but volitionally and directionally. Preaching the implications of the text provokes me to ask not: "How can I apply this word to my life?" but rather "Where will this text take me if I yield myself to it?"

Hebrews models preaching of the word from Scripture and gospel as a word that "*cuts deep*" (4:12), sharper than any two-edged sword, piercing to the division of soul and of spirit, of joints and of marrow, and discerning the thoughts and intentions of the heart.

The true preacher of the gospel works at depth, with a distaste for the superficial and the trivial, for the itsy-bitsy homilies that pass for preaching—what Paul Scherer calls "helpful hints for hurtful habits!"[39] We must preach deeply and concentrate more on the fundamental, ultimate issues of life. As Barth so rightly said:

> There is no wisdom in stopping at the next-to-the-last and next-to-the-next-to-the-last want of the people; and they will not thank us for doing so. They expect us to understand themselves better than they understand themselves, and to take them more seriously than they take themselves. We are unfeeling not when we probe too deeply into the wound which they carry when they come to us for healing, but rather when we pass over it as if we did not know why they had come.[40]

A mystery to ourselves, we need the word of God to understand us better than we know ourselves (Ps 139; 1 John 3:20). But however bad the diagnosis of our condition it is good news if it yields gospel remedies. Preaching like Hebrews dissects the interior workings of the heart, peels

---

38. See Johnson's fine book, *The Glory of Preaching*, especially chapter 7.

39. Scherer, *The Word God Sent*, 5.

40. Barth, *The Word of God and the Word of Man*, 109.

back the layers of self-deceit and self-defense, exposes the often unrecognized indoctrination of parents, teachers, and peers, excises the cultural accretions that compromise our testimony, and sets us free with truth. Because the gospel is salvation not self-help, preaching will always be more like surgery than therapy. The good news that we preach is that the "steel is plied" not by a butcher but a skilled surgeon, by our great high priest "beneath whose bleeding hands we feel the sharp compassion of the healer's art" (4:14).[41] Preaching aims to set up such deeply wounding but life-changing encounters with the Living God. Preaching in the spirit of Hebrews 4:11–13 initiates what Paul Scherer called a "radical transaction." The sword plunges "deep enough down to offend and far enough in to hurt; in where the quick is, and the needs that have to be stirred into consciousness before any need at all except the body's can be met, or life can issue from death."[42] Preaching that offers superficial answers to surface needs is bound to sell the truth short and risks the prophetic rebuke of healing the wounds of the people lightly. The humorist P. G. Wodehouse is reported to have said; "I believe there are two way of writing novels. One is mine, making a sort of musical comedy without music and ignoring the real world altogether; the other is *going right deep down into life and not caring a damn.*"[43] In Richard Lischer's words, "the spin doctors keep to the surface; the preacher is required to plumb the depths in order to impart a different view of the world."[44]

The vivid description here, of the word laying bare the heart of the hearers, leaving one's inner life *"naked and exposed,"* may variably be ascribed to the baring of the neck of a sacrificial animal prior to slaughter or to the pinning down by the neck of an opponent in wrestling. Either way, the implication is clear; the hearers do not stand in judgment over the word but stand under it, becoming vulnerable before it, and submitting to it. And to stand under the word is to begin to understand the word which is the prerequisite for drawing on its fruit-bearing life (cf. Matt 13:23).

The task of preaching then is not to extract a message from the text or, worse still, conjure up a message and bolster it with proof texts. Rather, the true task of preaching is *to let the text loose and to allow the*

---

41. Eliot, *East Coker.*

42. Scherer, *The Word God Sent,* 70.

43. Cited by Hall, *Bound and Free,* 127.

44. Lischer, "Resurrection and Rhetoric," 19.

text to have some of the same intended effect on contemporary hearers as it had on its original audience.

My working mantra in preaching from Scripture reads as follows:

Let the text speak.

Let the text do its work.

Let the text take the hearers in the direction it intends.

Appeal but don't manipulate; warn but don't nag; challenge but don't coerce. Be sure to proclaim, to herald, and to celebrate.

Above all, trust the gospel to evoke the response it deserves.

One final reflection: does the context in which we preach matter and can Hebrews offer any guidance here? I believe it does.

If Hebrews is an example of early Christian sermon, modeled in part on synagogue sermons, then it almost certainly finds its natural context in worship. Counter-intuitively, preaching in a true sense is directed to God in so far as it articulates on behalf of the church what the church surely believes and confesses. It is an act of worship, addressed to people but offered to God. Preaching is the "organized hallelujah of the ordered community."[45]

In this connection we may note the way in which Hebrews—like a typical synagogue sermon—follows the lectionary of Scripture and typically closes with a benediction (13:20–21). Its last word is "grace" (13:25).

But the preaching of grace in the context of worship does not seal us off from the world.[46] Grace first invites us to enter boldly the liminal space of God's holy and all-consuming fiery love in order to worship (4:16). That same preached grace then urges us to *"go outside the camp"* (13:13), to venture beyond our cultural comfort-zones into the dangerous and often hostile liminal space of the, as yet, unredeemed world in order to bear witness there to the One who despised the shame, finished the race of faith he had been given to run, and so successfully pioneered our own.

If we preachers allow it, this is where the preached text of Scripture intends to take us.

45. Forsyth, *Positive Preaching and the Modern Mind*, 95.

46. See my *Worship in the Best of Both Worlds*, especially chapter 3.

The Text Has More Than Enough Thoughts

Bonhoeffer's Lectures on Preaching

Ian Stackhouse

It was Eugene Peterson, I recall, who counseled young seminarians to find a few major theologians and to master their works. After all, you cannot read every theologian who has ever lived, he argued, so better to try to immerse yourself in a few. So, alongside P. T. Forsyth and Søren Kierkegaard, both of whom were already having a profound influence on me (and both of whom were a great deal to say about preaching), I decided to commit as a young student to the German theologian/martyr Dietrich Bonhoeffer. It wasn't difficult to do. There is something very immediate about Bonhoeffer, something deeply biographical about his theology that makes him very popular both in the academy and the church. I am not alone in having Bonhoeffer as a favorite. Who is not inspired by the radicalism of *The Cost of Discipleship*, which is basically a running commentary on the Sermon on the Mount, written in the vortex of Germany in the 1930s? And what more important theological book is there for our understanding of Christian community than *Life Together*? In my first year at Millmead we read through *Life Together* as a pastoral team, and each week we were struck by how utterly contemporary it all was.

When it comes to output, the Bonhoeffer corpus is considerable as well as varied: sermons, prison letters, poems, love letters, as well as fairly dense theological tomes make up his well-known works. But what is not so well-known is a series of lectures on preaching Bonhoeffer delivered each semester between 1935 and 1939 to his group of seminarians at Finkenwalde. In one sense all of Bonhoeffer's theology, it could be argued, was taken up with preaching. Theology that could not be preached was not worth having, as far as Bonhoeffer was concerned. He was a Lutheran whatever else he was (and the idea that you could separate theology and praxis was simply inconceivable to him). But in the lectures on homiletics—so helpfully retrieved for us by Clyde E. Fant in *Bonhoeffer: Worldly Preaching*—Bonhoeffer gives a full articulation of how he sees the ministry of the word in theological terms and, in the light of that theology, how practically we preachers should prepare and deliver our sermons.[1] Like *Life Together* (which was also written in the quasi-monastic setting of Finkenwalde), the lectures are surprisingly contemporary, mainly because the issues confronting homiletics in the inter-war period are still with us, not least the tensions between objectivity and subjectivity; deductive and inductive; ethos and pathos. I offer the lecture here in fairly lengthy quotes so that, first, we might get acquainted with what he actually said, and second, so that it might speak to our own situation.

The Sacrament of the Word

Foundational to everything we might want to say about the importance of Bonhoeffer's lectures for our own times is the fact that he believed preaching to be an utterly unique form of communication. Preaching for Bonhoeffer was *sui generis*, transcending the simple task of passing on knowledge, or mere learning, by virtue of the fact that it was for Bonhoeffer, in typically Lutheran terms, *sacramentum verbi*: the sacrament of the word. In short, preaching is encounter with the living Christ, and its rationale is not so much the cult and liturgy of the church, but the incarnation of Christ himself. In other words, preaching for Bonhoeffer derives not so much from our ecclesiology, the practices of the church, but Christology: "Through the Holy Spirit," he argues in the second lecture, "the incarnate Word comes to us from the scripture in the sermon. And it is one and the same Word: the Word of creation, the Word of the incarnation, the Word of the Holy Scripture, the Word of the sermon."[2]

---

1. Fant, ed., *Bonhoeffer: Worldly Preaching* (B:WP from hereon).
2. B:WP, 129.

This is a high view of preaching indeed. By means of the well-known distinction in sacramental theology between the *signum* (the sign) and the *res* (the thing itself), preaching for Bonhoeffer is not merely information, not simply pointing to something else, but is, in and of itself, the carrier of the thing to which it refers. In a very striking image Bonhoeffer argues that the "proclaimed word is not a medium of expression about something else, something which lies behind it, but rather it is the Christ himself walking through his congregation as the Word."[3] To put it in Pauline terms, the message of the gospel is not just *about* the power of God, it *is* the power of God unto salvation.[4]

In his opening couple of lectures, in which he explores, among other things, the differences between preaching, teaching, evangelism, and witness, it is quite clear that Bonhoeffer regards the sermon (in which he hopes all the various forms of Christian speech might be held together) as the "actualization of his [Christ's] acceptance and sustenance," and therefore should be done in such a way that the hearer places all their cares, needs and fears upon it. "This proclamation of the Christ," he argues, "does not regard its primary responsibility to be giving advice, arousing the emotions, or stimulating the will—it will do these things, too—but its intention is to sustain us."[5] Such is the intention of the word to do this that, importantly for Bonhoeffer, it carries its own momentum: a kind of self-movement of the word to the congregation.

Bonhoeffer returns to this idea later in an excursus on the factor of concreteness in preaching.[6] "The sermon is concrete," he argues, "only when God's word is really in it. God alone is the *concretissimum*." And without this concreteness in preaching, without the factuality of the Bible, all we do as preachers is create people according to our own ideals, rather than people in the image of God. Therefore, it is imperative that the preacher stands aside to allow the self-movement of the word to happen. For Bonhoeffer, the preacher is not there to apply the word, which in some homiletical schools is just about all the preacher is there for, but rather to get out of the way so that the word might do its work unimpeded. In a most striking image, Bonhoeffer sees that with the "introduction

---

3. *B:WP*, 127.

4. Rom 1:16

5. *B:WP*, 127.

6. *B:WP*, 140–42.

of the biblical word, the text begins moving among the congregation."[7] Christ is indeed the sermon.

It hardly requires comment that such a view of preaching flies in the face of so much negativity in recent years concerning the pulpit (although it must be noted that Bonhoeffer himself had his own grievances against mere oratory). Just how odd his views are, to say nothing of how offensive they might be, can be seen in the way he polarizes preaching and music. Unlike our own day where preaching is just about tolerated and music is celebrated, for Bonhoeffer it is the other way round: "Music and symbols [as the Berneuchen movement believed], do not make us without excuse," he argued, "they are not unequivocal and do not break down the will."[8] Preaching, on the other hand, is the means by which Christ is ushered into the congregation and confronts the human heart. Indeed, so vital is the word to the edification of the church that ordination for Bonhoeffer is not so much the call to pastor a congregation, although it includes that, but the call to preach.[9] To preach predates ministry, and outlives the pastorate. As far as Bonhoeffer is concerned preaching is prior to everything.

Some may not want to go that far in their understanding of preaching, or the office of the preacher for that matter. As with other radical iconoclasts, Bonhoeffer sets up some unnecessary dichotomies that render his view on preaching unpalatable for some. At times Bonhoeffer is guilty of the same kind of homiletical docetism that Barth has been accused of.[10] Just how the preacher is able to distance themselves from the emotions of say Paul's second letter to the Corinthians, in the way that Bonhoeffer counsels his preachers in the tenth lecture,[11] is something that presumably he alone knew about in terms of technique, because in reality it is well-nigh impossible to achieve, not to mention unrealistic. Surely a high view of Scripture, such as Bonhoeffer articulates, permits, if not requires, an immersion in the emotions of the letter rather than a distancing from them, as a way of honoring its intent? Indeed, there are

7. *B:WP*, 128.

8. *B:WP*, 129.

9. *B:WP*, 134. Although, it is important to note that Bonhoeffer also noted the connection between the work of the preacher and the work of the pastor: "Just as the sermon grows heavily out of the pastor's work among the congregation, it also provides opportunity for work among the congregation to be developed out of it." *B:WP*, 177.

10. For an interesting critique of Barth's anti-rhetoric in preaching and the impact it has had on the theory of communication see A. Resner Jr, *Preacher and Cross*, 58–65.

11. *B:WP*, 171.

times when Bonhoeffer can be quite irritating in the way he castigates the spontaneous element in religion. But then again, as with other crisis theologians, it is precisely the hyperbolic nature of his argument, the way in particular in which the word takes on a life of its own in Bonhoeffer's understanding of what happens in preaching, that forces the reader to reconsider his or her own subjectivity in preaching. In other words, we may not agree with Bonhoeffer's almost quasi-magic view of the word, but by wrestling with it, not least the radical juxtaposition of preaching alongside the other practices of the church, we are forced to reflect on the inconsistencies not to mention weaknesses, of our own day. For the rest of this chapter I intend to adumbrate the numerous ways in which these lectures speak to our current situation, and argue in the process that for all the questions that Bonhoeffer's theology of preaching raises, and for all the ways in which it can only be understood in the inter-war context of religious idolatry, nevertheless the lectures ought to be compulsory reading for anyone considering church-based ministry in the twenty-first century. To use the parlance of preaching itself, Bonhoeffer's lectures speak to our situation.

1. The Obsession with Relevance

First, they speak to our obsession for relevance. For as long as I have been preaching, which now spans four decades, relevance in the pulpit has been the single most important criteria in homiletics. If a sermon is not relevant, then a sermon is not real. For a sermon not to be practical, not to be in some way relevant to the ordinary everyday needs of the listener, is the cardinal sin of modern homiletics. Application is the *sine qua non* of all modern preaching, and a response, in its own way, to the charge of obscurantism that has been levelled against preaching in the classical form. As long as the preacher is relevant, it is argued, then preaching might still be conceivable as a practice of the church; hence, the preference, indeed dominance, of the inductive method. Inductive preaching, or topical preaching, is the homiletical corollary of a church that has become anxious about its place in the real world, so called.

For Bonhoeffer, however, the ascendency of relevance over and against the concreteness of Scripture is to place things the wrong way round. Such is the authority of the Bible, the poignancy of the questions it poses to the human condition, that for Bonhoeffer the criterion of relevance must always prove subservient to the need for the preacher to immerse oneself in what Barth called the "strange new world of the

Scriptures." The imperative for all preachers is to allow the Bible to pose its own questions, to speak on its own terms. "The contemporary situation," Bonhoeffer warns, "is not sufficient to determine the content of the sermon; the dealings of God with men, as they are testified to in the Bible and made known through the teachings of the church is sufficient."[12]

Such a stance for the Bible is not an argument for a naïve, literalistic biblicism, nor is it to be guilty of homiletical detachment. One only needs to read Bonhoeffer's sermons to know that he preached always with an awareness about what was happening around him. Likewise, he preached with all the force of his personality. For Bonhoeffer one cannot do otherwise. What he is warning preachers of, however, is the way that the immediate context can so often displace the immediacy of the text, the intra-mural world of the Scriptures. To put it in my own terms, by allowing the contemporary situation to overtake our exegesis, we can end up too easily with eisegesis, and thus end up not preaching the Bible at all. How many times does a preacher announce a text, have someone read it out aloud to the congregation, and then introduce the sermon by some recent news event in order to give the sermon a whiff of relevancy? Even though the one who employs such devices may indeed reverence the word (even Bonhoeffer recognized the validity of topical preaching), for Bonhoeffer this kind of preaching so often betrays our lack of trust in the word to create its own hearing.[13]

2. The Penchant for Rhetoric

Such is the primacy of biblical text in Bonhoeffer's understanding of the homiletical task that not only does his lecture speak to our predilection for relevance, but also our penchant for rhetoric. Again, it is not that Bonhoeffer denies the place of personality or charisma in preaching. Bonhoeffer has no truck with those who deliver dull, dispassionate sermons. "From what has been said about factuality, humility and discipline, it would be a false conclusion to elevate monotony and rigidity to the

---

12. B:WP, 138.

13. I am interested here in Robert Farrar Capon's urge to preachers to cut the inductive waffle at the beginning of the sermon and get to the text early. Contrary to the inductive method where the text is relativized for the sake of gaining the listeners interest, Capon argues that Christian preaching per force should take its initial cue from the Scripture itself: "Starting your sermon with anecdotes about your high-school gym teacher or your Aunt Helen's shopping habits is pre-emptying the Word's time." I find his comments persuasive, all the more so since Capon could hardly be called a conservative evangelical. Capon, *The Foolishness of Preaching*, 82–83.

ideal. . . . There is even the right for a certain amount of pathos in our speaking as well."[14] In fact, there is an amusing moment in one of the later lectures where Bonhoeffer, in an attempt to encourage genuineness in the pulpit, admits that it is "unnatural to prevent naturalness,"[15] which seems to be a case of wanting to have it every which way. But what he does warn us against is the tendency that is widespread these days to, in effect, apologize for Scripture by trying to spice it up with rhetorical flourish or emotional panache. Inadvertently perhaps, these methods we employ to present the word via predetermined rhetorical devices (not to mention the use of visual images) betray once again a lack of confidence in the word to do its own work.[16] Bonhoeffer encourages us to let go of these things. "By forsaking my personal ambition," he argues, "I accompany the text along its own way into the congregation, and thus remain natural, balanced, compassionate and factual. This permits the Word's almost magnetic relationship to its congregation. I do not give life to it, but it gives life to me and the congregation. The movement of the Word to its congregation is accomplished through the interpretation of it."[17] Precisely because the word is so concrete, it comes as no surprise in a later lecture that Bonhoeffer lambasts those who shout in the pulpit. For Bonhoeffer, shouting in preaching, as well as exhaustion following preaching, is the ultimate betrayal of the word, and a signal that one has not truly spent time in preparation, for if they had, the word alone would have been enough. "Good preparation" he argues, "allows the greatest amount of factual, direct preaching from the pulpit. Only the unprepared preacher has to use techniques of emotionalism, shouting, or influencing through pressure. These techniques betray his insecurity."[18]

In Bonhoeffer's view, the insecurity noted here derives from a need in the preacher to be personally identified with the word he proclaims, to come away from the event of preaching with people talking about the charisma of the preacher and not the power of the word.[19] But whereas

14. *B:WP*, 172–73.

15. *B:WP*, 172.

16. For a stinging critique of the use of visual media in preaching, powerpoint in particular, see Lischer, *The End of Words*, 24–27

17. *B:WP*, 138

18. *B:WP*, 149

19. At various times in the lectures Bonhoeffer draws the distinction between *anthropos pneumatikos* and *pseukikos*, significantly in the context of the evangelistic efforts of the National Mission movement. One senses his unease with a kind of

in a secular context this might be understandable, and even desirable, if the speaker is to make his mark, in a Christian context this is reprehensible. "In secular speeches—for example, political speeches—everything hangs upon the discernible *identity* between the speaker and his words. In the delivery of the divine word, however, everything hangs upon the discernible *distance*."[20] Precisely because we are dealing with the word of God, and not simply some political ideology or religious idea, the most important thing the preacher can do is to be as factual as he can, as concrete as the word itself.

3. The Reliance on Illustrations and Forms

It is true that Bonhoeffer is in reaction to, and even in denial of, the emotional component in preaching, not to mention the emotionalism that accompanies music and song. It is historically true that he scorned the emotionalism of the pietists, accusing them of offering nothing more via their emotionalism than a religious striptease and incapable, therefore, of offering a riposte to the idolatry of the German Christian movement.[21] However, the source of his antipathy to techniques, or coercive pressure, on the part of the preacher derives not just from a reaction to the worst excesses of subjectivism, but from a long-held conviction about the power of the word to create its own congregation. In this sense he has a great deal in common with P. T. Forsyth, who likewise encouraged preachers to trust the word, rather than embellish it.[22] Illustrations are all well and good. In recent years a veritable cottage industry of sermon illustration books has grown up, offering the preacher a whole range of stories, sometimes jokes, and even personal testimonies, to support the preachers point. But the problem is that so often the illustration ends up dominating more than the message. The thing the congregation remember is not so much the message as the anecdote. Indeed, I can remember

---

evangelism that appeals to the emotions, experience and religious immediacy. For Bonhoeffer, the conversions that are elicited from such campaigns are not truly of the Spirit because they are not rooted in the text. Even the evangelistic sermon, as far as Bonhoeffer is concerned, must be textual. See *B:WP*, 163–68.

20. *B:WP*, 171. The exception to this rule for Bonhoeffer would be the sermon as testimony such as we find in the testimony of Jesus before Pilate, as well as the testimony of Timothy before many witnesses. In these words, "the distinction between ministry and person is least suggested." *B:WP*, 124.

21. See Huntemann, *The Other Bonhoeffer*, 99–112.

22. For the most definitive work on P. T. Forsyth's theology of preaching see Forsyth, *Positive Preaching*.

a cartoon once, in *Leadership* magazine I think, where the preacher is at his desk, praying earnestly to God. "Dear Lord," he prays, "please give me a sermon for this illustration."

Anyone who has preached for any length of time will know how easy this is to do. Who has not found a sermon illustration or a joke and then succumbed to the temptation to squeeze it into the sermon regardless of whether or not it is apposite to the message. It is as if the modern preacher is over-burdened by the need to interest the congregation or, worst still, entertain. For Bonhoeffer, however, this fixation on illustrations is a betrayal of the preacher's task,[23] as is our predilection towards rhetorical forms and structures. To our tendency to impose upon sermons fixed forms, sermon templates, rhetorical formulas, as well as quaint illustrations, Bonhoeffer urges preachers towards a more faithful exegesis in which rhetoric is subservient to text, in terms of the message but also the form. "The goal of the individual sermon," he stresses, "is that the text might be orally expressed and that it, rather than the structure of the ideas, might be retained by the congregation; that it might be remembered, and not the problems proposed or the illustrations told."[24] He goes on: "The text gives the sermon its form. Artificial organizational schemes and sermon forms produce pulpit orators. We don't need model sermons; sermons that are according to the text are model sermons."[25]

The implications of this stance for the modern preacher can be adduced both negatively and positively. Negatively, it warns us against spending too much time trawling through the internet to find some sentimental preacher's story. It warns us also against pre-prepared sermon templates, such as the three-point sermon. For Bonhoeffer these templates are extraneous, and not germane to the way in which Scripture comes to us.[26] Positively, it urges us to take confidence in the power of Scripture to deliver its own message as well as its own form. As Bonhoeffer puts

23. "One should be very sparing in the use of stories, illustrations and quotations. These shift attention [from the text] and usually there is no time for that. The preacher should especially guard against worn-out illustrations and untrue stories." *B:WP*, 158.

24. *B:WP*, 157.

25. *B:WP*, 157.

26. Indeed, if I have a small criticism of Tom Long's highly influential *The Witness of Preaching* it is that his suggestion of a number of sermon templates towards the end of the book which runs contrary to, and to some extent undoes, in my opinion, the main thesis of the book which is all about the preacher going out from the congregation in order to discover the Scripture. For Long's discussion of this matter and the various sermon templates see Long, *The Witness of Preaching*, 126–30.

it (again, it is best to let Bonhoeffer speak for himself): "Strict textual preaching is the true way to overcome the constant demand for more sermons. The torrent of waiting for fresh ideas disappears under serious textual work. The text has more than enough thoughts. One really only needs to say what is in it."[27]

Again, we may not want to state things so austerely. I note Calvin Miller's remark that "All in all, it must be said that humor and wistful sentiment are teachers, and illustrations that grab an audience may come from any part of the human condition and the serve the world of truth."[28] By this, he is not pandering to the need to entertain. "Entertainment," he agrees, "is a spectator sport, whereas biblical exposition is the basic work of the kingdom."[29] But even so, he raises the question as to whether we shouldn't employ a touch of humor from time to time as a mercy to those who have to listen to us. Entertainment, Miller argues, can be a servant of truth. I am inclined to agree. It is not an either/or matter in the way that Bonhoeffer suggests. As long as an illustration serves the text, opens a window on the truth, and even provides some light interlude, then not only may it be regarded as permissible, it may also be positively advantageous. But why I think Bonhoeffer is important, and why his presentation of anecdote as the antithesis of text is so pertinent to our situation is because we live at a time when anecdote is sometimes all that is offered from the pulpit, and quite clearly this will not do. If we are to be able to say with all integrity that we are Bible-believing churches, then we will need to demonstrate this by the seriousness with which we take the text, both as the source of our message, but also its form.

For Bonhoeffer, this exhortation to stay with the text is not unrelated to the importance of having the original text before us. There is simply no substitute for the preacher than working with the original text, not least because the Greek and Hebrew texts are heavy laden with imagery which, if only we gave time for it to reverberate in our imaginations, would be an endless source of primary material for our sermons.[30]

27. *B:WP*, 158.

28. Miller, *Letters to a Young Pastor*, 206.

29. *B:WP*, 200.

30. For a very helpful explanation of the difference between an illustration that undermines the biblical text and an illustration that serves the biblical text see Barnes, *The Pastor as Minor Poet*, 128–31. Barnes makes a great deal of the fact that the Bible has relatively few illustrations but plenty of images. It is these images that the preacher needs to plunder.

Which is not to say that we should be quoting the Greek to our congregations, nor that we should make the Greek say more than it means. I knew a preacher once whose handling of the Greek made the *Amplified Bible* seem like the *Reader's Digest*.[31] But even so, since the Bible comes to us in ancient languages it behoves us as preachers to master them as much as we can.

Conclusion

Bonhoeffer's lectures on preaching are perhaps the strongest defence you will ever find of biblical expository preaching. Indeed, he sees no difference in the end between preaching and Bible study. And if by reading his lectures all we come away with is a greater passion for reading the Bible, as opposed to better techniques for preaching a good sermon, then Bonhoeffer would most certainly feel he had done his job. For sure, like all good preachers actually, he overcooks his point. There are dichotomies in Bonhoeffer's understanding of the church in worship that are unnecessary, and simply derive from the unique context he was in. In one sense, given the widespread capitulation of the German church to Nazi ideology he could do no other than to articulate a theology that stressed objectivity and emotional restraint. But why I think Bonhoeffer is essential reading for anyone about to embark on a preaching ministry in the church, and why I think seasoned preachers should read it at least once a year, is because he is relentless in his insistence that the heart of Christian worship is a proclamation. Without a word from God, then all we have is cult and liturgy, but not the formation of a Christian congregation in God's image. In fact, so great is Bonhoeffer's concern to let the word of God form the congregation that even the lectionary, which has often been a haven for those wanting to retain a healthy regard for the whole counsel of God, comes in for criticism: the reason being that the lectionary itself can impose artificial constructs on the word, thus ignoring vast chunks of Scripture. Hence, Bonhoeffer's preference, which is my preference in fact, for preaching through whole books of the Bible, because in this way the preacher is forced to consider not only the plain meaning of the text, but the whole thrust of the canon. "A preacher," he argues, "should not be afraid of continuous

---

31. For a useful guide to some of ways in which preachers can so easily mishandle the text see Carson, *Exegetical Fallacies*, 25–90.

preaching from whole books, including even Romans and the gospel of John. The *lectio continua* holds the middle ground between the pericope series and the free choosing of one's own texts"[32]

One of the delights about reading through Bonhoeffer's lectures is that in the midst of some fairly complex theological argumentation you come across some little piece of practical advice. Indeed, the last few lectures are fairly full of practical wisdom on all kinds of matters relating to the preacher and the congregation, and what it does is remind us, as if we needed reminding, that Bonhoeffer was working with ministers at the coal face rather than students in the academy. Many of these students would go on to lose their lives for the sake of the gospel. It reminds us also that Bonhoeffer was not without his own little peculiarities. For instance, (and maybe the fact that I am writing this in the season of Advent has something to do with my noticing this particular piece of advice), the Christmas sermon, he says, should be started no earlier than four weeks before Christmas "so that it will not be a message that is not in the Christmas spirit."[33]

Another amusing piece of advice is to do with that odd time that most preachers I know struggle with, namely the period before the delivery of the sermon. Not knowing oftentimes where to look and what to do during the liturgy, Bonhoeffer counsels his students to take care. "The congregation should be looked at calmly during the liturgy," he notes. "The preacher should neither stare at the ceiling or at the floor. But he should also not have a fixed stare at the congregation as if he is counting heads and checking over who is there."[34] I love this piece of advice, just as I love what comes next, because not only does it speak to our nervousness before the sermon, but also our weariness after it. To preachers, like myself, who find themselves hanging around after the sermon, anxious to know if anyone has connected with my words, Bonhoeffer takes us in hand and counsels us to let go. After all, if the word is truly the word, if it truly has a momentum of its own, then for all the comments of the sermon feedback committee (which sometimes comes in the form of some awkward person at the door afterwards) the truth is we have no idea how Christ has been present in the sermon. Therefore, the best thing we can do, says Bonhoeffer, is to go home. "You have done your work, leave and

32. *B:WP*, 160.

33. *B:WP*, 148.

34. *B:WP*, 152.

go and get your glass of beer and let the word of God take its free course; God will care for that."[35]

To read Bonhoeffer on preaching is to be forced to think counter-intuitively and for this reason alone I would commend him to aspiring preachers. In a culture where the word has been increasingly humiliated, to use a phrase of Jacques Ellul, where music and symbol have become the staple diet of many Christian congregations, Bonhoeffer forces us to return to the sources. To a church culture that has become obsessed with numbers, with statistics on church attendance, with trying to get bums on seats, Bonhoeffer is a voice crying in the wilderness. "Church going," he says, "must stand the test of whether or not the church is maturing in scriptural knowledge and in a growing ability to judge various doctrines."[36] The opening up of Bibles among the members of the congregation, in order that they might follow the text, is a far less deceiving indication of the work of the preacher, he argues, than any church attendance list. It is, after all, what preaching is all about. More important than the numerical size of the congregation is the fact that people are being transformed by the encounter with the Christ of the sermon.

35. *B:WP*, 176.
36. *B:WP*, 158.

3

Prophetic Preaching
from Old Testament Narrative Texts

Steven D. Mathewson

A FEW YEARS AGO, I stumbled onto an insight about the book of Judges that changed the way I preach the narrative texts of the Old Testament. The insight had to do with where Judges fits in the canon of Scripture. I grew up considering Judges to be one of the "historical books" because it resides in that category in the English Bible's classification of Old Testament books. To my surprise, though, I discovered that the Hebrew Bible categorizes it quite differently. The Hebrew Bible classifies Judges, along with Joshua, Samuel, and Kings as "former prophets." This insight created a shift in my thinking. I began seeing Judges as a prophetic book. To be designated as one of the "former prophets," I realized, Judges must convey a prophetic message just like the "latter prophets" such as Isaiah, Jeremiah, or Amos. The only difference lies in the kind of literature the prophet used in the "forth-telling" of his message. Judges and the other former prophets use narrative as the vehicle for communicating their prophetic message. It dawned on me that my preaching from Judges must be prophetic if I am to respect the author's intent.[1]

---

1. Block makes a similar point, arguing that "by classifying Judges as a prophetic work," it "carries a paraenetic/homiletical agenda" and "represent an extended sermon, or series of sermons" which "draws its 'texts' from the real historical experiences of the Israelites in the premonarchic period. But like a modern preacher, the biblical author selects, organizes, arranges, shapes, and crafts his material for maximum effect" *Judges, Ruth*, 52.

This insight got me thinking about how other narrative books or texts reside in the Torah, the first five books of the Hebrew Bible. While "Torah" is usually translated as "law," it is actually a broad term that means "teaching" or "instruction."[2] So the classification of the first five books of the Hebrew Bible deems them to be books of teaching or instruction. How is this teaching or instruction communicated? Once again, narrative literature plays a key role. Genesis is predominantly narrative. Exodus contains quite a bit of narrative. A few narratives appear in Leviticus, Numbers, and Deuteronomy.

What I am arguing is that the appearance of so many narrative books and texts in the Torah and former prophets sections of the Hebrew Bible tells us something about the purpose of these books and texts. While they communicate in story, these narrative texts communicate a prophetic message or at least convey instruction or teaching. Gordon J. Wenham concludes that there is "a normative claim in historical narrative that fiction for all its interest rarely makes."[3]

This means, then, that we cannot pit propositional against narrative. Nor can we assume that narrative texts do not contain propositions. Rather, we must recognize that the narratives of the Hebrew Bible communicate theology. To be sure, the communication is subtle. But we cannot confuse subtlety with non-propositional. As Wenham observes, "Old Testament narratives . . . seldom contain explicit moral judgements, but much more often leave the events to speak for themselves."[4] In this respect, narratives resemble a child's dot-to-dot picture. Despite initial appearances, there is a picture. But this picture does not emerge until the child connects the dots, drawing a line from one dot to another. Narrative works this way. The preacher must connect the dots. But at the end, rather than having a picture-less collection of dots, some kind of image emerges. The image has to do with how God's people worship and serve him.

If a narrative issues a prophetic challenge of some sort, how does a preacher go about discovering it and then preaching it? A decade ago, I presented a fairly detailed exegetical and homiletical process in my book, *The Art of Preaching Old Testament Narrative*.[5] Since that time, I have continued to preach from narrative texts and fine-tune my approach. The

---

2. Hupping, et al., *The Jewish Bible*, 2.

3. Wenham, *Story As Torah*, 12–13.

4. Ibid., 14.

5. Mathewson, *The Art of Preaching Old Testament Narrative*.

present chapter will walk preachers through this approach in order to help them preach these texts more effectively. Those who have not read *The Art of Preaching Old Testament Narrative* may wish to work through it at some point to gain more detailed insight into the process. Those who have read it will find this chapter worthwhile as it supplements, augments, and clarifies the approach I presented a decade ago.

Discovering the Prophetic Challenge by looking at the "ACTS" of a Narrative

The place to begin is studying the text itself. Stories work differently than wisdom texts or psalms or epistles. So preachers need to follow an exegetical process which tracks the way in which a narrative communicates. A decade ago, I proposed an exegetical process which pays attention to the conventions of narrative literature and leads a preacher to discover a story's "big idea."[6] Since then, I have latched onto an acronym which helps preachers summarize what they need to examine in order to discover the prophetic message communicated by a narrative text. I now counsel readers and preachers of Old Testament narrative texts to look for the "ACTS." That is a fairly easy acronym to remember if you think of a narrative as a play in several "acts"—as in Act 1, Act 2, and so forth. Each letter in the term "ACTS" represents a particular feature of an Old Testament Narrative text.

1. *A is for Action.*

When I read an Old Testament narrative through the first time, I begin by looking at how the action or the plot develops since these stories focus more on the action than on the development of particular characters.[7] Furthermore, as Israeli scholar Shimon Bar-Efrat observes, "The plot serves to organize events in such a way as to arouse the reader's interest and emotional involvement, while at the same time imbuing the events with meaning."[8] Basically, Old Testament narratives follow the flow of stories from all times and cultures by working the axis of crisis and resolution. So, a wise preacher will read a story and ask: what is the crisis and how is it resolved? The crisis may be a problem, an opportunity,

6. Ibid., 31–90.

7. Ska, "*Our Fathers Have Told Us,*" 17.

8. Bar-Efrat, *Narrative Art in the Bible*, 93.

or a challenge. The resolution may be a happy ending (in which case the story is labelled as a "comedy") or a tragic ending (in which case the story is labelled as a "tragedy"). Prior to the crisis, there is a section which literary scholars call "exposition" which provides the information to set up the story. This section may run for a few sentences or entire paragraphs. A few stories may include a conclusion, or dénouement, which summarizes the implications of the resolution for the characters.

2. *C is for Characters.*

Of course, it is the people who make the stories interesting. Wise preachers will pay careful attention to the characters and how they relate to each other. Literary scholars have devised various sorts of schemes to account for how characters function and relate to each other in a story. My counsel to preachers is to keep it simple and look mainly for "protagonists" (central characters who are most indispensable to the plot), "antagonists" (main adversaries or forces arrayed against central characters), and "foils" (characters who heighten the central character by providing a contrast or occasionally a parallel).[9] When I ask students to give me the name of the story recorded in 1 Samuel 17, they typically reply: "David and Goliath." On a literary level, however, this story is the story of "David versus Saul." Goliath is the challenge both characters face. David is the protagonist, while Saul functions both as the antagonist and foil. In this story, "the future king and present king respond differently to Goliath, revealing their fitness to occupy the throne of Israel."[10]

3. *T is for Talking.*

The statements or speeches made by the characters are worthy of a separate category of analysis. As Robert Alter observes, "Dialogue is made to carry a large part of the freight of meaning."[11] So preachers should look to what the characters say for clues as to the author's intended prophetic message. A classic example is Joseph's statement in Genesis 50:20 which summarizes the meaning of the entire Joseph cycle as well as the immediate story in Genesis 49:29—50:26: "You intended to harm me, but God intended it for good to accomplish what is now being done, the saving of many lives."

9. Mathewson, *The Art of Preaching Old Testament Narrative*, 58.
10. Ibid. See also Brueggemann, *First and Second Samuel*, 124–25.
11. Alter, *The Art of Biblical Narrative*, 37.

4. *S is for Setting.*

A final feature for consideration is the setting of the story. Wise preachers will look both at a story's historical-cultural setting and its literary setting for clues to its meaning. A preacher analyzes the historical-cultural setting by asking, "Where did the story happen? Is there any significant geographical movement within the story? When did this story take place? During what season or time of year? What was happening in Israel's history at the time?"[12] Equally crucial is an understanding of a narrative's literary setting. This has to do with an episode's location and role within a larger narrative. For example, the 1 Samuel 17 narrative takes place early in a "dynastic defense" section running from 1 Samuel 15 to 2 Samuel 8. This section defends the replacement of Saul's house with David's house on Israel's throne.[13]

Proclaiming the Prophetic Challenge in a Gospel-Centered Sermon

Once a preacher has done the exegetical work, the hardest part of the sermon preparation task begins. In this respect, preaching an Old Testament narrative text resembles climbing Mount Everest. David Brashears, the first American to scale Mount Everest twice, claims: "Getting to the summit is the easy part; it's getting back down that's hard."[14] The difficulty preachers face is proclaiming the prophetic challenge in a sermon that is gospel-centered and points listeners to Christ. So we need to consider how a preacher is to proceed with crafting a gospel-centered sermon once the exegetical work has been completed.[15]

A helpful place to begin is a 1970 doctoral dissertation, *Sola Scripture: Problems and Principles in Preaching Historical Texts*, by Sidney Greidanus.[16] His dissertation explored a controversy which raged in the Reformed churches in Holland just prior to World War II over how to

12. Mathewson, *The Art of Preaching Old Testament Narrative*, 68.

13. See Wolf, "Implications of Form Criticism for Old Testament Studies," 303–6.

14. Krakauer, *Into Thin Air*, 277.

15. The material in the remainder of the chapter first appeared in and has been adapted from Mathewson, "An Exercise in Theology and Ethics," an unpublished paper delivered to the Old Testament Narrative Literature Section of the Evangelical Theological Society at its annual meeting in New Orleans, Louisiana, on November 19, 2009.

16. Greidanus, *Sola Scriptura*.

preach "historical texts"—that is, Old Testament narrative texts. Within these Dutch Reformed churches, some preachers advocated an "exemplary approach" in which the characters provide models to imitate or avoid. Others in these same churches argued for a "redemptive-historical approach" (or "Christocentric" approach) which proclaims how the story points forward to the person and work of Christ, the eternal Logos who is at work throughout history. Greidanus essentially argued for a mediating position. He agreed with the redemptive-historical side that a sermon on a historical text must be *theocentric* (God-centered) because these texts intend to proclaim the acts of God. He also agreed with the exemplary side that this proclamation must be *relevant*, communicating the "ethical thrust" of a passage within the light of the author's theocentric framework.[17] Greidanus has since argued for a much stricter Christ-centered approach in his 1999 work, *Preaching Christ from the Old Testament: A Contemporary Hermeneutical Method*. He now counsels preachers to move from the Old Testament text to the incarnate Christ.[18]

The approach, or model, I propose aligns roughly with the mediating approach suggested by Greidanus in his 1970 doctoral dissertation and further developed in his 1988 work, *The Modern Preacher and the Ancient Text: Interpreting and Preaching Biblical Literature*.[19] My model asks three key questions once the exegetical work on a narrative text has been completed.[20]

1. *What theological message does this story communicate?*

Here the goal is to identify the theology communicated by the narrative. Daniel Block argues: "The key to authoritative preaching from Old Testament narratives is to discover the theology that is reflected and expressed in the text."[21] Such a discovery is possible because "Biblical narrators were concerned not only to describe historical events, but also to interpret them. Indeed, it is in the authors' interpretation that we find the permanent message."[22] This interpretation will align, of course, with the overall message of a book.

17. Ibid., 224–26.

18. Greidanus, *Preaching Christ from the Old Testament*, 36; 233.

19. Greidanus, *The Modern Preacher and the Ancient Text*. See pages 188–226 for his discussion of "Preaching Hebrew Narratives."

20. For a thorough description of the exegetical process used to study an Old Testament narrative, see Mathewson, *The Art of Preaching Old Testament Narrative*, 31–90.

21. Block, "Tell Me the Old, Old Story," 413.

22. Ibid.

One of Haddon Robinson's categories can help preachers answer this first question. Robinson counsels preachers to look for "the vision of God" in a text—that is, the aspect or attribute of God's character which the biblical writer highlights.[23]

2. *How does the story's theology connect with the Bible's larger story or meta-narrative?*

This second question enables a preacher to prepare a gospel-based, Christ-centered sermon without drawing dubious lines from the story to Christ. Bryan Chapell's perspective is worth pondering:

> Even if a preacher does not specifically mention an aspect of Christ's earthly ministry in a sermon, it can still be Christ-centered. As long as a preacher explains the ways in which God uses a text to reveal his plan, purposes, and/ or reasons for redemption, the sermon leads listeners away from human-centered religiosity. Exposition is Christ-centered when it discloses God's essential nature as our Provider, Deliverer, and Sustainer whether or not Jesus is mentioned by name.[24]

So, this second question links the theology of a story with the gospel because the Bible's larger story *is* the gospel. The Gospel Coalition frames the story of the Bible like this: *God providentially brings about his eternal good purposes to redeem a people for himself and restore his fallen creation, to the praise of his glorious grace.*[25] To state this another way, the Bible is the story of God re-establishing his presence among his people.[26] This restoration of God's presence is accomplished through the twin elements of the gospel—the death and resurrection of Jesus Christ (1 Cor 15:1–8).

3. *What admonition or exhortation does this story offer?*

---

23. Robinson, *Biblical Preaching*, 94.

24. Chapell, *Christ-Centered Preaching*, 303.

25. This statement appears in The Gospel Coalition's "theological Vision for Ministry" in II, 1 (http://thegospelcoalition.org/about/foundation-documents/vision/).

26. This statement of the Bible's storyline does not deny that the Bible is the story of redemption. It simply presses the issue further by asking: "From what and to what are God's people redeemed?" We are redeemed from sin's bondage to life in the presence of God. On the presence of God as a unifying theme in the Bible, see Beale, *The Temple and the Church's Mission*, 23–27; 365–402. See also Dempster, *Dominion and Dynasty,* 45–50; 231–34.

If the first question identifies the theological message of the story and the second question identifies how the story and its theological message connect to the overall storyline of the Bible, this third question identifies the prophetic challenge issued by the story.

This third question reflects my disagreement with a strict Christ-centered approach when it says: "We do not confront men with Christ by preaching theological ideas nor by ethical exhortations, but by rehearsing the saving events witnessed in Scripture."[27] But this approach is, I believe, unnecessarily reductionistic. When the apostles spoke of the gospel and rehearsed its saving events, they issued a call for nonbelievers to believe (see Acts 2:38–41 and 1 Cor 15:1–2) and a call for believers to align their behavior with the gospel (see Gal 2:14).[28] The following statement by D. A. Carson is worth pondering. He insists on gospel-centered preaching, and he encourages preachers to locate texts of Scripture—including narrative texts—within the redemptive flow of Scripture. Yet, in a recent interview conducted by R. C. Sproul, Carson commented:

> Many Christian preachers have preached series from the life of Abraham or the life of David, and it has been not uncommon [for them] to preach almost moralizing sermons. David was good here, let's be good. David was bad there, let's not be bad. And that's about all you see from it whether from Abraham or Daniel or David. Everything becomes a moralizing lesson and that's all. Then they become aware of biblical-theological categories and see how David is the beginning of the Davidic dynasty and how . . . through the promises given to Abraham all the families of the earth will be blessed. So they begin to preach in these broader categories and forget the moral categories. But then you . . . remember how Paul in 1 Corinthians 10:1–13 can read Israel's history and draw moralizing lessons. In other words, one of the ways that the Old Testament is read on occasion is precisely to draw moralizing lessons. Elijah was a man as we are, yet he persevered. We should be prayer warriors as he was. There's no deep typology. It

27. Donald G. Miller as quoted by Greidanus, *Preaching Christ*, 235–36.

28. Conversely, a sermon is sub-gospel and sub-Christian when it calls listeners to be or to do something without presenting it as a response to God's grace in the power that God's grace provides through the finished work of Jesus Christ. So then, gospel-centered preaching does not preclude imperative. Rather, it always grounds the imperative (what you must do) in the indicative (what God has done for you in Christ).

is an argument by analogy. He's somebody to imitate. It's application.[29]

Preachers, then, need not pit a redemptive approach against a didactic approach. The two can and should coexist in our preaching. As Wenham concludes, "Old Testament narrative books do have a didactic purpose, that is, they are trying to instill both theological truths and ethical ideals into their readers."[30]

An Example: Preaching Jephthah's Vow in Judges 11:29–40

To help preachers move from theory to practice, I would like to apply the methodology I have suggested to the narrative of Jephthah's vow in Judges 11:29–40. This episode appears in the larger Jephthah story in Judges 10:6—12:7.

Here is a brief exegetical summary of the story. In terms of the *Action* or plot, this story is a tragedy which begins in prosperity and descends into tragedy. The crisis has to do with the battle Jephthah prepares to undertake as well as a vow he makes. As Jephthah prepares to advance against the Ammonites, he vows to offer whatever comes out of the door of his house as a burnt offering if he returns victorious. The resolution takes place in two stages. First, Jephthah returns victorious. But then the story takes a tragic turn. His daughter comes out of his house when he returns, and it ends up that "he did to her as he had vowed. And she was a virgin" (Judg 11:39). Jephthah's line, then, has ended since she was an only child.

There are two main *Characters* in the story: Jephthah and his daughter. Jephthah is clearly the protagonist, having been introduced as a "mighty warrior" (Judg 11:1) and appearing as another one of the deliverers God raised up to save his people from enemy oppression. It is hard to know whether to classify Jephthah's daughter as an antagonist or a foil. This is where literary labels can break down since they cannot always describe precisely a character's role. It is interesting to note that Jephthah's daughter is not named, perhaps a reflection of her tragic situation. She takes her father's vow as seriously as he takes it and insists that

29. "R. C. Sproul Interviews D. A. Carson on Biblical Exegesis," Taylor on April 7, 2011 on his "Between Two Worlds" blog on The Gospel Coalition website. The quoted section of the interview, which I have lightly edited for style, runs from about 21:22 to about 23:08. Carson's answer is in response to a question on canonical interpretation.

30. Wenham, *Story As Torah*, 3.

he fulfil it. Whether right or wrong (and I will discuss this matter below), she is complicit with him in his action.

Moving on to the *Talking* or dialogue, there are three main statements. The first is Jephthah's actual vow in Judges 11:30–31. The second is Jephthah's expression of grief in Judges 11:35. The third is his daughter's instructions to carry out his vow, yet to give her time to roam the hills and grieve with her friends in Judges 11:36. What these statements establish is the absolute seriousness with which Jephthah and his daughter took this vow. The latter two statements reflect the grief which accompanies its fulfilment.

Finally, when examining the *Setting*, we find that the historical-cultural and literary settings overlap. This story happens later in the "cycles" section of Judges—a series of cycles which spiral downward as life in Israel further deteriorates with each new deliverer who has been raised up to deliver the people from enemy oppression. With the Jephthah cycle, Israel has reached a new low which will only be eclipsed by the final cycle in which Samson is the deliverer. The story continues the theme in Judges, then, that God's people disintegrate when they become like their Canaanite neighbors.

What, then, is the prophetic challenge of this story, and how should a preacher preach it? Quite frankly, this is one of the most challenging stories in Judges to interpret. To pull out exegetical threads together and identify the story's big idea, we must wrestle with the three key questions presented earlier.

1. *What theological message does this story communicate?*

The answer to this question hinges on our view of Jephthah's vow. Should we understand the making and fulfilment of this vow in a positive or negative light?

John Sailhamer argues that Jephthah did not offer his daughter as a burnt offering but dedicated her to the Lord for lifelong service. Sailhamer notes that the vows in Leviticus 27:1–13—dedicating a person to the service of the Lord (27:1–8) and dedicating an animal for an offering to the Lord (27:9–13)—"*are* virtually identical to Jephthah's situation and use the same terminology."[31] Jephthah's vow, Sailhamer concludes, "entailed the alternative of dedication to the Lord or burnt offering, and in the case of his daughter he fulfilled it by dedicating her to the Lord for

31. Sailhamer, *NIV Compact Bible Commentary*, 211.

life."[32] He finds further support in "the recurring theme of 'dedication to the Lord,' found throughout the subsequent narratives."[33]

This theme of "dedication to the Lord" aligns with other clues—the question of Jephthah's legitimacy, Jephthah's lack of an inheritance from his father or through his daughter, and Jephthah's conviction that ownership of the land does not rest on inheritance on the will of God (see Judg 11:24)—to reveal a central theme in the Jephthah narrative. Sailhamer writes: "It appears, then, that a central theme of the Jephthah narrative is the sovereign will of God in choosing and using those whom he pleases. Jephthah's claim to rule in Israel was not based on birth, tact, or judgment. It was rather based solely on his zeal to trust God and do his will."[34]

However, most Hebrew Bible scholars today offer a negative assessment of Jephthah. They argue that Jephthah, influenced by pagan religion, made an inappropriate vow and actually offered his daughter as a burnt offering. Several lines of reasoning, I believe, support this negative assessment and conclusion regarding Jephthah's vow.

First, the downward spiral of Israel into moral decline throughout the so-called "cycles section" (3:7—16:31) extends to the judges or "saviors" as well. David Janzen notes that "the six major judges become progressively less effective and less faithful. . . . The judges are progressively less able to bring out troops for battle, and at the end Samson will fight alone."[35] Block says: "The placement of the Jephthah cycle immediately after the story of Abimelech also invites a negative comparison with this man."[36] By this point in the "cycles' section," then, readers can only expect that Jephthah will continue the downward trend.

Second, when Jephthah's vow is viewed in light of this decline in the judges/ saviors as well as in the nation, it appears to accommodate paganism rather than expressing allegiance to Yahweh. K. Lawson Younger Jr. concludes: "There is little doubt that Jephthah's vow is nothing short of making a deal with the deity, an attempt to exert control over God—a practice familiar to pagans, who believe in the manipulation of the gods for human purposes."[37]

32. Ibid.

33. Ibid.

34. Ibid., 210–11.

35. Janzen, "Why the Deuteronomist Told about the Sacrifice of Jephthah's Daughter," 343.

36. Block, *Judges*, 378.

37. See Younger Jr., *Judges, Ruth* , 262.

Third, this interpretation is the most natural reading of the text. A literal translation of the final two clauses of Judges 11:31 reads: "and it will be to Yahweh, and I will make it go up as a burnt offering." Some want to translate the Hebrew conjunction "and" (Hebrew, *we*) at the beginning of the second clause as "or." This turns the two clauses into two alternatives: dedication in case of a human being or a burnt offering in case of an animal. However, it is appropriate to translate "and" as "or" only when the items joined by "and" are clear alternatives such as in Judges 1:33 (Beth-Shemesh *or* Beth-Anath) or in Judges 5:8 (shield *or* spear). Besides, Hebrew has another conjunction, "or" (*ŏ*), which clearly distinguishes between items. The narrator even uses "or" (*ŏ*) in Judges 11:34 ("no son *or* daughter"), as well as in Judges 18:19, 19:13, 21:22. So he could have easily used it in Judges 11:31 had he wanted to distinguish between dedication and burnt offering. Additionally, the language in Judges 11:31 is similar to the prophet Jeremiah's description of child sacrifice in Jeremiah 19:5: "to burn their children in the fire as burnt offerings to Baal." Furthermore, while the vow's fulfilment in Judges 11:39 does not use "burnt offering" language as in 11:31, it is nevertheless specific: "and he did to her his vow which he vowed." This terse report "reflects the narrator's hesitation to speak of such a horrible, detestable act."[38]

Fourth, Jephthah's endowment with the Spirit need not result in a vow which was made and fulfilled honorably. Barry Webb has demonstrated the presence of two sequences in the story of Jephthah's vow. In the first (A), Jephthah's endowment with the Spirit leads to his victory over Ammon. In the second (B), Jephthah's vow plus his victory over Ammon leads to the fulfilment of the vow. Webb concludes: "While the victory is *causally* related to the Jephthah's endowment with the Spirit, it is only *incidentally* related to the vow. . . . While divine determinism operates in sequence A it is not clear whether or not it operates in sequence B."[39] Furthermore, "Jephthah has received no visitation, as Gideon, nor any prophetic word, as Barak (4:6–7)."[40]

Fifth, the offering of Jephthah's daughter as a burnt offering certainly fits with the slaughter motif in the previous story (Abimelech) and the following episode (Ephraimites). Block observes: "Abimelech had sacrificed his Israelite half-brothers at the altar of his own ambition so he

---

38. Mathewson, *Joshua and Judges*, 179.
39. Webb, *The Book of the Judges*, 63.
40. Ibid., 65.

could rule over his Canaanite half-brothers. Jephthah did one better—he sacrificed his own daughter and with her himself that he might rule over a tribe of his Israelite half-brothers."[41] Robert O'Connell suggests that "Jephthah's slaughter of his daughter (11:39–40) parallels microcosmically Gilead's slaughter of its tribal 'brother' Ephraim (12:1–6)."[42]

Sixth, "it is hard to imagine how the fate of Jephthah's daughter would lead to a four-day annual festival of lament if she had simply been dedicated to the lifelong service of Yahweh as a virgin. A response of this magnitude suggests a more tragic end."[43]

So if Jephthah actually sacrificed his daughter as a burnt offering, what then is the theological message of this story? Janzen's assessment provides a good starting point:

> The portrayal of the sacrifice fits the pattern of moral decline in the book of Judges, and it forms an integral and interconnected part of the story of Jephthah as a whole. Moreover, as part of this whole it reflects an important theme stressed elsewhere by the history: *when Israel sacrifices like foreigners do, it will act like foreigners, as well.* This is why the story of Jephthah's sacrifice is followed immediately by the story of the tribe of Ephraim, which acts just like the Ammonites, the foreign nation in this account, by invading Gilead.[44]

But we must press this assessment further. How does this story reflect this theme? Why does Israel sacrifice and worship like foreigners? Why does Israel continue down the path of being Canaanized? Why do God's people continue to self-destruct by disobeying God and adopting their values from their pagan neighbors? The answer is ignorance of Torah. Several scholars see this as a key idea, if not the main idea, in the story. Lillian Klein believes that the sad outcome could have been prevented "had Jephthah 'known' his faith."[45] Comparing Jephthah to Samson, she writes: "Jephthah is uninformed and Samson is unthinking."[46] Similarly, Block observes: "Jephthah lacked understanding of the theological origins of his nation and had no appreciation for Israel as a community—a

---

41. Block, *Judges*, 378.
42. O'Connell, *Rhetoric of the Book of Judges*, 189.
43. Mathewson, *Joshua and Judges*, 179.
44. Janzen, "Sacrifice of Jephthah's Daughter," 339. The italics are mine.
45. Klein, *The Triumph of Irony*, 92.
46. Ibid., 131.

community of blood, descended from one ancestor, and of faith, united in the worship of Yahweh their redeemer."[47] O'Connell also comments on Jephthah's ignorance: "Given the reader's knowledge that Jephthah's vow achieves nothing toward his success against the Ammonites—*knowledge to which Jephthah was never privy*—Jephthah's sacrifice of his daughter can only be pathetic."[48] Younger offers this assessment of the story: "The irony is stark. Jephthah delivers the Israelites from the Ammonites, who along with their neighbors sacrifice their children to their gods; then he sacrifices his daughter to Yahweh, who does not accept human sacrifice! In this way, Jephthah exhibits his ignorance of God's Law (Torah)."[49] Younger makes a further comment about Jephthah's responsibility to fulfil his vow: "While it was a sin to break a vow (Num 30:2), God did provide for the redemption of vows, vows made without full reflection of their ramifications. Tragically, had he known about this, Jephthah could have redeemed his daughter (Lev 27:1–8)."[50]

To summarize, the story of Jephthah's vow advances the storyline of Judges with its moral and societal breakdown. Israel is self-destructing by disobeying God and adopting the values of its pagan neighbors. Rather than wiping out the Canaanites, the Israelites are wiping out each other! Shalom is increasingly elusive. The story of Jephthah's vow highlights a major cause: ignorance of Torah. The ignorance of Torah takes God's people farther down the path of towards ruin.[51]

2. *How does the story's theology connect with the Bible's larger story or meta-narrative?*

When we think about the story of Jephthah's vow in its larger context, we encounter a Scripture passage which challenges the interpretation I

---

47. Block, *Judges*, 387.

48. O'Connell, *The Rhetoric of the Book of Judges*, 185. The italics are mine.

49. Younger, *Judges*, 262.

50. Ibid., 265.

51. Is this the only way to understand this story? Webb cautions interpreters that "the text is highly resistant to any simplistic, reductionist form of interpretation" due to the "implicit, indirect means" through which meaning is conveyed (Webb, *Judges*, 77). I am not claiming that the meaning of a rich text like the story of Jephthah's vow can be reduced to a single sentence. But I do believe that the main theological message into which and from which all the other ideas flow can be summarized in a single sentence. This becomes critical for preaching. I have often heard Haddon Robinson, the dean of the "big idea" approach to preaching, say: "The problem with some sermons is not that they contain too many ideas. The problem is that they contain too many *unrelated* ideas."

have presented. Hebrews 11:32 cites Jephthah as an example of faith. The full list includes Gideon, Barak, Samson, Jephthah, David, Samuel, and the prophets. Does this not require us to interpret the story of Jephthah's vow in a more positive light? No. In fact, we run the risk of misinterpreting the story of Jephthah's vow when we start with Hebrews 11:32 and work backward rather than starting with the Jephthah story and working forward. We must wrestle with how the original audience would have understood the Jephthah story before moving to Hebrews 11:32.

How, then, can such a tragic figure as Jephthah be cited as an example of faith? We should note that the representative list of actions in Hebrews 11:33ff. accomplished by these men "through faith" deal largely with military exploits and endurance in suffering.[52] Certainly Jephthah belongs in the category of those "who became powerful in battle and routed foreign armies" (Heb 11:34). Obviously, the writer of Hebrews had no problem citing men with major moral flaws as examples of faith because of what they accomplished on the battlefield. After all, Gideon was an idolater, Samson used his privileges largely for self-indulgence, and David committed both adultery and murder. John Calvin's comment on the examples in Hebrews 11:32 still provides a helpful perspective:

> Everything praiseworthy that they did the apostle has attributed to faith, although there was none of them whose faith did not falter. . . . Jephthah rushed headlong into making a foolish vow and was over-obstinate in performing it, and thereby marred a fine victory by the cruel death of his daughter. In every saint there is always to be found something reprehensible. Nevertheless although faith may be imperfect and incomplete it does not cease to be approved by God.[53]

So then, we do not need to reinterpret Jephthah as a virtuous man, overestimating his spiritual sensitivity to the law of Moses, particularly its prohibition of child sacrifice (see Deut 12:31; 18:10) and its provision for the redemption of vows (Lev 27:1–8).

If the story of Jephthah's vow communicates a theological message about the ignorance of Torah and the disaster this creates, then it reinforces a developing theme within the canon. This is the theme that knowing and obeying God's word leads to life and blessing, while disregarding God's word leads to ruin. This is a prominent theme throughout

---

52. See Attridge, *Epistle to the Hebrews*, 348. See also Lane, *Hebrews 9–13*, 385.

53. Calvin, *Hebrews and The First and Second Epistles of St. Peter*, 182.

Deuteronomy.[54] It also stands at the beginning of the book of Joshua. In Joshua 1:7, the second of three commands from Yahweh for Joshua to "be strong and courageous" ties in specifically to the purpose of obeying Yahweh's law.[55] The opening clause in Joshua 1:7 should be translated "Only be strong and very courageous to be careful to do all the law." The two infinitives—"to be careful to do"—specify the way in which the two imperatives should be executed.[56] This theme also stands at the beginning of the book of Psalms. Psalm 1 contrasts the blessed man with the wicked, and the blessed man's delight and meditation in Yahweh's law plays a key role in his success. Moreover, this theme continues into the new covenant. It reaches its zenith, perhaps, in 2 Timothy 3 where Paul reflects on terrible times in the last days (3:1–9) and charges Timothy to continue in the holy Scriptures which make a person wise for salvation and equipped for every good work (3:10–17).

The story of Jephthah's vow has another poignant connection with the book of Judges and the developing story of the Hebrew Bible. Yahweh's people seem unwilling and unable to obey his law. They need something more. Certainly the rhetorical effect of Judges leaves the reader crying out for something more when the book ends with an episode containing another ill-advised vow. This time, Israel took an oath not to give their daughters in marriage to the Benjamites (Judg 21:1). But when the Benjamites are all but wiped-out, the elders of Israel respond in a manner reminiscent of Jephthah. They elevate the keeping of their oath over their regard for human life. They solve their problem by encouraging the Benjamites to kidnap Israelite girls who attend the annual festival of Yahweh in Shiloh (Judg 21:15–22)! The nation has reached an all-time low. How will Israel escape her downward spiral into ruin?

Indeed, something more is needed. "This realization prepares the reader for the later promise of a new covenant which will provide the increased spiritual resources needed for obeying God's commands."[57] Jesus

---

54. See especially Deut 28:1–68 and 32:46–47.

55. Mathewson, *Joshua and Judges*, 22.

56. For this use of the infinitive construct, see Van der Merwe, Naude, and Kroeze, *A Biblical Hebrew Reference Grammar*, 155.

57. Mathewson, *Joshua and Judges*, 219. See especially Jeremiah 31:33 and Ezekiel 36:26–27. We should note that the provision of the new heart, the placement and writing of the laws upon the heart, the gift of the Spirit, and the power to walk in God's statutes do not diminish the need for new covenant believers to study and learn the Scriptures (2 Tim 2:15; 3:14; 4:2).

the Messiah inaugurated this covenant through his death.[58] Ironically, "a key minister of this new covenant will be the Apostle Paul (2 Corinthians 3:6)—a descendant of the very Benjaminites who salvaged their future by gaining wives through bloodshed and kidnapping (see Romans 11:1; Philippians 3:5)."[59]

3. *What admonition or exhortation does this story offer?*

Preachers have detected a wide variety of admonitions or exhortations in the story of Jephthah's vow.[60] For some who interpret Jephthah's vow positively, the story encourages believers to trust in God's power to overcome their past so that he can change them and use them. Those who view Jephthah negatively sometimes preach the story as a call to accept God's grace instead of working to compensate for our unworthiness before God. Others see in this story a challenge to honor the commitments we make to God regardless of the cost. Have you kept your promises? This question became the title for one preacher's sermon on Judges 11:29–40. Alternatively, some preach the story of Jephthah's vow as a warning to believers about making rash, foolish vows. For others preachers, the story calls God's people to stop their attempts to control or manipulate God to do our will since this betrays a lack of faith in God. If God had already empowered Jephthah, no vow was necessary. A strict Christ-centered approach does not look for an exhortation but views either Jephthah or his daughter as a type of Christ. For some, Jephthah is an anti-type, sacrificing his daughter's life for his own good while Christ sacrifices his own life for the good of God's children. Jephthah's daughter, then, serves as the real type of Christ, the one who willingly gave his life for us on the cross.[61] But if viewed positively, Jephthah typifies Christ's willingness to give up everything to bring salvation for God's people. Just as Jephthah's made a

---

58. See Luke 22:20; 1 Corinthians 11:25.

59. Mathewson, *Joshua and Judges*, 219.

60. An internet search of sermons on Jephthah will attest to this. In fact, most of the following examples come from internet searches I conducted in the summer and fall of 2009. I decided not to provide specific citations since the web-sites providing these sermons—mostly local churches and theological institutions—frequently change and update their content.

61. In a sense, a strict Christ-centered approach does lead to an admonition or exhortation: receive Christ as your Savior because Christ, like Jephthah's daughter, was willing to lay down his life.

sacrifice to secure the deliverance of God's people from the Ammonites, so Jesus' sacrifice delivered God's people from sin.[62]

What, then, shall we preach? As the above survey illustrates, it is not easy to pin down the prophetic challenge of the story. J. P. Fokkelman is right when he says: "He [the narrator] is rarely willing to disclose the 'moral of the tale' at the end of his story. . . . A good narrator does not want to make things easy for us by sermonizing himself all the time."[63] So, what admonition or exhortation best accounts for all of the data with the least amount of difficulty?

If the theological message of this story is that the ignorance of Torah takes God's people farther down the path towards ruin, then this story calls God's people to know the Scriptures so that they can truly know God and experience the blessings of his presence. A distorted view of God leads communities of faith—and the individuals in them—to self-destruction. "Ignorance is not bliss but disaster!"[64] Gary Inrig comments:

> I have met many Christians who think their God is like Jephthah's false view of God. He is a stern and sadistic God, a legalistic God, who squeezes the joy out of life and delights in the unpleasant. He is a God who must be bargained with, and whose favor must be earned, whose presence cannot be counted on. But that is not the God of the Bible. Unless we know God in truth, we cannot live in truth.[65]

Christopher Wright observes, "Theology and ethics are inseparable in the Bible. You cannot explain how and why Israelites or Christians lived as they did until you see how and why they believed what they did."[66] This dictum cuts both ways. Poor theology leads to poor ethics. Right theology, rooted in a careful understanding of Scripture, leads to the kind of ethics which result in the glory of God and the good of God's people. The story of Jephthah's vow communicates the urgency of knowing God truly. Yes, right theology matters because a distorted view of

---

62. Again, in a positive understanding of Jephthah's vow, his sacrifice is the dedication of his only child to life-long service as a virgin to Yahweh. This effectively ends his lineage.

63. Fokkelman, *Reading Biblical Narrative*, 148–49.

64. This is Younger Jr's sermon title for the Jephthah story. He shared it with me in a March 2007 conversation.

65. Inrig, *Hearts of Iron, Feet of Clay*, 195–96.

66. Wright, *Old Testament Ethics For the People of God.*

God leads to self-destruction.[67] Or, as Haddon Robinson puts it, "God overlooks ignorance, but ignorance can do great damage."[68]

The church urgently needs to hear this message today. Although knowledge can lead to pride (1 Cor 8:1), believers need constant reminders of God's truth (2 Pet 1:12–15).[69] Without right theology, we can miss God's grace and end up living out of guilt or trying to manipulate God.[70] Without right theology, we can end up abusing God's gifts—specifically money, sex, and power—for selfish purposes instead of kingdom purpose.[71] The effect is that we, like Jephthah, end up tearing down community instead of building up community.[72] In his classic, *Knowing God*, J. I. Packer wrote: "Disregard the study of God, and you sentence yourself to stumble and blunder through life blindfolded . . . with no sense of direction and no understanding of what surrounds you. This way you can waste your life and lose your soul."[73] But those believers who take great pains to understand Scripture and the theology it communicates will "grow in the grace and knowledge of our Lord and Savior, Jesus Christ. To him be glory both now and forever! Amen."[74]

67. This is my "big idea" or "preaching idea" for the story of Jephthah's vow.

68. See Robinson's sermon on Judges 10:1—11:40, "The Danger of a Strong Faith and a Weak Theology," on the PreachingToday.com website. The first part of Robinson's idea—"God overlooks ignorance"—deals with Hebrews 11:32 which lists Jephthah as a man of faith. Robinson emphasizes that God does not overlook unbelief. But, as Robinson notes in the second part of his idea, "ignorance can do great damage" as evidenced by the fate of Jephthah's daughter.

69. Some argue, too, from James 1:22 that the church today does not need more Bible knowledge ("hearing") as much as it needs to act on that knowledge ("doing"). However, we cannot solve the "hearing-but-not-doing" problem by de-emphasizing the "hearing" aspect. As a pastor serving in a very biblically literate congregation, I am still surprised how much confusion reigns. People still need the intake of Scripture even as they need to work on doing it.

70. Keller does a fine job correcting our misunderstanding or ignorance of God's grace in *The Prodigal God*.

71. For a helpful corrective to this problem and the idolatry behind it, see Keller, *Counterfeit Gods*.

72. This problem becomes more apparent in Jephthah's handling of the Ephraimite rebellion in the episode following the story of Jephthah's vow. Whereas Gideon had handled a previous instance of Ephraimite anger with a well-crafted diplomatic reply (Judg 8:1–3), Jephthah shows no mercy when he leads the men of Gilead against the Ephraimites (Judg 12:1–7). Although the Ephraimites had provoked the military confrontation, the narrator attributes the response of Gilead to the Ephraimites taunt that "You Gileadites are renegades from Ephraim and Manasseh" (Judg 12:4).

73. Packer, *Knowing God*, 15.

74. 2 Pet 3:18. This conclusion to Peter's second epistle flows out of a challenges to

A Final Plea

The Jepthah story certainly shows why preachers avoid Old Testament narrative texts. They are often quite difficult and demand rigorous thought and preparation from preachers. Yet, the Jephthah story also reveals why preachers cannot afford to ignore them. Old Testament narrative texts contain prophetic messages which the people of God need to hear as much today as when these texts first appeared. Preachers who ignore the stories of Genesis or Judges or 1 Kings do so to their own peril, depriving themselves and their listeners of the prophetic instruction of at least one-third of the Old Testament. May God raise up a new generation of preachers who are so committed to preaching the whole counsel of God that they preach Ruth or 2 Samuel as regularly and as faithfully as Colossians or Romans or any section of the Bible's grand story.

---

be on guard against error (3:17) which grows out of the distortion of Scripture (3:16).

4

Preaching the Darkest Psalm

Psalm 88

David M. Howard, Jr.[1]

THIRTY YEARS AGO, WHEN I began my teaching career at Bethel Seminary in St. Paul, Minnesota, I was asked to teach an elective class on the book of Psalms. Since I had never even *taken* a course on Psalms—let alone taught one!—it was something of a challenge. Yet, I immersed myself in the book of Psalms and the secondary literature that summer and managed to make my way through the term without prompting a student revolt. And, in the process, I learned much more than my students did, things that I treasure to this day.

Among the things I read was Walter Brueggemann's seminal essay on "Psalms and the Life of Faith: A Suggested Typology of Function,"[2] in which he proposed to look at the psalms through a completely different lens from the one that form criticism had used for the better part of the twentieth century.[3] He spoke of three "orientations," each of which takes

1 This essay first appeared in *Preaching Magazine,* Sept/Oct 2012, 38–43, and is used with permission.

2. Brueggemann, "Psalms and the Life of Faith," 3–32. A more accessible presentation of this typology may be found in his *Spirituality of the Psalms.*

3. The father of form criticism was Hermann Gunkel, who laid out the classic form-critical categories—praise, thanksgiving, lament, etc.—in his magisterial *Einleitung in Die Psalmen*; English translation: *Introduction to the Psalms.* A more accessible presentation is his *The Psalms: A Form-Critical Introduction.* His work has been refined by many, including Westermann, *Praise and Lament in the Psalms,* and

into account what the worshiper's stance (or "orientation") toward God is as he (or they) prays. The three categories are as follows:

1. Psalms of *orientation*, where the psalmists are in tune with God, life seems to be clicking on all cylinders, and all is well (represented primarily by creation, Torah, and wisdom psalms[4]).

2. Psalms of *dislocation* (or *disorientation*), where the psalmists feel estranged from God, life seems to have been turned upside down, and nothing seems to make sense (represented mainly by the laments).

3. Psalms of *reorientation* (or *new orientation*), where the psalmists are reconciled to God, life is good and well ordered again, and the emotional highs are palpable (represented by the thanksgiving and praise psalms). The difference from the psalms of orientation is that the psalms of reorientation usually acknowledge the tragedies of life, but from the perspective of their having been overcome by God's actions (thanksgivings), and they usually reflect an exuberance toward God that is mostly absent in the psalms of orientation (especially in the praise psalms).

In Brueggemann's discussion of the psalms of disorientation, he took particular note of Psalm 88 as the most extreme example of such a psalm. In contrast to the other psalms of disorientation, which typically end with some expression of trust or thanksgiving or praise, this psalm has none of these elements. It is a very dark psalm, and it simply ends on a very dark note.

It was the first time I had noticed what seemed to be the utter hopelessness of the psalm, and it was somewhat unnerving. What should I think about such a psalm? What could I say to my students about such a psalm? How could I preach such a psalm?

I had no answers, so I did the next best thing: I completely ignored the psalm and hoped that my students would not ask any questions about it. And it worked! For almost a decade, I managed to get through discussions on the Psalms without having to discuss this one.

Gerstenberger, *Psalms, Part 1; with an Introduction to Cultic Poetry* and *Psalms, Part 2, and Lamentations.*

4. In this essay, Brueggemann included also the hymns, since "they anticipate or remember no change," i.e., they reflect an orderly status quo (p. 7). In his later writings, he included most hymns in the third category, psalms of *reorientation* (e.g., *Spirituality of the Psalms*, 55–57).

Cowardly as it was, my avoidance of this psalm—and others like it—was not too far from what most Christians prefer to do regarding such psalms. I do not recall ever hearing a sermon from any lament psalm that addressed the lament itself head-on, except perhaps Psalm 22 as it applies to Christ's suffering, or scattered, out-of-context references to particular verses from one of these psalms. The church seems to be loath to address the full force and implications of the psalmists when they express anger with their situations, or even, it seems, at God himself.

Sheila Carney has addressed this concern in a provocatively titled article in which she pleads for an honest handling of such psalms in the context of the community of believers.[5] Speaking of unbelievers who would utter the blasphemous words of her title, she says, "For such persons, the community provides no stability, God is no anchor, the covenant has no meaning." Her point is that for believers, the opposite is true: the believing community *does* provide stability, God *is* an anchor, and the covenant is all-important.

In such a context of community, the church should welcome the difficult psalms into church life, and pastors should not shrink (as I did) from preaching from these psalms. Perhaps an exclusive diet of these psalms in public worship is not what is called for, but certainly their bold proclamation from the pulpit occasionally, and their use in other settings, including the counseling room, can help believers to embrace the full counsel of Scripture, including the difficult psalms.

So the longer I ignored Psalm 88, the more my conscience spoke to me that I should stop being such a coward, that I needed to tackle this psalm head-on in order to help my students and laypeople deal with such a difficult text. So finally, when I was asked to preach a two-part series in my home church one summer, I decided to do so. I preached the first week on "Praising God in the Good Times," choosing as my text, Psalm 113, one of the great praise psalms, and the second week on "Praising God in the Bad Times," choosing Psalm 88 as the text.

I worked hard on that sermon, undertaking my own original translation from the Hebrew three months in advance of the date when I was

---

5. Carney, "God Damn God: A Reflection On Expressing Anger in Prayer," 116–20. I certainly do not endorse her title—but neither does she, in fact: she is simply quoting what some people feel about God sometimes. Nor do I endorse some of her individual points, but her central thesis that the "cursing psalms" are undeservedly ignored in the church is well taken, as are some of her suggestions for a holistic approach to the psalms and a healthy appropriation of even the most difficult psalms.

to preach.[6] In those three months, Psalm 88 was never far from my mind. Finally, during the week before the sermon, I organized my thoughts, and then sat down to write the sermon on Saturday evening (ever the procrastinator!). Six hours later I was done.

I had coordinated with the worship team about the sermon, and so one of the hymns we sang that Sunday morning was Horatio Spafford's "It Is Well with My Soul." It is a wonderful hymn of trust in God. To the uninitiated, it might sound like the product of someone who knows nothing of the hardships of life. But in reality, Spafford wrote this hymn after he had suffered great loss: he lost his four-year-old son to scarlet fever in 1871 and that same year his business was completely destroyed in the Great Chicago Fire. Then, scarcely two years later, his four daughters perished aboard a ship that sank in mid-Atlantic. Incredibly, Spafford conceived of this hymn shortly after this, as he was on board another ship and passing over the very spot where his daughters had died.[7]

I preached the sermon on that Sunday morning, and it was received enthusiastically. Three to four times the number of people who would normally thank me for a sermon came to me to thank me for this one, many deeply moved and with tears in their eyes. I have preached it a number of times since, and I now routinely use it in my classes when we discuss the Psalms, and the feedback is very much the same.

And so, I present that sermon below, unchanged since it was first preached at Liberty Community Church in Lindenhurst, Illinois on July 14, 1991 (except for the later addition of the Romans 8:26 reference).

My prayer is that it will help others to see and experience God even in the hardest of times.

"Praising God in the Bad Times"

Joe and Marylou Bayly were a real-life couple whom God tested beyond what I think I could ever begin to endure. Joe was in the Lord's work, working in a Christian organization with students and writing for

---

6. That translation may be found in the scholarly essay that I recently published on the psalm: "Psalm 88 and the Rhetoric of Lament," 132–46; the translation is on p. 138.

7. The story of "It Is Well With My Soul" is well known and easily accessible in books such as this one: Osbeck, *101 Hymn Stories*, 126–28. It also is told in any number of Internet sites, such as this one: http://thegospelcoalition.org/blogs/justintaylor/2011/11/01/the-true-story-behind-the-hymn-it-is-well-with-my-soul/ (accessed January 16, 2012).

Christian magazines. They had a happy family. They had three sons, and a daughter.

Then, tragedy struck. One of their young sons developed leukemia. At the age of five, he died.

As Joe tells it in a book he wrote afterwards, Danny died in his own bed, with his mother and father next to him, comforting him, loving him, and telling him about Jesus' love and heaven.[8]

The family had always spoken of these things, and Danny had responded with the simple faith of a child in what his parents said.

But, this day, Danny did not want to go to heaven. He wanted to stay, to be with his mom and dad, his brothers and his sister, in his own home. He didn't want to leave all that he knew.

But, he did. He did leave. He died that day.

Then, God gave the Baylys the hope of new life again. They were expecting another baby, and they rejoiced. But, when the day came, the baby was born with a severe handicap. They named him John, but on the second day of his life, he too died.

The Baylys had lost two children. It has been said that the most severe trauma a parent can suffer is to undergo the death of a child. Statistics show that divorce rates skyrocket in families in which a child dies, when neither parent can reach out to the other beyond his or her own grief. Yet, the Baylys lost two sons.

But, God was not finished with them yet. A few short years later, their eighteen-year-old son, Joe, had a freak sledding accident. He was a hemophiliac, and he bled to death.

Seven years. Three sons. Three deaths.

Joseph Bayly wrote a poem after the death of his son Joe. Here is part of it:

> Let me alone, Lord, you've taken from me what I'd give your world. I cannot see such waste that you should take what poor men need. You have a heaven full of treasure; could you not wait to exercise your claim on this? O spare me, Lord, forgive, that I may see beyond this world, beyond myself, Your sovereign plan, or seeing not, may trust You, Spoiler of my treasure. Have mercy, Lord, here is my quitclaim.[9]

---

8. Bayly, *The Last Thing We Talk About*, 34; originally published as *The View From a Hearse.*

9. Bayly, *Psalms of My Life*, 40.

Introduction to Psalm 88.

Our psalm for today is a psalm for the bad times, for people in spots like the Baylys found themselves in. There are many psalms that teach us how to praise God in the good times, and, indeed, that's what many people think of when they think of the psalms: praising. But, it is interesting to note there are just as many psalms that teach us how to relate to God in the bad times as in the good times. The book of Psalms does not hide from the difficult issues of life.

These psalms for the bad times are called "laments," and roughly half of the Psalter is made up of them. A typical pattern is that the psalmist addresses God, tells God of his overwhelming troubles, asks God to hear his prayer, and then thanks God for hearing and answering his prayer. This last part is either from the perspective of expressing confidence that God will do this, and so he is promising to thank and praise God when he does answer, or else from the perspective of God's actually having answered the prayer; it's as though a time gap is there, and in the last verses of the psalm, the psalmist thanks God for his deliverance.

Psalm 88 is a lament, and it fits the lament pattern somewhat. But, it is unique in the Psalter—there is no other psalm like it—because it presents such a bleak picture. It *has* no praise at the end. It just ends. It ends on a very depressing note. It ends with a horrible groan. One commentator has called it the "darkest corner of the Psalter."[10]

Let's Read Psalm 88 (Please Follow Along as I Read It)

Cry of Distress (vv. 1–2)

The psalm begins with an anguished cry of distress (vv. 1–2). We should notice two things here. First, it is addressed to the Lord, "the God of my salvation" (v. 1a [RSV]; NIV: "the God who saves me"). Despite the fact that the psalmist is in a position where he feels overwhelmed by life—and even by God—he still acknowledges that this is *his* God, the God of his salvation (or deliverance).

Second, we should notice that this psalm is a "prayer" (v. 2a). Despite the overwhelmingly despairing note in the psalm, it is still a prayer, and it is addressed to God (see also v. 13).

10. White, *Evangelical Commentary on the Bible*.

Both of these points show us that the psalmist is not an atheist. He still prays to God, to *his* God.

The psalm quickly moves on, though. The psalmist is not interested in affirming this God, but rather in pouring out his troubles before him, and even in questioning him.

The Psalmist's Troubles (vv. 3–5)

In verses 3–5 we have his first recital of his troubles, and it is an impressive list. This section is permeated with images of death (Sheol, the Pit, the grave, the dead, the slain, defiled bodies). The psalmist has not died, but he uses these images to illustrate how serious his troubles are. It's an overwhelming picture of darkness and despair painted here.

God's Afflictions (vv. 6–9)

The psalmist now points to God as the source of his problems in verses 6–9. *God* has brought him down, down to the very depths (v. 6). Here again we have the darkest images imaginable: God has brought down to the lowest pit, the dark places, the depths (v. 6). The psalmist feels the weight of God's wrath, of his angry breakers crashing over him (v. 7).

And, perhaps worst of all, God has removed his friends from him; there is no one he can turn to! He is utterly alone in life (v. 8). We ourselves know from experience that the support of family, friends, and church people is crucial in helping us through the crises of life. But this psalmist feels as though he has none of these (and he states this even more forcefully at the end of the psalm, in v. 18).

The psalmist feels overwhelmed: he is trapped, and he cannot get out (v. 8c). He can't see: his eye is dimmed with grief (v. 9a). He calls out to God, in a seemingly futile attempt to get him to listen (vv. 9b-c).

Questions for God (vv. 10–12)

As a result of all of this, the psalmist turns to the only one he can, to God, and he has a series of six questions for God in verses 10–12. They all are variations on one theme: the dead do not praise God. Each question in these verses mentions the realm of the dead, along with something about God's goodness.

There are two assumptions in these verses. The first is that the psalmist feels troubled even by the threat of death, either literally or metaphorically. A second assumption, more importantly, is that the psalmist equates praising God, testifying to his goodness—his steadfast love, his faithfulness, his righteousness, his wonderful works—with *life*. One commentator has noted that, for the psalmists, the relationship between praising and not praising was the same as that between living and not living.[11] If you were alive, you were praising God.

This thought is expressed a little more clearly in a passage from Psalm 30 (another lament) (Ps. 30:9): "What gain is there in my destruction, in my going down into the pit? Will the dust praise you? Will it proclaim your faithfulness?"

In this passage we can see that the psalmist assumes that while he is alive, he will praise God. So too in Psalm 88, this assumption is behind the questions in verses 10–12. The psalmist's request for deliverance is not self-centered or self-serving, some sort of instinctual primal scream that displays the survival instinct of our species. No, it is an anguished and tormented request—yet a reasoned one—that he be spared, *so that he can praise and glorify God*! It comes out of an experience in the past where there was a better relationship with God. It is a request born out of faith in God as one who *could* deliver him, and as one whom the psalmist *wants* to praise, even if he cannot bring himself to do so right now.

Final Cries of Distress and Affliction (vv. 13–18)

The psalmist concludes the psalm by giving another desperate litany of his troubles in vv. 13–18, crying out to God and describing in more detail the ways in which God is afflicting him. The psalmist uses almost every image imaginable to get his point across. He speaks of God rejecting him, of his being afflicted—and even dying—from the days of his youth (vv. 14–15), of God's terrors, his burning anger, his dreaded assaults (vv. 15–16), passing and swirling over him (vv. 16–17).

The psalmist ends on a depressing note (v. 18), that God has taken away his closest supports, and all he has left is darkness. English translations differ on how exactly to translate the last verse of the psalm. For example, the NASB reads "You have removed lover and friend far from me;

---

11. Westermann, *Praise and Lament in the Psalms*.

my acquaintances are in darkness." The NIV reads "You have taken my companions and loved ones from me; the darkness is my closest friend."

I would suggest something similar, but I note that the text ends with a single word—"darkness"—that can easily and legitimately be seen as a final gasp or moan, a final cry of desperation, as follows: "You have removed far away from me the one who loves me and the one who is my friend, namely, those who know me!" The psalm then ends with this one stark, anguished word, a despairing cry: "Oh, Darkness!" It is like the character in Joseph Conrad's novel, *Heart of Darkness*, who, as he faced death and looked back over a totally corrupt life that he had lived, uttered his dying, despairing words: "The horror! The horror!" Darkness is all that the psalmist can see as he looks out around him. There is nothing left for him, it seems.

Conclusion

So, what can we learn from this psalm? Is there anything to learn from such a sad and bleak text?

Yes, we can learn from this psalm. I believe it teaches us at least two things. *First,* it shows us that, even in the midst of the worst circumstances, it still is possible to talk to God, to have a relationship with him. Remember, for one thing, that the psalmist is "praying" here (vv. 2, 13). He is not praying very happy thoughts, but he is still praying—he is still talking to God. In spite of his perception that God has caused his troubles, he still believes God is close enough to hear him. Remember also that the psalmist still affirms his relationship with God: he calls him the "God of my salvation" (v. 1). Despite the strain and the distance, the psalmist still acknowledges God. Finally, remember that the psalmist assumes that praise is the normal mode of life, and he wants to return to that mode (vv. 10–12). He mentions God's attributes, such as his steadfast love, his faithfulness, his righteousness, his wonderful works.

So, even this saddest of psalms affirms God.

But, we would be dishonest to the text if we were to say that this is the full message, or even the major message, of the psalm. The glimpses into the praise of God in this psalm are only that: fleeting glimpses. What this psalm gives us a much clearer picture of is lament, distress, depression, darkness, despair. These images are clear, powerful, and unrelenting. The psalm paints a dark picture over and over again, and it ends on this dark note.

So, a *second* thing we learn from this psalm is that it is part of a believer's experience in life to feel depressed, even to feel so depressed as to have nothing good to say to God. The psalmist can barely gasp a few hints about his positive feelings toward God; his true feelings are overwhelmingly negative.

In the mid-1980s, my wife Jan and I went through some very dark times. We were wanting to start a family, but it was not happening. We applied to an adoption agency, but things seemed to move at a snail's pace. We prayed consistently about this, but it seemed as though the Lord was not answering us. Well, as it turned out, he did indeed marvelously answer our prayers, giving us the two daughters that we now have, via adoption, and we wouldn't trade them for the world! They are more precious to us than life itself.

But, the depth of the despair in the time of waiting was very real. It was indeed a dark time for us, especially for Jan, who comes from a family of *nine* children. All we wanted was *one*!

Jan felt overwhelmed by God, even angry with him. She tells me of one time when we were going to have a time of prayer together, and I asked her if she wanted to pray. She was at a point where she felt she had nothing left to say to God, that she was spiritually and emotionally drained. She felt in some ways the way that the author of Psalm 88 felt, and so she said no, she didn't want to pray.

Now I've done a lot of things wrong in our marriage over the years, but one thing I did right was on that day (I know it was right, because Jan has told me so). My response was quick and short, but it was obviously the right one for that moment: "OK, I'll pray." Jan says she felt a big release, and a measure of understanding, that, when she couldn't summon the energy to pray, in some way it was OK.

It was OK with me, because I knew she had not abandoned her faith. She (and I) had many questions, but she was not turning her back on God. She just couldn't face him directly at that time, and she certainly couldn't mouth the great praises of God that are present in so much of the Psalter. She would not have felt comfortable reading some of the great praise psalms in the Psalter; she would have felt much better reading Psalm 88. But, she sat through our prayer time together, by her very presence silently affirming her relationship with God, even though at that time she could barely understand this God, this God who seemed to be blocking us from what we so earnestly desired.

There is much to be said about silence and pain. Sometimes we hear God more clearly in our pain. C. S. Lewis said (in an excellent book entitled *The Problem of Pain*) that "God whispers to us in our pleasures, speaks in our conscience, but shouts in our pains: it is [God's] megaphone to rouse a deaf world."[12] And, God himself helps us in our weakest hours. Paul writes in Romans 8:26: "In the same way, the Spirit helps us in our weakness. We do not know what we ought to pray for, but the Spirit himself intercedes for us with groans that words cannot express" (NIV).

But, we ask, what right does God have to inflict or to allow such pain, such distress, as was experienced by the Bayly family, or by the psalmist of Psalm 88? What does he know of pain?

The answer is that God does indeed know of pain. He subjected himself to it on our behalf. He himself gave his own Son, his only Son to be tortured and killed. As a father, God must have suffered unspeakable pain at some level. And, God the Son obviously suffered. He knows what our pain is like.

Yet, God also knows our limitations. Psalm 103:14 says that "he knows how we are formed, he remembers that we are dust." We may very well have times in which we cannot bring our lips even to utter a word to God, certainly not a word of praise to him. The words get stuck in our throats. Yet, the very fact that Psalm 88 is in the Bible—that it wasn't "censored" and deleted from the Bible as some sacrilegious aberration from what should be the "correct" way of relating to God—this very fact tells us that it is OK to be silent or to question God severely in our distresses.

What are your distresses today? The nice thing about the psalms is that they are so general; we can plug in our own individual troubles in the appropriate spots, and pray right along with the psalmists.

Have you ever felt like Joseph Bayly did at the death of his son Joe? Then pray a prayer like he did: "O spare me, Lord, forgive, that I may see beyond this world, beyond myself, Your sovereign plan, or seeing not, may trust you." Pray a prayer like Psalm 88. Ask God to help you trust him, even when you can't see the big picture. Don't feel guilty that you can't pray the great praises found elsewhere in the Psalter. Those are for another time, and they will come in time. Just don't let go of God completely. Remember the words of the writer of "It Is Well With My Soul," whose story we heard about this morning, who lost his family at sea.

12. Lewis, *The Problem of Pain*, 93.

Remember, too, the mature faith of Daniel's three friends, when they were to be thrown to their deaths in a fiery furnace if they would not bow down to the Babylonian king's statue. Here's what Daniel's friends said (Dan 3:17–18, NIV): "If we are thrown into the blazing furnace, the God [whom] we serve is able to save us from it, and he will rescue us from your hand, O king. But even if he does not, we want you to know, O king, that we will not serve your gods or worship the image of gold you have set up."

"*Even if he does not.*" That is the nature of the "praise" that we are to offer up to God in our weakest hours. God does not require us to sing, with Bobby McFerrin, in his Grammy-Award-winning song of a few years ago, "Don't Worry, Be Happy!" He only wants us not to abandon him; he wants us to cling to him, "the God of our salvation," so that in due time, when we can, we may again praise him.

Postscript

The above sermon was written to minister to people who are in the "disorientation" mode of life. It is a legitimate mode in which believers may find themselves, and the insights from Psalm 88 should help such persons.

But, praise be to God, believers do not need to remain in such a mode forever. The psalms and Christian experience both give abundant evidence of God's grace and a "way out" of such a mode. My wife and I can testify today that we would not trade the painful experience of infertility even if we could. For one thing, we never would have met our two daughters, who are now in their twenties and whom we still love more than life itself. We cannot imagine life without them. For another, that searing experience helped shape who we are today. In contrast to our relatively self-sufficient lives up to that point, this experience showed us that we did not have full control of those lives. We could not fix our own situation (and the attendant feelings), so we were forced into more dependence on God. Today we rejoice in the lessons of dependence on him that we learned—and are still learning!—hard as they were (and are). And, finally, the experience opened our eyes to many hurting people whom we might have looked right past had we not had this experience, and we have been able to minister to such people because of what we thought of as our travails and God's "unfairness" to us. Not in our own strength, of course, but in the spirit of comfort that Paul wrote about in 1 Corinthians 1:3–4:

"Praise be to the God and Father of our Lord Jesus Christ, the Father of compassion and the God of all comfort, who comforts us in all our troubles, so that we can comfort those in any trouble with the comfort we ourselves receive from God."

So, Jan and I now live in a mode of "new orientation," having learned many lessons. But, that does not obviate the need for the church to address those who are not there yet, who are living in the deepest disorientation. In the words of the sermon, "[God] only wants us not to abandon him; he wants us to cling to him, 'the God of our salvation,' so that in due time, when we can, we may again praise him." For those in great distress even Psalm 88 can offer some measure of comfort and hope.

5

Gender Sensitive Preaching

Reading as a Woman

Emma Ineson

A Word about Difference

I HAVE BEEN TELLING people that I am writing a book chapter about reading and preaching the Bible text as a woman. Some of them look slightly puzzled and ask, "But how is preaching as a woman any different from preaching as a man?" That's a very good question. In fact, in some respects I understand those bewildered people who are not sure whether there is even anything to be written about what it means to read and preach Scripture as a woman. I have grown up in a church that has increasingly come to accept the ministry of women in most areas (although we have still a way to go in some). I know the issues. I have heard all the arguments and mostly I now just want to get on with it. I am not often eager to have myself singled out as "a woman minister" or "a woman lecturer" or a "woman preacher." I just want to be a minister, lecturer, and preacher. When I stand up to preach on Sundays at my church or on weekdays at the college where I teach, uppermost in my thoughts is not my gender. The fact that I am a woman is part of what I bring to preaching (and this chapter will go on to discuss how so), but I stand there simply as a preacher and I preach my sermon as me.

However, I am also aware that my being a woman is part of who I am and therefore what I bring to preaching: who I am as an individual woman, of course, but also my femaleness, my gender, which may even have more significance than what a man might bring with his maleness. This is because in preaching as a woman I bring the experience of women who have not always been able to preach. I bring the voice of the half of humanity whose contribution to the world of biblical studies, preaching, and church life in general has not always been recognized. I still bring "difference." But what kind of difference? How important is gender in the construction and reception of preaching?

It is all too easy to slip into well-rehearsed generalizations; a woman is bound to be more empathetic, more rooted in the experiences of every-day life, more inclined to use stories, more in touch with feelings, and so forth. Susan Durber wonders whether it means that women "will thump less and evoke more?"[1] In talking about the difference between men's and women's preaching, there is the danger of falling either way into the same traps that must be avoided when talking about the differences between men and women in general. It is possible to both overplay and underplay the extent and significance of difference. Alice Matthews highlights the problems inherent in talking about gender difference: "When differences are exaggerated people are often reduced to sets of roles and are denied their full personhood. When differences are denied, God's purposes in creating humanity as male and female may be thwarted."[2]

To do the former and exaggerate difference highlights a failure to recognize that not all women (or all men) are the same. We can fail to see that there may be as much diversity within a group of women or men preachers as between the two. Some women might be more like some men than other women in their characteristics, and in their preaching. For instance, I am sometimes told that my preaching style is more "male" and appeals to men. I am a teacher and logical patterns and clear points are the way I prefer to approach things (although calling this a "male" way of doing things is, in itself, somewhat of a stereotype). Some women also say they relate well to my preaching. Others relate better to the preaching of my husband who tends to be less structured in his sermons, use more stories and cry more readily. We must be careful not to group all women or men together; other factors, such as upbringing, background, theological standpoint, individual personality, and so on, will influence the way women and men receive and prepare sermons as much, and possibly more, than their gender.

1. Durber, Preaching Like a Woman, 12.
2. Matthews, *Preaching that Speaks to Women*, 23.

In a study of sermons from within the black tradition, Cheryl J. Sanders found that women's and men's sermons were generally alike in most respects—namely the form the sermon took (textual, narrative, expositional, or topical), the range of biblical texts used, and the theme of the sermon. They differed slightly in the tools they used to achieve their purpose.[3] Women were found to be more slightly more inclined to tell stories and use personal testimony than men, who were in turn more disposed to offer social criticism. The main difference was in the extent to which male and female preachers used inclusive language for God and humanity. Sanders draws the conclusion that women and men generally preach the same sorts of sermons but with different "accents."[4]

On the other hand, to deny any difference at all might lead to a significant missed opportunity. Those who see an obvious, distinctive difference encourage the exaggeration of the uniqueness of women as preachers. Women preachers, they say, have an important task in "re-gendering" preaching, for the sake of women, the church, and the task of preaching itself. Elaine Graham, for instance, points to the importance of difference (she calls it "alterity") as a theological category. This is not so much that women have a inherently different way of preaching but that by their very selves preaching they in turn affirm anyone who is considered "other" (in categories of race or ability, for example) such that, "speaking out of difference therefore becomes a positive and powerful strategy."[5] Durber does not see women as having an essentially different way of preaching, and is keen to reject stereotypes of the women are more [fill in the blank] kind. Nevertheless, she insists that women bring a difference borne of "newness." Given that women have come more lately to the pulpit women preachers might still have a "different reception from male preachers given the way in which gender is under construction within both culture and the church."[6] What it means to "preach like a woman," to quote the title of her book, is still open to debate. But she suggests that women can make a conscious choice to "preach in forms, styles and words that come from their experience as women who live in patriarchal

---

3. Sanders, "The Woman as Preacher," refers to these devices as the "homiletical task." Examples include affirming, celebrating, criticizing the church, exegeting Scripture and so on, 214ff.

4. Ibid., 222.

5. Graham, *Transforming Practice*, 178.

6. Durber, *Preaching Like a Woman*, 1.

cultures and churches."[7] Women bring to preaching a fact that is almost too obvious to state; the fact that we are women—that we live in women's bodies with all that inhabiting the body and gender and sexuality of a woman in our current cultural context entails. Gender identity, how we experience ourselves as male or female, is one of many factors inherent in a person's make-up that is influenced by their culture. Our ideas, feelings and values[8] are all shaped by our sex and our gender to some degree or other and even if we refuse a deterministic viewpoint, it is hard to deny that a woman is shaped by living in a woman's body in the world. As I approach, exegete, and preach Scripture, I bring who I am to that task— and who I am is a woman. As Childers puts it: "where better to start a conversation about the preachers' creative process than with the segment of the population who live in bodies that remind them constantly of creativity's rhythms?"[9] But this book and therefore this chapter is not just about preaching generally. It is specifically about reading and preaching from the Bible. How does a woman approach Scripture in order to preach it? Does she see Scripture differently? Does she notice different things? What emerges in her preaching? I have chosen to explore this by using a biblical text as a framework for exploration. I have chosen a story (a typical female thing to do, some might say!) as a way in to the subject. It is the story of Mary approaching the tomb to find that Jesus has risen from the dead (John 20:1–18).[10] In this framework, Mary represents for us the woman preacher. The empty tomb (more specifically the fact of Jesus' resurrection) represents the Bible text to be preached on. Mary's announcement of the resurrection can be seen as the sermon preached. The resurrection is, in this sense, a "text" to be discovered, encountered, and understood. How did Mary "read" it?

Mary's encounter with the risen Jesus at the tomb is all about different ways of seeing. The Greek words reflect this.[11] Firstly she sees the plain fact—the empty tomb. Then she sees Jesus but doesn't recognize

7. Ibid., 9.

8. Matthews, *Preaching that Speaks to Women*, 21.

9. Childers, *Birthing the Sermon*, x.

10. Slightly differing versions of the account are found Matthew 28:1–10, Mark 16:1–8, and Luke 24:1–8.

11. V. 1 *blepo*—to see physically, to notice, to glance at; v. 14 *theoreo*—to observe carefully, to observe intensely, to contemplate, observe, scrutinize; v. 18 *eido*—to perceive, pierce with intelligent comprehension, to understand, to perceive the significance of.

him, and finally she reports to the other disciples that she has seen the Lord, with full realization of the implications of her seeing. As we approach Scripture as women, seeking to understand it and to read it well in order to be given a vision we can share with others, Mary's seeing seems like a good place to start.

Approaching the Text

"Early on the first day of the week, while it was still dark, Mary Magdalene came to the tomb and saw that the stone had been removed from the tomb." "Early on the first day of the week, while it was still dark" is a good description of starting out on the process of sermon preparation. In studies of women preachers, many mention starting to think about the sermon well before it is to be preached.[12] One says: "A certain fear of the Holy task ahead is important, but better if faced earlier in the week."[13] Most also confess to finishing it off on the morning of the event itself! There is something about coming to the text quietly, before things get too hectic, before the clamor starts, metaphorically speaking, "at dawn." As Mary came to the tomb that morning, she was expecting to find nothing more than a sealed tomb and a dead body. As I approach the text for my next sermon I admit that my expectations are sometimes quite low. I know God's calling on me to preach. I know that something will emerge in the end that brings life and good news to my hearers, but when I first approach the task in the dark it can seem a daunting task.

Mary came to the tomb to find the stone rolled away. At that point, she had no idea what that meant, but her mind must have been racing. There is a sense when I approach Scripture for the first time that I do not know what I will find. I "see" the text. It may even be a very familiar one, perhaps one I have preached on before, but each sermon is different and unique, and at this initial stage of approach I do not know what it will "mean" for this particular congregation, this time. It is a common experience for women preachers to describe that sense when the text is first met and read of "something brewing:" "I feel something within but it is in the nebulous part of me just beyond reach. It is like the early

---

12. E.g., Childers, *Birthing the Sermon.* This may not be a particularly "female" phenomenon. It is worth noting that at least one (male) author in this volume also refers to the same process.

13. Linda Carolyn Loving in Childers, *Birthing the Sermon,* 108.

stages of pregnancy or after seeds have been planted. I know there is new life, but I cannot locate it in the ultrasound of my mind."[14] It is important to live with the text for a while before forming any hard and fast ideas about how to preach it. I like to mull it over, letting it come to me in odd moments (usually in the shower, or walking to work, or cooking, or engaging in activity that occupies my body but frees my mind). I get to know the text, become familiar with it, and become friends with it. I wonder if this is a particularly female thing to do. I expect many men would say they do the same thing, but I have heard several women speak of this phase as like pregnancy.[15] In this early phase, I hold the text somewhere in an inmost place, as the Psalmist might say, where it is growing and forming, but not yet ready to be born, where the Spirit is feeding it and helping the connections to be made. Purvis-Smith quotes one woman preacher saying: "It's coming from out of me. It has to be a very close thing. The thing is in process for me always. It's sort of like having a baby.[16] The pregnancy and birth metaphor for preaching is not a new one. Even Calvin (who would probably take a dim view of women in the pulpit) compared preachers with wet nurses.[17]

During this early approach to the text, before I have consulted anything "official" like a commentary, I like to talk others about my sermon. I get a bit obsessed with the developing, growing sermon and, like a new newly pregnant mother or someone who has just fallen in love, I tend to tell everyone about it. This often leads to new insights. Shortly before last Easter, for example, I told a fellow woman minister I met at a conference that I was planning to preach on John 20. My new friend was also "brewing" her sermon for Easter and we talked together about how we might develop our preaching. I was able to help her with some details about the Greek and she had some good ideas about how the sermon might speak to children. There began an email exchange between us in which we virtually wrote our sermons together, helping each other, sharing ideas. I'll often mention what I'm preaching on in group conversations—at my home group, in the staff room at college, at meals with friends, and wait to hear the contributions others have to

---

14. Teresa L. Fry Brown, in Childers *Birthing the Sermon*, 16. Several of the women in Childers' anthology use images of pregnancy to describe sermon preparation.

15. Ian Stackhouse describes a very similar approach to the sermon in his chapter in this volume.

16. Purvis-Smith, "Gender and the Aesthetic of Preaching," 226.

17. In a sermon on 1 Timothy 4.6–7, cited in Childers, *Birthing the Sermon*, ix.

make. I like to think of it as the homiletical equivalent of a baby shower! Is it possible that women may be particularly prone to this kind of communal sharing in sermon preparation?

As pregnancy is always an anxious time, as well as a hopeful one, part of this sermon gestation period involves wondering what I will do with the text and what it will do to me. For women this takes on a particular significance, a certain apprehension even.[18] This sense of anxiety or fear is not necessarily a bad thing. It might actually benefit our preaching: "For many of us anxiety is not only an inescapable part of preaching it is a necessary component."[19]

So what is this anxiety or fear, exactly? It may take several forms.[20] Firstly, there is the fear of preaching itself. The jury is still out about the relevance and effectiveness of preaching as a valid method of communication for today. Some see the very act of preaching as patriarchal, favoring instead a more conversational, communal gathering around Scripture.[21] I firmly believe that good preaching can be effective, relevant and communal and is truly a "female" thing to do, but the lurking fear may still be there for women.

Add to this the fear of preaching as a woman. Leaving aside questions about whether women should preach at all (we should), there is often among women preachers a fear that we will not be able to live up to the weight of expectation; that we must not only preach well for ourselves, but as representatives of all womankind. We have ringing in our ears opinions like that of Samuel Johnson: "Sir, a woman's preaching is like a dog's walking on his hind legs. It is not done well; but you are surprised to find it done at all," and we feel the pressure to do a good job, not just for ourselves but for all our sisters.[22]

Thirdly there is the fear of what the Bible might hold for a woman who preaches. For some, the Bible has been encountered as a patriarchal

18. Most of the women in Childers' anthology speak of the fear, stress and anxiety of sermon preparation, using words and phrases like "challenge," 153; "love/hate relationship," 101; "doesn't always go easily," 51; "costs me plenty," 36; "makes me anxious," 36.

19. Ibid., 36.

20. Durber outlines several reasons why women may be anxious about the process of preaching, *Preaching Like a Woman*, 3ff.

21. See, e.g., Purvis-Smith, who examines how the very architecture of preaching, the high-up pulpit, the tone of delivery, etc., has been a very "male" space. She cites the example of a church that meets in a home and discusses the text together: "preaching is more who they are than what they do," "Gender and the Aesthetic of Preaching," 229.

22. Boswell, Croker, Wright, *The Life of Samuel Johnson*, 252.

document representing oppression, violence and irrelevance. It is indeed impossible to deny the difficulty of some parts of the Bible for women. As Durber says, "We can be almost certain that all the biblical texts were written by men and they all have an androcentric basis."[23] She goes on to outline various feminist approaches to scriptural interpretation.[24] Heather Walton calls the Bible "a powerfully dangerous resource,"[25] and examines the options open to women interpreting scripture—to read the "good" stories and ignore the "bad," or to reclaim and rewrite the bad stories, retelling the history of the text "in memory of her." But she says the Bible is still deeply misogynist and so prefers to tell as "scripture" the stories of women outside the Bible. Elizabeth Schussler Fiorenza[26] and Rosemary Radford Ruether[27] would see the Bible as oppressive but also liberating for women, containing plenty that shocks and evokes fear, but also hidden "better news," a golden thread.[28] Phyllis Trible brings to the fore the oppressive texts (the rape of Tamar, in 2 Samuel 13.1–22, for instance) and exposes them, in the hope that they might be shamed and inspire repentance.[29] Ostriker asserts that text can be "broken open" and rewritten to contain good news for women.[30]

All of these different ways of approaching the Scripture betray the reader's posture in relation to the text. How do we view the authority, or otherwise, of the Bible in relation to our lives? Feminist critics would say that as women preachers we have a duty to approach the Bible warily. Smith says, for example, "A feminist, critical interpretation begins with a hermeneutic of suspicion rather than with a hermeneutic of consent and affirmation."[31] However, Ostriker talks instead of "hermeneutic of desire."[32] By this she means that the Scripture may not readily offer up its liberating power for women, but that our task is to continue to seek

23. Durber, *Preaching Like a Woman*, 18.

24. Foskett, *Interpreting the Bible*, includes a helpful summary three modes of feminist critique and four modes of feminist construction of the biblical text, drawing on the work of Anderson and Moore, *Mark and Method*.

25. Walton, "Breaking open the Bible," cited in Durber *Preaching Like a Woman*, 23.

26. Schussler Fiorenza, *In Memory of Her*.

27. Radford Ruether, *Sexism and God-Talk*.

28. Radford Ruether quoted in Durber, *Preaching Like a Woman*, 20.

29. Trible, *Literary Feminist Readings of Biblical Narratives*.

30. Ostriker, *Feminist Revision and the Bible*.

31. Smith, *Weaving the Sermon*, 95.

32. Ostriker cited in Durber, *Preaching Like a Woman*, 22.

it, and then we will find it. Durber speaks of approaching the Bible texts "with careful, affectionate attention."[33]

As a woman preacher I firmly believe that the Bible can be a liberating force for women, but that we must allow ourselves to assume a humble posture in relation to it. This is different from settling for a literal reading or taking its more difficult passages at face value. We are obliged to delve deeper (more of that in a moment). But our initial posture should be one of submission to the word of God and what it has to say in us and though us. In one sense, although not the sense endorsed by feminist commentators, I should be afraid; very afraid. It is indeed a Holy Bible and will always be dangerous. It is very likely to challenge me, as well as affirm me, to inspire me to a different way of living, to disturb my comfort and to lead me closer to Jesus, who challenged and disturbed, as well as comforted. I cannot avoid preaching from certain texts (for example the Epistles that appear to prohibit women speaking in church, or the texts from the Old Testament that present appalling acts against women) because I am afraid what I might find there.[34] Martin Luther spoke of being "taken captive by the word of God," a theme Volf picks up in the title of his book about the using the Bible in doing theology, and in which he asserts that approaching the Bible as a genuinely sacred text demands a "hermeneutic of respect."[35] This is recognition that the Bible is bigger and more powerful than I am. It is also bigger and more powerful than my enemies, and that includes my enemies as a woman. Mary's first approach to the tomb caused her to weep. The Bible may do that to us sometimes. But, like Mary, we must not settle for tears without expecting the text to reveal some more liberative answers.

Understanding the Text

"So she ran and went to Simon Peter and the other disciple, the one whom Jesus loved, and said to them, 'They have taken the Lord out of the tomb, and we do not know where they have laid him.'" Faced with the fact of the empty tomb, in her state of fear and panic, Mary did not understand what she had "read," and her instant reaction was to run to

33. Ibid., 181.

34. Indeed some of the sermons in anthologies of women's sermons deliberately use precisely these texts.

35. Volf, *Captive to the Word of God*, 34.

Peter and John for advice and help. As a woman encountering the text for preaching, it is all too easy to "run and fetch my brothers" too quickly. I can readily experience a crisis of confidence, for all the reasons cited above. Then I am inclined to panic and run to the internet (in my worst moments) and commentaries (in better ones) for help. Don't hear me wrong, commentaries are an indispensable resource for preachers, and even the internet has occasionally been a source of inspiration and help. But when my seeking help is borne out of a panicky loss of confidence, it is rarely a good place to start. It is much better to begin by approaching the text for myself, reading and living with it for a while. I wonder what Mary was doing while Peter and John were rushing in and out of the tomb? Where was she? What was she thinking? As soon as I ask for help from the experts, the tendency is for them to rush in and take over, as Peter and John did. To go too quickly for others might crowd out the quiet voice of the Spirit speaking to me.

And then they were gone. The other disciples took off home again and Mary was left with the text, still wondering what it meant. Given what we have just said about approaching the Bible with a hermeneutic of respect, it seems appropriate to notice that Mary "bent over" to look into the tomb. As we bend over to peer through the gloom into the text is what I see there likely to be in any sense different to what a man might see? What is the exegetical task like for women preachers?

When Mary first encountered the empty tomb she saw the fact of its emptiness but did not understand what that meant. Through a process, in which she was questioned by the angels and told them why she was weeping, and in which she had a conversation with a Jesus she did not yet recognize, she pieced together the reality of the situation. This process of questioning the text and allowing it to also question us is an important one. Durber speaks of the need to "interrogate the text like a detective."[36] This process of looking harder and asking questions is often described as wrestling. Childers speaks of "wrestling Luke to the ground."[37] Ostriker says, "It is what we wrestle with all night and from which we may, if we demand it, wrest a blessing."[38] Foskett speaks of the "reader's" authority to engage the text faithfully, even to the point of wrestling with it with no less ferocity than Jacob showed

---

36. Durber, *Preaching Like a Woman*, 181.

37. Childers, *Birthing the Sermon*, 44.

38. Ostriker quoted in Durber, *Preaching Like a Woman*, 22.

in his own struggle at Penuel."[39] Even with a posture of humility and submission to the text, I can still engage robustly with it, wrestle with it, fight it even. The Scriptures may "capture" me, but I can still wriggle. Jesus was not dismissive of women who did this with him. The Syro-Phoenician woman (John 4:1–30) gave as well as she got in her robust exchange with Jesus, questioning his assumptions (some might even say his rudeness) and demanding an adequate response. The Samaritan woman at the well (Mark 7:25–30 and Matt 15:21–28) engaged in a most unseemly exchange with Jesus. Yet both of these women respected Jesus, came to see him as the Messiah, received healing and affirmation from him. As women we can take the same approach to Scripture. It is not disrespectful to question, to probe, even to disagree. Some of those I wrestle with most ferociously are those I respect most keenly.[40]

What forms might the wrestling take? There are certain perspectives we might bring to exegeting the text as women. As I have said, this is different from saying that women preach in a certain way, or that women are more inclined to do one thing or another in their preaching. But in the reading of the text, there are ways of seeing the Bible and its narratives that are more likely to be mine by virtue of the simple fact that I am a woman.

Firstly, I will have the perspective of living in a woman's body. I feel what it is like to have the body of a woman, rather than the body of a man, and I will bring that to my reading of the text. So, for example, when as a woman I read about Jesus healing the woman with a hemorrhage (Mark 5:21–34), possibly when I am menstruating myself, I can identify bodily with the pain in a way that a man cannot.

Added to this, I bring the perspective of my standpoint of a woman. This means that as I read a Bible text, especially the narratives, I will have the perspective of the women in the text. This does not mean that I will identify in my lived experience with all the women in the Bible. At this stage in my life, I do not know what it is like to be old like Anna or childless like Hannah or to be raped and abused like Tamar. It is not that all women identify with all women but that, as a woman, I am more likely to take the standpoint of the women in the stories. As someone who is unemployed, or living in a war zone, or disabled, or a refugee will notice

39. Foskett, *Interpreting the Bible*, 58.

40. Durber describes this kind of relationship with the text and says, "in the cracks and fissures of this text, I find a space still to be, whether to fight and resist or receive grace beyond dreams." *Preaching Like a Woman*, 23.

different things in the text simply by virtue of who they are and what their experiences have been, so when I hear the narrative of the birth of Jesus, I am more inclined to see myself standing next to Mary, rather than Joseph. When I hear about David looking at Bathsheba, I might picture myself in the bathroom with Bathsheba rather than on the rooftop with David. It is a matter of perspective, or vantage point. I once heard a husband and wife team preaching together on the story of Ruth and Boaz. She took the perspective of Ruth and he Boaz and what we encountered was a thoroughly "alive" version of the story. They were expounding Scripture rather than acting out or telling the story, but the whole thing had the feeling of being in a soap opera! Their perspectives as male and female brought the story to life.

I bring to my process of wrestling with the text the perspective of being female. I cannot get away from the fact that Jesus was male (and therefore different to me), and so I will react to the stories about him from that perspective. I recently heard a sermon on the woman who anointed Jesus feet with perfume (Luke 7:36–50). The preacher was extolling the woman's extravagant expression of worship, passion, and love for Jesus as a good example for us. I understood the preacher's point. But I have to confess that as he painted this picture of this outrageously, shamefully confident woman, my instant, unformed reaction to her was, "Attention-seeker!" My (probably sinful) reaction was borne out of a kind of jealousy toward this woman, who approached the Savior (whom I also love) with such outpouring of devotion. This was my sexuality speaking. Not my sexuality in the sense of sexual expression, but my sexuality in the sense of being female, experiencing the world and the text as female.

I am also more able to see and appreciate the perspective of the outsider in the text. As a woman approaching a text that was largely written by men, in patriarchal cultures and in which a "frequently androcentric" perspective has shaped the literary world of the text as well as the history of its reception, interpretation and use."[41] I will bring the perspective of one who has been excluded from this world. In the Bible, as still in much of the world, the male is the norm and the woman provides the difference. So I may be more inclined to notice where the power lies and to question the assumptions apparent in an initial reading of the text.[42] This morning

41. Foskett *Interpreting the Bible*, 59.

42. Foskett cites Carter Shelley's re-interpretation of the parable of the woman and the judge, seeing her not as nagging until the Judge gives in under the pressure, but as persistent and therefore an excellent role model, *Interpreting the Bible*, 58.

in our college chapel service we had a reading from Matthew 22.23–27 in which the Pharisees question Jesus, asking what happens after the resurrection to a woman who has been married to each of seven brothers? Whose wife will she be then? The preacher spoke about the nature of marriage and resurrection and heaven and whether the Pharisees had a point and the doctrinal implications of it all. All I could think was "That poor woman! Being passed from one husband to the other. No wonder she was dead at the end of it!" I know she was not a real woman but merely a made-up example, but my "noticing" was very firmly focused on her (and women like her who may actually exist). Durber asserts, "This technique of reading a text from a different place, noticing an apparently marginal character, can provide a new entrance to the story and stir new ways of seeing and understanding it."[43]

As a woman reader of texts for preaching my wrestling will take a very deliberate form with some parts of the Bible. These are the texts that have something directly to say about my nature and calling as a woman. I am thinking particularly of passages like 1 Timothy 2.8–15 that apparently prohibits me from preaching at all. I can honestly say that far from wishing it wasn't there, this text has become one of my favorites. That is because I have wrestled with it hard and long and now I have received a blessing from it. I have a strong and firm relationship with that scripture, and it is a pleasure to preach from it whenever I am asked. I do not have room here to go into the nature of this blessing, but through careful exegetical study, lexical analysis, and historical exploration of the original context in which it was written, I have found this text to say something all together more liberating and helpful than first appeared. I believe this text contains some truly "golden threads" about what it means to live peaceably together as male and female in the church. Sometimes the text says to us—why are you weeping? This is not as bad as it looks.

When I am preparing a sermon, there is often that moment of realization, when it all comes together and I know what it is God has put on my heart to say. Just as Mary worked through the process of weeping at the empty tomb, seeing Jesus standing there without recognizing him, and eventually seeing him for who he is, there comes that moment when God calls my name from the text and I know and recognize what it is that God wants to say through my sermon. Then I am able to call the text "Rabboni," my teacher, and I know have something to go and tell others about.

43. Durber, *Preaching Like a Woman*, 26.

Preaching the Text

> Jesus said to her, "Do not hold on to me, because I have not
> yet ascended to the Father. But go to my brothers and say to
> them, 'I am ascending to my Father and your Father, to my God
> and your God.'" Mary Magdalene went and announced to the
> disciples, "I have seen the Lord"; and she told them that he had
> said these things to her.

Mary's response to her encounter with the "text," the risen Lord, is to want to cling on for dear life. Translations that render it "Do not touch me" are inaccurate. Jesus does not dismiss Mary's intimate and loving touch. To say "Do not hold on to me" implies that she is already clinging to him. Mary and her Lord in a loving embrace. Sometimes it feels like that when I've finished writing my sermon. I have come to know it and my relationship with the message, the word God has put on my heart is strong and alive. It is then that the imperative is to go and tell others, to preach it.

In Matthew's account of this story we are told that Mary went "with fear and great joy."[44] That is a good description of what it's like to preach. There is the sense of great joy that I have a message to deliver, coupled with that ever-present fear that I may not do justice to what God has given me, fear of how the message (or I) may be received, fear that I may have gotten it wrong. As Mary went to tell the disciples that day, her message was not only the fact of the resurrection, but herself, Mary, with everything that Jesus has been for her in the past, bringing it to them: I have seen the Lord. She is telling them as Mary, bringing who she is to the task of telling. Again it seems almost too obvious to state, but as women we bring to our preaching our own experiences and selves. Purvis-Smith says this may be a particularly female thing to do. She quotes a woman preacher as saying: "I think we females are much more inclined to start with our own experience."[45] I am not sure I agree that we start with our own experience. I think we start with Scripture, but we bring our own experience. This may mean using stories and links and illustrations that relate to our lives as women. Nancy Beach, Teaching Pastor at Willow Creek church, says: "As a woman communicator, it is hugely significant for me to listen to my life—from my female perspective—and to share

---

44. Matt 28:8.
45. Purvis-Smith, "Gender and the Aesthetic of Preaching," 226.

the stories that are unique to me."[46] When I bring into my sermons stories about the joys and challenges of being a mother, about the pressures of work/life balance, about what it feels like to live as a woman in my society and culture today, I am more likely to speak more audibly into the lives of women hearers. Likewise male preachers can do the same for men. Graham points to the importance of naming the experiences of women previously hidden: "The invisibility of women's experience, and especially of unaddressed areas of pastoral need, seek some redress; but as women speak about previously unspoken lives they redefine the nature and function of pastoral preaching."[47] She names the examples of incest and abuse, but it need not only be the more serious issues that affect the lives of women. I read a commentary recently on the Annunciation, which drew upon the painting by Fra Angelico, in which the (female) commentator raised the possibility that a strange black line that ran through the picture may actually be the washing line, and that this was an image of God breaking into the mundane and ordinary. It is that sort of naming that women might bring to preaching? We may also want to be careful to use women as well as men as examples and illustrations in our sermons. When we talk about the heroes of faith, do we name Sarah and Miriam as well as well as Abraham and Moses? When we are telling inspiring stories of faith at work in history, do we mention Josephine Butler as well as William Wilberforce? Jesus' hearers might have been surprised to find him using women as protagonists in some of his stories. The woman in the story of the lost coin is one example.

So Mary went and announced her news to the disciples. How did she do that? How did she announce? We can be sure that the disciples heard her voice, out of breath and tremulous as it may have been, telling them the most important news they would ever hear. For women preachers, finding our authentic "voice" as women is a key task. Durbar talks about: "Women finding and developing ways to speak with voices that [are] self-consciously their own; speaking from the experience of a woman's body, speaking clearly of the women of the faith from the past, speaking of the Bible in ways learned from biblical criticism alert to questions of gender."[48] Beach draws on the work of Jane Stephens to affirm the importance of a woman preacher finding her own unique

---

46. Beach, *Gifted to Lead*, 123.

47. Graham, *Transforming Practice*, 173.

48. Durber, *Preaching Like a Woman*, 1.

voice and using it with confidence. Stephens describes voice thus: "Voice is an artesian well, the best resource of each person. Their most genuine, vital expression and energy, fueling the organization's best and wisest work. It is what happens when we are working at the center of our vocation—our calling, 'The place where our own deep gladness meets the world's deep need.'"[49]

This chapter started out with a discussion about what, if anything, is the difference between women's biblical preaching and men's. As we return to the question perhaps the answer might be found most fruitfully in this idea that women will simply preach with their own, authentic voice. Of course, at one level this means preaching with our physical voices, which sound different to those of men. Sometimes when I preach in a place where women's voices have been less often heard (as I do quite often. I tend to get invited to churches that are not sure about women's preaching, but want to "try it out"), I am aware of the impact of my female voice in the physical space. It's almost a spiritual feeling. I find it moving that this building may not have heard the voices of many women and it is as if my voice somehow fills the space in a new way. This is often reflected in people's comments to me afterwards: "It's nice to hear a woman's voice." But when we speak of the voices of women we do not refer only to their vocal chords. We mean also their expression, their way of saying things their unique style. Durber draws out this point: "If you really want to 'preach like a woman . . .' you will have a degree of self-awareness and an understanding of the impact that your woman's life, body, voice, and story have on others as they listen to the gospel from your lips and body."[50] So the question is perhaps not whether women will bring more of this or that to the task of reading and preaching Scripture, but whether a woman will choose to find and preach with her own authentic voice. That voice will sound different for each of us, but it is above all to be a voice that proclaims, "I have seen the Lord!" and goes on to tell others what he has said to us.

49. Stephens and Zades, *Mad Dogs, Dreamers and Sages*, cited in Beach, *Gifted to Lead*, 186.

50. Durber, *Preaching Like a Woman*, 179.

PART TWO

HISTORICAL

6

Jonathan Edwards on Preaching

Oliver D. Crisp

IN THE POPULAR IMAGINATION Jonathan Edwards is synonymous with
the hellfire preaching of the revivals that comprise the Great Awakening
in Colonial New England of the 1730s and 1740s. His rhetorical style is
easily identified by his most famous (or infamous) sermon, "Sinners in
the hands of an angry God," which is a staple of anthologies on American
literature.[1] In it Edwards paints a vivid picture of the appalling fate await-
ing those who fail to repent. Speaking directly to the congregation, he
explains that God holds them over the pit "much as one holds a spider,
or some loathsome insect over the fire." This wrathful Deity, "abhors"
Edwards' auditors, and is "dreadfully provoked." His wrath "burns like
fire"; God looks upon the members of the congregation "as worthy of
nothing else, but to be cast into the fire." For God is "of purer eyes than to
bear to have you in his sight." Indeed, says Edwards, his parishioners "are
ten thousand times more abominable in his eyes, than the most hateful
venomous serpent is in ours."

This is not a sermon for the fainthearted. Although it does reflect a
strain of hellfire preaching in Edwards' work, its declamatory language

---

1. "Sinners," as it is often called, may well rank as one of the most famous sermon
texts ever preached. It can be found in, e.g., *The Norton Anthology of American Literature*, eds. Baym, Franklin, Gura, Krupat, and Levine, a widely used textbook in American Literature courses that reproduces it alongside another of Edwards' sermons, "A
Divine and Supernatural Light." A representative sample of Edwards' sermons, including both of these sermon-texts, can be found in *The Sermons of Jonathan Edwards*,
eds. Kimnach, Minkema, and Sweeney, the edition from which I quote "Sinners" here.

does not distinguish it from other such Puritan sermons, where the jeremiad or mournful complaint of the preacher was a common component of congregational diets. Although Edwards made a lasting contribution to this genre, it is not representative of his homiletics as a whole. For this reason it is unfortunate that it has become the one sermon-text by which he is remembered and the means by which the myth of the Hellfire Edwards has been kept alive.[2]

Edwards' Manner of Preaching

It is no surprise, then, that when one thinks of Edwards the preacher, the image conjured up is usually that of a tall, cadaverous man of stern, uncompromising visage, wearing a black Genevan gown, with starched clerical bands and a powdered periwig atop his high, receding brow. That is how he is presented in the standard portrait of Edwards painted from life by Joseph Badger and reprinted on endless book covers. If he is remembered as the preacher, it is standing in the high New England pulpit somber, serious, holding in the palm of his hand a small rectangular prompt-card, on which is written in his crabbed, spidery hand the skeleton of the sermon he is reading. It is reported that in his preaching Edwards made little or no use of physical gesture; that he was not particularly demonstrative. Instead, he stood still, intoning each word with care and precision in order that his congregation would hear and understand the sentences he uttered. His sermons were not so much proclaimed as delivered: they were often works that would make as much sense written as read.[3] In fact, a number of the works by which he is remembered began

2. Although there is more work to be done on this score, in recent years our understanding of Edwards' homiletics has been greatly enlarged by the editorial introductions to the relevant volumes of the Yale University Letterpress Edition of Edwards' Works, especially vols. 9, 10, 14, 17, 19, 22, and 25. Wilson H. Kimnach has been the most important recent interpreter of Edwards' homiletics and editor of the key vol. 10 in this edition of Edwards' works, which gives a general introduction to his sermon *corpus* as a whole. In this regard Kimnach's "The Sermons: Concept and Execution" in *The Princeton Companion to Jonathan Edwards*, 243–57, is also worth consulting. The aforementioned *The Sermons of Jonathan Edwards* has a helpful editorial introduction to Edwards' homiletics as well, with a greater focus on the shape of Edwards' sermons than this chapter.

3. There is an important issue here, having to do with the convoluted relationship between the sermon as an oracular form and the sermon-text as the written document preserved for posterity. As any preacher knows, the two are not synonymous. Edwards preserved examples of polished written sermon-texts as well as sermon skeletons

their lives as sermons preached to his congregation.[4] An instructive report of Edwards the preacher is given by one of his closest disciples, the theologian and minister Samuel Hopkins. He writes,

> His appearance in the desk [i.e., in the pulpit] was with a good grace and his delivery easy, natural and very solemn. He had not a strong, loud voice; but appeared with such gravity and solemnity, and spake with such distinctness, clearness and precision; his words were full of ideas, set in such a plain and striking light, that few speakers have been able to command the attention of an audience as he. His words often discovered a great deal of inward fervour, without much noise or external emotion, and fell with great weight upon the minds of his hearers. He made but little motion of his head or hands in the desk; but spake so as to discover the motion of his own heart, which tended in the most natural and effectual manner to move and affect others.[5]

The content of Edwards' sermons could be characterized as relentlessly logical. The outline was made "visible" to the mind's eye of his auditors through careful explanation and the (sometimes) elaborate use of headings and sub-headings in order to break up the text as it was delivered. The structure of his sermon-texts followed the Puritan scheme of three broad sections: Text, Doctrine, and Application. The text was usually no more than a verse or sentence, from which a doctrine was taken. It was stated as a sort of thesis for what followed. Then he usually set about a close and careful analysis of the text, particular emphasis being placed upon the literary form of the passage and its propositional content. This part of the sermon was usually conceptually laden, with reference being made to larger systematic issues in which the particular text was situated. This in turn was "improved"—a Puritan term for the close pastoral application of a text. Puritan ministers were renowned for

---

or outlines. But care must be taken in assessing these documents precisely because sermon-texts are not identical with the preached word. There is always much more to a sermon that the text preached, even if that is a complete text that is read in full before the congregation (as Edwards on occasion did). Similarly, there is a great difference between the text of a play and the performance of that text even though the actors speak only the words of the playwright.

4. For instance, the *Religious Affections* or *Charity and its Fruits*.

5. Hopkins, *The Life of Jonathan Edwards*, 52. Earlier in the same passage Hopkins reports that Edwards "wrote most of his sermons out in full for near twenty years after he first began to preach; though he did not wholly confine himself to his notes in his delivering of them." Hopkins, *The Life of Jonathan Edwards*, 50.

the forensic way in which they attempted to apply Scripture to the lives of the congregation with considerable psychological insight and existential nuance. The section of the Puritan sermon concerned with such application was usually peppered with direct appeals to the listener: "*you* need to do this," "*you* are the one this passage is speaking of," "*your* situation is directly in view here," and so on. Edwards' work was representative of such sermons. These appeals included the prophetic overtones of cajoling and upbraiding the congregation, as well as denouncing sin. But this was intermixed with appeals designed to soothe, restore, and encourage the burdened soul. The delivery of the sermon lasted at least an hour. It was not unheard of for a sermon to be double that length. In a society in which there were no radios, no televisions, and no computers, the preached word constituted the weekly public broadcasts. They were taken very seriously, and everyone in the town or village would have been expected to be present on a Sunday, even if they were not themselves professed believers or members of the church.

The popular cameo of Edwards the scarecrow-like preacher is accurate as far as it goes.[6] As was typical in the period, Edwards wore clerical garb in the pulpit, and he always preached from there—speaking from a lectern would have been an almost unthinkable act of liturgical dereliction for a Congregational minister of the period. These formal accoutrements were a fixture of his career as was the liturgy in which the sermon was the climax. The colonial society in which Edwards lived was, after all, founded in order to be a place in which the plain style of Reformed worship could flourish.[7]

His mode of preaching did change during his lifetime, however. He was influenced in midlife by the much more histrionic style of the Anglican itinerant, George Whitefield, whom he befriended on his

6. Edwards was emaciated. His health was rather fragile after a serious sickness in his days as a student at Yale, and he often fasted. Hopkins tells us that Edwards worked up to thirteen hours a day in his study. But this single-minded pursuit of ideas was made possible by a household managed by his wife, the redoubtable Sarah Pierrpont Edwards; a large family; and slave labor. His otherworldliness had an important moral cost that should not be lost on contemporary admirers of his work ethic or output.

7. The service of worship each Sunday in Northampton would have involved unaccompanied psalmody and a sermon. There was no place for musical instruments. The liturgical calendar was deliberately shunned as indicative of "popery." The whole style of worship was representative of the austere aesthetic approved of in Puritan worship. A near modern equivalent are the services of the Kirk and the Free Church of Scotland in the Western Isles.

evangelistic tours of the eastern seaboard of what is today the United States.[8] Whitefield visited Edwards on several occasions and preached in the Northampton pulpit that Edwards usually occupied. But Edwards was not Whitefield, nor was he an aspiring Methodist. Whitefield was a born actor, who honed his public speaking skills in open-air arenas, preaching extemporaneously for several hours at a time often to crowds of thousands. By contrast, Edwards was a man of a scholarly disposition and his pulpit habits betrayed the retired existence he lived. Unlike Whitefield, he never preached in the fields or byways, but only in the church of which he was minister, or, with some frequency as his fame spread, at the invitation of brother pastors in other townships. The settled order of Congregational New England was not something Edwards sought to overturn.

In fact, for all his admiration of Whitefield's manner and attempt (during the revivals of the Great Awakening) to be more extemporary in his preaching, Edwards was not really at home in that more immediate mode of delivery. He did move from the full text sermons of his early ministry to the use of small flashcards that could be "palmed" for a more apparently natural delivery. But in later life when important occasions arose he still wrote out his sermons in full. It may be that Edwards felt his natural gifts were less effective or impressive than those of Whitefield. But it may also be that the pressure of constant work as a minister, as well as additional invitations elsewhere meant that the more economical way of writing up his sermons was something of a practical necessity. Whatever the reason for the gradual change to the manner of his preaching (and these different pressures are by no means mutually exclusive), the fact that he never felt entirely at home in the "extemporary" mode, and that he returned to his more natural full-script preaching at important moments later in life are, I suggest, not insignificant. They indicate something important about the disposition of the man behind the text.

Edwards was a preacher for almost his entire adult life. He was a minister by profession, which meant that sermon preparation was one of the staples of his weekly routine. He preached weekly, twice on Sundays, as well as delivering mid-week "lectures," which were really disquisitions on some biblical text. When one adds up the amount of preparation and writing this involved (where Edwards was writing out his text in longhand), it is equivalent in literary output to the production of three

8. The most comprehensive account of Whitefield's life is still Dallimore's hagiography, *George Whitefield*. There are two excellent recent critical biographical studies. These are Stout, *The Divine Dramatist* and Lambert, *"Peddler in Divinity."*

book-length chapters a week or an entire monograph in a month! Such devotion to the preached word required a significant amount of routine study. As an heir to the Puritan tradition of plain preaching and analytical exegesis, Edwards thought the exposition of the text of Scripture one of the central tasks of the preacher. But he did not indulge in hand waiving or physical motions. He did not think these important in effective ministry—despite the obviously successful example of exactly that sort of delivery in the dramaturgy of Whitefield. In many ways, their two approaches to the delivery of sermons reflected their different ideas about the task of the preacher. Whitefield sought by use of his considerable oratorical gifts and a mellifluous and powerful voice, to persuade his hearers. He was an evangelist through and through. Moral change was the desired outcome, and often this was accompanied by physical and emotional outpourings. He was a dramatic and arresting speaker who drew similarly dramatic and arresting responses from those who listened to him.

Edwards was no mean preacher either, and on occasion his sermons elicited spectacular responses. (The most celebrated example is the reaction to the second preaching of his "Sinners" sermon at Enfield, where the congregation were grasping hold of the pillars of the church and wailing so loudly in fear of being cast immediately into hell that Edwards was unable to finish his sermon). But, although he was an apologist for the revivals that swept through Colonial New England, he did not put much store by physical or hysterical responses to his sermons. In fact, he thought these no sure indicator of any real spiritual awakening. What was needed was moral change, wrought in the heart by the secret work of the Spirit of God. Only that was lasting and only that would be of real benefit to his hearers. In the knowledge that preaching must convert the soul and equip the saints, Edwards directed his energies towards the goal of uncovering and laying bare ideas before the minds of his congregation in the full expectation that God would honor the preaching of his word by regenerating "those appointed for salvation," or encouraging and building up the faith of those already on the way to the eternal city.

Edwards on Preaching as Power

This brings us to the rationale for preaching, as Edwards understood it. Perhaps it comes as no surprise for someone who regarded himself as a representative of the Reformed tradition that Edwards had a very high view of those ordained to minister word and sacrament. Not only was the sermon the liturgical apogee of every Sunday service at which Edwards preached, in common with the established order of New England Congregationalism; he clearly thought that preaching was his primary responsibility as a minister.

More than a thousand of Edwards' sermons or sermon skeletons have been preserved and painstakingly transcribed in the modern edition of his works. We also have his numerous notebooks, including volumes devoted entirely to biblical exegesis and to harmonizing the two biblical testaments. Edwards even had in mind a work of systematic theology that would have been cast as a narrative, which would have enabled him to set out the biblical story of salvation history. This work, incomplete at his death, was one of the great works to which he had hoped to devote his mature years. It supplanted an earlier projected system of doctrine that was to be called *A Rational Account*, which was more obviously a philosophical and apologetic work. To this end, he preached a series of sermons to his congregation at Northampton— a sort of first attempt at setting forth some of the ideas he hoped to develop in his larger project. These have been published as his *History of the Work of Redemption*, a fascinating overview of the whole biblical drama. Evidence of Edwards' deep entanglement with Scripture can also be found in his typological works. He wrote a great deal about the way in which the Old Testament prefigures the New, in various types and "shadows" that are fulfilled in Christ. But he took this much further than some of his contemporaries, elaborating an entire system of signs in the created order, which he thought could be decoded or understood through deep study of Scripture. (Some examples are fairly jejune, like the sun, its light, and its rays as an image of the Trinity; others are more complex, like his claim that the whole creation is a mere shadow of the spiritual world, which is infinitely more real than the one we inhabit).[9] In his hands the Bible was a both a textbook for salvation and a grammar for understanding God's work in creation as well as the source of great personal spiritual comfort and delight.

All this is pertinent to the question of how Edwards thought about the nature and purpose of preaching because it shows how deep and systematic his involvement with Scripture actually was. His biblical interests bleed into every area of his thought, including his most abstruse

---

9. See Edwards, *Typological Writings*.

philosophical theology. In light of this, it comes as no surprise that Edwards regarded the preaching of Scripture as a task of fundamental importance. In an early entry in his *Miscellanies* notebook, he records how he thinks that preaching is really about *power*:

> Without doubt, ministers are to administer the sacraments to Christians, and that they are to administer them only to such as they think Christ would have them administer them. Without doubt, ministers are to teach men what Christ would have them to do, and to teach them who doth these things and who doth them not, that is, who are Christians and who are not, and the people are to hear them as much in this as in other things; and that so far forth as the people are obliged to hear what I teach them, so great is my pastoral, or ministerial, or teaching power. And this is all the difference of power there is amongst ministers, whether apostles or whatever. Thus if I in a right manner am become the teacher of a people, so far as they ought to hear what I teach them, so much power I have.[10]

Warming to his theme, he goes on to say:

> And if it was plain to all the world of Christians that I was under the infallible guidance of Christ, and [that] I was sent forth to teach the world the will of Christ, then I should have power in all the world: I should have power to teach them what they ought to do, and they would be obliged to hear me; I should have power to teach them who were Christians and who not, and in this likewise they would be obliged to hear me.[11]

This passage appears to be an exercise in megalomania, and no doubt there is something of this present in the writing of the young, Yale-educated minister. But what is just as interesting for our purposes is the way in which Edwards conceives of the task of the preacher. True preaching has to do with what we might term the *rhetoric of power*, that is, with words that change their hearers by the attending work of the Holy Spirit. Edwards was certainly not of the view that "sticks and stones can break my bones but words can never harm me." He believed that words have the power to save or to damn. If that is the case, then, from a certain point of view, preachers of the gospel are the most powerful of people. For this reason, Edwards thought expository preaching was imperative. For the power of the preacher is derived from the authority upon which she or

10. Edwards, *The "Miscellanies,"* 222.

11. Ibid.

he preaches. To the extent that the preacher rightly divides the word of God, she or he delivers words of power that can be the means by which the eternal destiny of her or his auditors is secured.

This is an important factor in rightly understanding Edwards' view of the nature of preaching. It is also borne out by his practice of reading his sermons, and explains why it is that he was never really at home in a purely extemporary style, such as that which marked Whitefield's ministry. As John E. Smith puts it in his reflections upon Edwards' homiletics "[i]t is not surprising to find that by all accounts Edwards's talents were far more literary than oratorical. His weak points appear to have been in voice, gesture and rhythm; his great power was in his masterful use of language."[12] Edwards played to his strengths as a scholar-pastor. But his method was not driven by pragmatic concerns about his own limitations as a preacher, but by his views about the nature of the homiletical task. Edwards' idea of the nature of preaching was very much a logocentric, or word-orientated approach, which elevated the rhetorical component of preaching over other more practical or dramaturgical aspects, such as bodily gesture.

The effects of this approach to preaching were significant. One example comes from the reminiscence of Dr. West of Stockbridge, whom Edwards' early biographer Sereno Dwight quotes the following effect, "On one occasion, when the sermon exceeded two hours in length, he told me that, from the time that Mr. Edwards had fairly unfolded his subject, the attention of the audience was fixed and motionless, until its close; when they seemed disappointed that it should terminate so soon. *There was such a bearing down of truth upon the mind, he observed, that there was no denying it.*"[13] The rhetorical tone reported here is unmistakable.

Preaching Naked Ideas

But Edwards' analysis of the nature of preaching did not stop there. He had views about how rhetorical power could be maximized based upon his analysis of preaching as laying bare the idea one wanted to convey to one's listeners. This notion of "laying bare the idea" was something Edwards learned from his reading of the English philosopher, John Locke. Famously, Locke had defined "ideas" as "Whatsoever the Mind

---

12. Smith, *Jonathan Edwards*, 139.

13. Dwight, *Life of President Edwards*, 604, emphasis added.

perceives in itself, or is the immediate object of Perception, Thought or Understanding."[14] In one respect, Edwards took hold of Locke's definition and applied it to homiletics. This can be seen early on in his intellectual development in his Cover-Leaf Memoranda to his notebook *"Natural Philosophy,"* in which he writes the following: "When I would prove anything, to take special care that the matter be so stated that it shall be seen most clearly and distinctly by everyone just how much I would prove; and so to extricate all questions from the least confusion or ambiguity of words, *so that the ideas shall be left naked.*"[15]

The Harvard historian Perry Miller thought this an important indication of what he called Edwards' rhetoric of sensation, according to which ideas were not merely concepts but the vehicles of *emotion* used by Edwards to galvanize and reorient his congregation.[16] But that cannot be right. Edwards wrote about religious *affections,* not religious *emotions*; the two are not synonyms. Whereas emotions can be thought of as equivalent to mere passions to which we are subject, affections have to do with the apprehension of a thing, "the response of the self to an *idea*."[17] In other words, unlike emotions, affections involve the understanding. An affective knowledge of a thing involves acquaintance with that thing; it requires experience of that thing as well as comprehension of it. Edwards maintained that the believer is given a "new sense of things" in conversion, including "a new simple idea" of his or

14. Locke, *An Essay Concerning Human Understanding,* II. VIII. 8.

15. Edwards, *Scientific and Philosophical Writings,* 193. Interestingly, in the same passage Edwards reminds himself to be plain in his speech, so as not to wear his learning on his sleeve. He says, "be very moderate in the use of terms of art. Let it not look as if I was much read, or conversant with books or the learned world" (ibid.) In light of these latter remarks, one wonders what he would have made of the common modern homiletical practice of referring to "the original Greek" when speaking to audiences with no understanding and little interest in matters of philology.

16. "Edwards great discovery, his dramatic refashioning of the theory of sensational rhetoric, was his assertion that an idea in the mind is not only a form of perception but is also a determination of love and hate. To apprehend things only by their signs or by words is not to apprehend them at all; but to apprehend them by their ideas is to comprehend them not only intellectually but passionately. For Edwards, in short, an idea became not merely a concept but an emotion." Miller, *Errand into the Wilderness,* 179. But Miller overstates matters when he goes on to say, "For Edwards it [i.e., his 're-fashioning of the rhetoric of sensation'] was the most important achievement of his life and the key to his doctrine and practice." A more sure-footed account of Edwards in this regard can be found in Kimnach, "Jonathan Edwards's Pursuit of Reality," 102–17.

17. Smith, *Jonathan Edwards,* 33.

her relationship to God. The preaching of Scripture is what "activates" this in the believer. It is what brings about a moral reorientation of the sinner. He writes, "Something is perceived by a true saint, in the exercise of this new sense of mind, in spiritual and divine things, as entirely diverse from anything that is perceived in them, by natural men, as the sweet taste of honey is diverse from the ideas men get of honey by only looking on it, and feeling of it."[18]

Edwards' desire to reach his congregation with homiletical power meant that he made a concerted effort to craft sermons that would be affecting. And since, by his own admission, affections were roused when a person apprehended an idea, it was only natural for him to think that he ought to spend his sermons laying bare those ideas, making them as clear as possible, so as to be as transparent a vehicle for the susurrations of the Holy Ghost as he could make them. As he says in his *Some Thoughts Concerning the Present Revival of Religion,*

> I think an exceedingly affectionate way of preaching about the great things of religion, has itself no tendency to beget false apprehensions of them; but on the contrary a much greater tendency to beget true apprehensions of them, than a moderate, dull, indifferent way of speaking of 'em. . . . I should think myself in the way of my duty to raise the affections of my hearers as high as possibly I can, provided that they are affected with nothing but truth, and with affections that are not disagreeable to the nature of what they are affected with. . . . Our people don't so much need to have their heads stored, as to have their hearts touched; and they stand in the greatest need of that sort of preaching that has the greatest tendency to do this.[19]

On "Plain Style" and "Subtile Distinctions"

Edwards published only one series of sermons in his lifetime under the rather prosaic title *Discourses on Various Important Subjects.* They were prepared for the press at the behest of his congregation, as a sort of memorial to the recent spiritual awakening (already receding into the past by the time they were printed). Taken from the 1740s, the period in

18. Edwards, *Religious Affection,* 206. See also Edwards' sermon, "A Divine and Supernatural Light" in which this analogy with honey is spelled out, in Edwards, *Sermons and Discourses,* 405–26.

19. Edwards, *Some Thoughts Concerning the Present Revival of Religion,* 386–88.

which he was most active as a minister, they comprise an interesting set of polished Edwardsian gems.

In the Preface to these sermons, Edwards offers some comment on the style of the sermons that have an important bearing upon his views about the nature and purpose of the sermon form. In reflecting on the complexities involved in one of the sermons on justification by faith, he writes that divines that have championed this doctrine have been criticized by fashionable eighteenth-century theologians who argue that the classical doctrine is encumbered by "speculative niceties" and "subtile distinctions" which only serve the cause of further dispute. Against such work, these early modern theologians had set up a more "plain, easy, and natural account of things." But to these theologians Edwards has a ready answer. Many "are ready to start at anything that looks like nice distinction, and to condemn it for nonsense without examination." But, observes Edwards with more than a hint of sarcasm, upon "the same account, we might expect to have St. Paul's epistles, that are full of very nice distinctions, called nonsense, and unintelligible jargon, had not they the good luck, to be universally received by all Christians, as part of the holy Scriptures."[20] Logical rigor—even hard concepts, carefully explained— are not things Edwards thought should be absent from a well-formed sermon. Progress in the Christian faith implies progress in our knowledge of God. So it is important, from an Edwardsian point of view that the minister feed her or his flock with expository material that helps the more advanced as well as the immature.

He goes on to offer this comment on the sermons he prepared for the press:

> If the distinctions I have made use of in handling this subject are found to be inconsistent, trivial, and unscriptural niceties, tending only to cloud the subject, I ought to be willing that they should be rejected; but if on due examination they are found both scriptural and rational, I humbly conceive that it will be unjust to condemn them, merely because they are distinctions, under a notion that niceness in divinity never helps it, but always perplexes and darkens it.[21]

In a veiled attack upon the "modern divines" to which he referred earlier in the Preface, Edwards explains that he has adopted a "plain" and

---

20. Ibid.

21. Edwards, *Sermons and Discourses*, 796.

"unfashionable way of preaching," the fruits of which have been blessed in the Awakening. Although he appears to worry about the lack of "such ornaments as politeness, and modishness of style and method" that his sermons display, it is clear from the context that Edwards is criticizing his opponents, not apologizing for the "plain" manner of his own preaching.

Weighing Edwardsian Homiletics

Let us take stock. Edwards thinks that the preacher really concerned to effectively communicate to his congregation will endeavor to speak clearly, plainly, without ornament, without artifice, and without ostentatious display of his or her learning. The pulpit is not the place for "polite" or "fashionable" ideas. It is the place at which God's word is declared. For this reason sermons should be clear, well formed, and, where it is possible, simple and to the point. This does not necessarily mean that sermons should avoid difficult or convoluted doctrine, however. Edwards is clear that good preaching involves attending to the different needs of one's hearers, ensuring that those who have made some progress in the faith are ministered to as much as those who are just starting out. Presumably, he would not be a fan of the modern development of so-called "seeker" style preaching in which the gospel is simply declared every week and no attempt is made to develop or "improve" the great doctrines of the Christian faith through systematic exposition. Rather, Edwards is of the view that the pastor has a responsibility to equip the saints through teaching them the whole counsel of God—even when that involves hard or complex material, of the sort Edwards covers in his sermon, "Justification by Faith."

We have also seen that Edwards conceives of the sermon as an exercise in rhetorical power, or what Perry Miller calls the rhetoric of sensation. Such power is achieved through the clear presentation of the ideas that lie behind the passages of Scripture that are preached. This is Edwards' debt to Locke, although his semi-technical use of the category of "ideas" is more ontological than epistemological, that is, has more to do with the uncovering of how things are rather than what we know (although progress in knowledge can, of course, lead to the uncovering of how things are). The aim in laying bare the ideas of Scripture is to affect those that hear the sermon, so as to bring about a complete moral reorientation (in the case of those who are unconverted), and the introduction (via divine grace) of a new simple idea by means of which the regenerate are able to see things in a whole new light, from a God's eye point of view. Those who are already believers may also benefit from such affecting doctrine, in their encouragement and progress in understanding the faith. Little wonder that Edwards thought of the sermon in what I have called a logocentric (i.e., word-centered) fashion.

However, his approach to homiletics is not without its shortcomings and there are important ways in which the retrieval of what Edwards says about preaching must be tempered for a very different contemporary context. There are several obvious ways in which how Edwards approached his preaching differs significantly from his modern counterparts.

For one thing, the length and doctrinal complexity of his sermons would simply be practically impossible in a modern context. This is not simply because in a world of instant telecommunication, where people are bombarded with media of many different kinds on a daily basis, it would be unwise to presume that many congregations would tolerate a theological disquisition of this duration on a regular basis. A more fundamental gulf that separates Edwards from modern congregations has to do with the fact that his was a world saturated with biblical language and idioms, where his hearers had developed a tolerance, even delight in, the sermon. Harriet Beecher Stowe, a product of the New England formed by the theology of Edwards and his disciples, immortalized this culture in her novels.[22] She writes, "Never was there a community where the roots of common life were shot down so deeply, and were so intensely grappled around things sublime and eternal."[23] The intricate metaphysical systems theologians like Edwards and his disciples built in their studies and then preached from their pulpits were

> discussed by every farmer, in intervals of plough and hoe, by every woman and girl, at loom, spinning-wheel and washtub. New England was one vast sea, surging from depths to heights with thought and discussion on the most insoluble of mysteries. And it is to be added that no man or woman accepted any theory or speculation simply as a theory or speculation; all was profoundly real and vital—a foundation on which actual life was based with intensest earnestness.[24]

22. See Stowe, *The Minister's Wooing* and *Oldtown Folks*, both of which place New Divinity theologians—that is theologian-pastors schooled in the Edwardsian theology—at the centre of their narratives.

23. Stowe, *The Minister's Wooing*, 332.

24. Ibid., 334.

But clearly this is a far cry from the culture that has formed congregations in the complex liberal democracies of the modern western world. Retrieving Edwardsian principles for contemporary preaching must begin by acknowledging this gulf.

More may be tempted to the retired scholarly life that Edwards adopted in order to preach effectively. This has much to commend it, but comes at considerable cost—a cost most modern preachers will find too great. Edwards was a singular individual, but his life of almost monastic retirement did not help him to be an effective pastor. After all the revivals in Northampton, he was ejected from his living and spent the last years of his life as a missionary on the frontier. At least part of the problem (though by no means all) was his failure to attend to aspects of his vocation other than scholarship.

Finally, even if we balk at the extent to which Edwards' conception of preaching is logocentric, or worry that a sermon that is read is no sermon at all, there is much to commend Edwards' idea of preaching as the rhetoric of sensation aimed at laying bare the ideas of Scripture in order to affect those that hear it. Here too, he seeks to transcend what is often, and mistakenly, perceived to be a disjunction with which the preacher is faced: *either* an affecting (or worse, emotionally appealing) sermon, *or* a reasoned discourse. According to Edwards rightly dividing the word of God requires both.

The Bible for the Masses

The Popular Preaching of C. H. Spurgeon

Peter J. Morden

Introduction

ON 28 JULY 1878 Charles Haddon Spurgeon (1834–92) conducted an open air service in Rothesay, on the Isle of Bute, off the west coast of Scotland. The news that Spurgeon would be speaking on the island had created much excitement. Many had caught one of the steamers that worked the river Clyde, travelling "doon the watter" from nearby Glasgow in order to hear him. These joined the holiday makers who were already packing into Bute, a Victorian seaside resort popular with the urban working classes. According to one observer, "Every scrap of information concerning the service was eagerly devoured." When the time came for Spurgeon to preach, a staggeringly large crowd had gathered, with estimates suggesting that as many as 20,000 people were present for the open air service. The message was delivered with what our observer said was "marvellous power." Many of the hearers were so moved that they later perched along the harbor wall in their thousands, waving goodbye as the boat carrying the speaker made its way out of the bay.[1]

---

1. Spurgeon, *Autobiography*, 1.371–72. The observer was A. G. Short, a minister who had trained at Spurgeon's Pastors' College. Spurgeon's visit to Bute coincided with the traditional "Glasgow Fair Fortnight." Many factories were closed, hence the large

This incident is suggestive of Spurgeon's status as the foremost popular preacher of his era. In an age of great pulpiteers he was the best known of them all, becoming something of a Victorian "celebrity." Born and brought up in rural Cambridgeshire, he came to London to minister in 1853 whilst still a teenager and soon became the preaching sensation of the capital. His fame quickly spread and, through reports of his ministry and the transnational circulation of his printed sermons, he became a global phenomenon. As early as 1858, when he was still only twenty-four, the *North American Review* was reporting that Americans returning from a trip to England were invariably asked two questions, namely: "Did you see the Queen?" and "Did you hear Spurgeon?"[2] There were some in the 1850s who thought his fame would resemble that of a comet—he would blaze brightly for a short while and then fall from view just as suddenly as he had appeared. But they were proved wrong. In 1861 his congregation relocated to the specially built Metropolitan Tabernacle, which had a seating capacity of just over 5,000. Spurgeon would fill the building to overflowing Sunday-by-Sunday for the rest of his long London ministry.[3]

One of the reasons for this popularity was an exceptional combination of gifts. He had an extraordinary voice, immensely powerful whilst at the same time modulated and clear, so that some referred to it as musical.[4] This gave him the capacity to address vast crowds such as the one at Rothesay and still be heard to great effect. His approach to sermon preparation was extraordinary too. With regard to his regular Sunday ministry, the only written preparation he engaged in was a few hours on Saturday night (for the Sunday morning), and a few additional hours on Sunday afternoon (for the evening service).[5] Thousands of his sermon outlines survive, many little more than brief lists of headings and sub-headings, some written quite literally on the backs of envelopes.[6] From these scanty notes he would preach messages full of vivid language and telling imagery which repeatedly left his congregation spellbound. This ability to communicate was heightened by his highly dramatic, extempore style of delivery. His approach was reminiscent of the eighteenth-

---

numbers able to be present to hear him.

2. *North American Review,* 275.

3. For a more detailed biography of Spurgeon, see Morden, *C. H. Spurgeon.*

4. Fullerton, *C. H. Spurgeon,* 323; cf. 321.

5. Spurgeon, *Autobiography,* 4.65, 73.

6. "C. H. Spurgeon's pulpit notes," (L2.1).

century evangelist George Whitefield, and comparisons between the two
men were often made.[7] So, in Spurgeon a number of remarkable gifts
came together in a way which helps explain his effectiveness.

But, while it is important to recognize Spurgeon's unusual gifted-
ness, crucial additional reasons for his impact—especially amongst the
working and middle classes—can be adduced. This chapter explores
three of these: firstly, the connections between his preaching and popular culture; secondly, his commitment to preach the biblical text; and,
thirdly, his deep love of Scripture and his desire to be shaped by it and to
live it out, what I am calling his own, personal "indwelling" of the text.[8]

Spurgeon and Victorian Culture

First of all, the relationship between Spurgeon and various currents in
Victorian culture can be examined. He is sometimes regarded as a man
upon whom the Victorian era left little imprint, an English Puritan "born
out of due time" who stood resolutely against contemporary trends. Ernest Bacon provides an example of this approach. In his biography of
Spurgeon, subtitled *Heir of the Puritans*, Bacon states that his subject
"was completely molded and fashioned by those spiritual giants of the
sixteenth and seventeenth centuries, the Puritans. He stood in their noble
tradition, in the direct line of their theology and outlook."[9] It is true that
Spurgeon owed a substantial debt to the Puritans; indeed evidence of
this is shot through his books and published preaching. For instance, his
survey of biblical commentaries and expositions, entitled *Commenting
and Commentaries*, reveals the high regard he had for Puritan literature.[10]
I have written elsewhere and at length about Spurgeon's relationship to
Puritanism and analyzed some of the ways it shaped his ministry.[11] But
to say Spurgeon was "completely molded and fashioned" by the Puritans
ignores both the selective way he drew from Puritanism and the range of
more contemporary influences which marked him.

7. See, e.g., Magoon, ed., "*The Modern Whitefield*."

8. For the use of the term "indwelling" in respect of the Scriptures, see Colwell,
"The Church as Ethical Community," 222. Colwell encourages a "transformative indwelling of Scripture's story."

9. Bacon, *Spurgeon: Heir of the Puritans*, 102.

10. Spurgeon, *Commenting and Commentaries*, 185; 190; 132–33.

11. Morden, "*Communion with Christ and his People*," 16–46.

One of the most important cultural influences can be treated here by way of example, namely Romanticism. This was the nineteenth-century cultural "mood" that in Britain was often associated with the lake poets, Samuel Taylor Coleridge and William Wordsworth, the historical novelist, Sir Walter Scott, and the art critic, John Ruskin (whom, incidentally, Spurgeon knew personally).[12] Romanticism became increasingly pervasive in Britain as the nineteenth century wore on. Arising partly as a reaction against the Enlightenment, particularly Enlightenment rationalism, Romantics tended to dwell on concepts such as emotion, mystery, wonder, and awe. In addition, heroism was highly prized, as was a love of the wilder side of nature.[13] What Douglas Hedley describes as the "noumenal seas, mountains and lakes" of Coleridge's *The Rime of the Ancient Mariner* are deeply revealing of the Romantic temper.[14]

To argue that Spurgeon was influenced by this cultural movement is not usual.[15] This is partly because he did resist several "Romantic" trends in Victorian religious life, not least the tendency to regard Scripture as inspired only in the same rather vague and nebulous way that poetry is inspired.[16] Nevertheless, as Romanticism became less of a movement of high culture and began to percolate down through Victorian society he was shaped by it, and in a number of different ways. His communication was certainly influenced. On returning from a trip to Italy he declared, "I saw the other day in an Italian grotto a little fern which grew where its leaves continually glistened and danced in the spray of a fountain. It was always green, and neither summer's drought not winter's cold affected it. So let us abide under the sweet influence of Jesus' love."[17] This was a way of waxing lyrical about nature and using it to illustrate spiritual truths which was imbued with Romantic sensibility.

He also exalted the "heroic," doing so in a distinctly Romantic vein. In a sermon preached at the Metropolitan Tabernacle in 1885 he declared,

---

12. See, e.g., John Ruskin to C. H. Spurgeon, 25 November 1862, (D.1.8); Spurgeon, *Autobiography*, 1.94–95. The two men were especially in touch in the late 1850s and early 1860s.

13. Morden, *Communion with Christ and his People*, 113; Bebbington, *Holiness in Nineteenth-Century England*, 13.

14. Hedley, "Theology and the Revolt Against the Enlightenment," 30.

15. Although see Hopkins, *Nonconformity's Romantic Generation*, 252; 256–57.

16. Morden, *Communion with Christ and his People*, 114.

17. Cited by Thielicke, *Encounter with Spurgeon*, 95.

> We count that man happy who has passed through trial and hardship with a brave endurance. Such life is of an interesting and manly kind; but life without struggle and difficulty is thin and tasteless. How can a noble life be constructed if there is no difficulty to overcome, no suffering to bear? . . . Studying the lives of eminent men, we come to this conclusion, that on the whole it is good for a man to bear the yoke; good for a man to breast the billows; good for a man to pass through fire and through water, and so to learn sublime lessons. When we see what poor, paltry things those are who are nursed in the lap of luxury and consequently never come to a real manhood, "we count them happy that endure."[18]

This extract from "The Pitifulness of the Lord . . ." has a Romantic tincture in the way that it consistently evokes a heroic ideal. The faithful Christian is one who passes through "trial" and "hardship" with "brave endurance," battling through fire and water, learning invaluable, character building lessons along the way. Some of this imagery is redolent of John Bunyan's *The Pilgrim's Progress*,[19] but the spirit and tone is also shaped by a popular Romanticism which idealized the heroic. The Christian believer was like Sir Walter Scott's Ivanhoe, nobly battling through against the odds. Spurgeon wrote elsewhere, as knights were made "by a stroke from the sovereign's sword," so Christians would "become princes in Christ's realm" as Christ laid "his cross on their shoulders."[20] As Spurgeon warmed to his theme in "The Pitifulness of the Lord . . ." he drove his point home with a phrase borrowed from the American Romantic poet Henry Wadsworth Longfellow, "life is real, life is earnest."[21] This was a heroic, Romantic vision of the Christian life.

The passage from "The Pitifulness of the Lord . . ." is also significant for the way Spurgeon contrasted the experience of someone bravely passing through suffering with the leisurely lifestyle of the dandified élite, which he regarded as shameful. His Romanticism was not that of high culture, rather it was a Romanticism of the people, one that resonated

18. Spurgeon, "The Pitifulness of The Lord and The Comfort of The Afflicted," James 5:11, 327–28.

19. For the importance of Bunyan to Spurgeon, see Morden, *Communion with Christ and His People*, 26–30.

20. Spurgeon, *The Gospel of the Kingdom*, 248.

21. Spurgeon, "The Pitifulness of the Lord," 328. "Life is real! Life is earnest! / And the grave is not its goal" are lines from Longfellow's *A Psalm of Life*. See, e.g., Longfellow, *Favourite Poems*, 12. I am grateful to David Bebbington for this reference.

with the middle and working classes who flocked to hear him and who read his printed sermons. He habitually championed the common people, a stress which is highly significant. The cooling of Spurgeon's relationship with Ruskin was partly because the latter regarded the former as too common.[22] This emphasis on the common people shows him tapping into another movement that was important in Victorian society.

In siding with the hardworking lower and middle classes (Spurgeon spoke most often of the "common man") over and against the pampered élite, he was engaging in a significant debate that was taking place in Victorian life. There were others in Victorian culture who were making similar points to him. Elizabeth Gaskell, in her novel *North and South*, critiqued the mannered ways of "gentlemen" (identified with the south of England), with a more vigorous, "manly" lifestyle (identified with the industrial north of the book's hero, John Thornton).[23] Another voice— more influential at the time than Gaskell's—was Samuel Smiles, whose hugely popular work *Self Help* had sold over 250,000 copies by 1904. Smiles preached a gospel of thrift, hard work and perseverance in the face of adversity.[24] Spurgeon was an open admirer of Smiles, describing him as "one of the ablest authors of our time."[25] It was quite natural that the pastor of the Metropolitan Tabernacle should commend him (evangelical dislike of the novel would have precluded a similar regard for Gaskell). Spurgeon himself railed against anything that smacked of "culture" (by which he meant high culture) or affectation and consistently affirmed the hard-working agricultural and urban poor and middle classes.

This emphasis repeatedly surfaces in his preaching and writing. For example, when setting out his approach to holiness, he frequently declared that the path to sanctification was especially fitted for the "common man." In a sermon entitled "The Holy Road," preached in 1886, he painted a picture of the way of holiness as a "plain way," and as such a way which was eminently "suitable for [the] common and unlearned." Whereas some commentators spoke of religion as if it were "a very difficult thing" only to be understood by the "cultured few," Spurgeon took the opposite view. To illustrate his basic point "The Holy Road" included a story which exalted the simple piety of an "old farmer" which was from

22. Ruskin to C. H. Spurgeon, 25 November 1862. Ruskin's instinct was to withdraw from the masses, Spurgeon's was to remain among them, indeed to champion them.

23. Cf. Bebbington, "Spurgeon and the Common Man," 68.

24. Smiles, *Self Help*, vii.

25. Spurgeon, *Autobiography*, 1. 7. Cf. Kruppa, *Charles Haddon Spurgeon*, 167.

the "heart" and expressed in "plain speech." This was contrasted favorably with the "learned" definition of faith offered by an Archbishop, which was couched in high flown words and phrases.[26] Repeatedly, in sermons and books, Spurgeon talked up the piety of ordinary people, those who were "every-day saints." Farmers and laborers featured often in his stories of those making progress in the life of holiness.[27] As an extension of this theme, his "John Ploughman" books contained simple homilies self-consciously written for the "toiling masses" in a "rustic style." Spurgeon's stated aim in these popular books was to eschew "refined taste and dainty words" and instead rely on "strong proverbial expressions."[28] If "The Holy Road" was especially fitted for the common people then his preaching and writing were well suited to encourage them and to guide them along the way.

On one level, then, it is not surprising that the working and middle classes, both agrarian and urban, heard him and read him in such overwhelming numbers. He was both shaped by and in tune with different movements in Victorian society, particularly those which resonated with ordinary people. This is far from being the whole story, as I will seek to show, but it does explain his popularity in part.

Preaching the Biblical Text

If analysis of Spurgeon's career shows that various currents in Victorian life flowed through his ministry, it also shows that he was deeply committed to preaching the biblical text. His essential theological framework was Calvinistic, and in adopting this he was influenced by both the Puritans and by eighteenth-century Calvinistic evangelicals.[29] But he refused to be bound by any one system. Writing in his magazine *The Sword and The Trowel* in 1874, he stated that "the truth of God is wider than either of the two great systems [i.e., Calvinism and Arminianism]." He went on to observe that "Calvinism, pure and simple . . . is not perfect, for it lacks some of the balancing truths of a system which arose as a remonstrance against its mistakes." If the truth lay "in the valley between two camps"

26. Spurgeon, "The Holy Road," Isaiah 35:8, 415.

27. See, e.g., Spurgeon, "The Saint of the Smithy," 118.

28. Spurgeon, *John Ploughman's Talk*; Preface.

29. See the chapter, "A Defense of Calvinism" in Spurgeon, *Autobiography*, Vol. 1, 167–78.

then that truth should be followed—wherever it might lead.[30] One of the factors which drove him to this position was his passion for evangelism. He is reported to have once prayed in a prayer meeting, "Lord, hasten to bring in all Thine elect—and then elect some more."[31] But fundamental to his theological stance was his desire to be faithful to the Scriptures, wherever they led. If a text spoke of election he preached it; if it spoke of Christ dying for the whole world he preached that too, urging all people to "come to Jesus."[32] He summed up his approach in the following way, "I like to read my Bible so as never to have to blink when I approach a text. I like to have a theology which enables me to read it right through from beginning to end, and to say, 'I am as pleased with that text as I am with any other.'"[33] Spurgeon was, above all, a *biblical* preacher. For him it was the Bible that was authoritative, not a theological system.

It is worth emphasizing Spurgeon's commitment to the authority of the Bible. For him it was the word of God and, he believed, "untainted by any error."[34] The Bible as originally given was "infallible," and it gave correspondingly "infallible" direction for believers.[35] Tradition and human reason were not authoritative, any more than a theological system was. It was the Bible, and the Bible alone, that was the authority for the church and for individual Christians in all matters of doctrine and practice. This conviction undergirded his preaching. The overarching theme of the book in which this essay takes its place is the central importance of preaching the text of Scripture. Spurgeon's ministry is certainly in tune with this.

What role did Spurgeon ascribe to the human authors of the Bible? The "humanity" of the Scriptures was in fact very important to him. This emphasis was especially to the fore in his teaching on the Psalms. In 1869 he began publishing a multi-volume commentary on the Psalms, *The Treasury of David*. The production of the seven volumes which eventually made up the completed *Treasury* spanned over sixteen years and in many ways the commentary was Spurgeon's *magnum opus*.[36] Writing in

30. Spurgeon, "The Present Position of Calvinism in England," 49–53; cf. "High Doctrine and Broad Doctrine," John 6:37, 49–50.

31. Fullerton, *Spurgeon*, 182.

32. See, e.g., Spurgeon, "High Doctrine and Broad Doctrine," 56.

33. Spurgeon, "General and yet Particular," John 17:2, 237.

34. Spurgeon, "The Bible," Hosea 8:12, 110–12.

35. Spurgeon, "The Talking Book," Proverbs 6:22, 590.

36. Spurgeon, *The Treasury Of David*.

his Preface to Volume Six, he described the book of Psalms, taken as a whole, as the "tongue of saints." By this he meant that the book helped the Christian give voice to feelings which otherwise would have "found no utterance." The Psalms said what Christians themselves "wished to say," helping them vocalize feelings of praise, thankfulness and petition which might not otherwise have found appropriate voice.[37] It also helped believers express their penitence for sin. In his Preface to Volume Two of the *Treasury*, Spurgeon wrote of his experience of commenting on Psalm 51. "The Psalm is very human," he declared, "its cries and sobs are of one born of a woman."[38] For him, the human author of this Psalm was unquestionably David and the occasion which had led to its composition was the exposure, by the prophet Nathan, of the act of adultery committed by the king with Uriah's wife, Bathsheba.[39] In Spurgeon's exposition of Psalm 51 he identified strongly with the penitent king both in his sense of sinfulness and in his trust in God for forgiveness.[40] Taken as a whole, the Psalms provided a "map" of spiritual experience, one which traversed the valleys as well as the high points of the Christian life.[41] In expounding the Psalms in a way that emphasized their humanity he was careful to affirm that they were the word of God. Psalm 51, while being authentically "human" was also "freighted with an inspiration all divine." Indeed, it was "as if the Great Father were putting words into his child's mouth."[42] Nevertheless, the experience of frail, indeed fallible human authors who gave voice not only to their triumphs but also to their failures provided a pattern for Christian believers whose own pilgrimage would also run the whole gamut of spiritual experience.

Spurgeon firmly believed in the importance of the Bible's own "language world." As well as teaching and preaching the Psalms in a way which drew the reader or listener into the world of the Psalmist, he resolutely insisted on the importance of biblical concepts and language. Sinners, he maintained, needed to be justified,[43] redeemed,[44] reconciled

37. Spurgeon, *Treasury Of David*, 6. vii; "The Singing Pilgrim," Psalm 119:54, 181–92.

38. Spurgeon, *Treasury of David*, 2. v.

39. 2 Samuel 11.1–12.14; Spurgeon, *Treasury of David*, 2.449.

40. Spurgeon, *Treasury of David*, 2. 449–56.

41. Ibid., 2. vii.

42. Ibid., 2. v.

43. Spurgeon, "Messrs. Moody And Sankey Defended," Galatians 5:24, 327.

44. Spurgeon, "The Common Salvation," Jude 3, 200.

to God,[45] and forgiven.[46] These terms were often carefully and thought-fully explained, but there was never any question of their not being used.

Spurgeon was committed to this use of biblical language and con-cepts even when he was aware this commitment might offend Victorian sensibilities. His preaching on the atonement can be taken as an example. Over and against those who objected to the "idea of substitution and vi-carious sacrifice," he insisted that on the cross Christ bore "divine wrath in our stead," adding dramatically, "I nail my colors to the cross."[47] He was explicit in condemning those who backed away from the Bible's teaching and language about the atonement because they regarded it as difficult or offensive. As far as he was concerned, he was not going to "shift his ground," nor "adopt any other phraseology." These last comments came in a sermon entitled "The Sacred Love-Token," preached in 1875. In this message he also stated,

> We stand to the literal substitution of Jesus Christ in the place of his people, and his real endurance of suffering and death in their stead, and from this distinct and definite ground we will not move an inch. Even the term, "the blood," from which some shrink with the affectation of great delicacy, we shall not cease to use, whoever may take offence at it, for it brings out the fun-damental truth of the power of God unto salvation.[48]

The comment, that some "shrink" from the cross "with the affecta-tion of great delicacy" showed Spurgeon once again attacking the pur-veyors of high culture. But his distaste for such "refined" attitudes was not the central reason he insisted on the use of a word like "blood" when expounding the atonement. The chief reasons for its continued use were that it was the Bible's own word and that it set forth essential gospel truth.

45. Spurgeon, "Plain Directions," Psalm 4:4, 5, 391.

46. Spurgeon, "Bankrupt Debtors Discharged," Luke 7:42, 493; 499–502; *Autobi-ography*, 1.108, 110.

47. Spurgeon, "Redemption By Price," 1 Cor 6:19–20, 469–70. Spurgeon was thus firmly committed to penal substitution. I am of course aware of the recent debates as to whether this is, in fact, a biblical way of speaking about the cross. For some of the different approaches as they were debated in the UK context, see Tidball, Hilborn, and Thacker, eds. *The Atonement Debate*. My own view is that penal substitution is an important, biblical way of understanding the atonement, although it is not the only way. Spurgeon himself once said, "I feel . . . substitution does not cover the whole of the matter . . . no human conception can completely grasp the whole of the dread mystery." Quoted by Fullerton, *Spurgeon*, 181–82.

48. Spurgeon, "The Sacred Love-Token," Exod 12:13, 483–84.

Never mind if the cultured elite (or someone from the working or middle classes for that matter) objected to the use of the term "blood." It was biblical and it was crucial to the gospel. Consequently, nothing would deter him from using it.

How does such an approach help account for Spurgeon's popularity? Of course, it put some people off. Those who were repelled by his preaching included the novelist, George Elliot, who declared that Spurgeon held to a "grocer's back-parlor view of Calvinistic Christianity,"[49] and Matthew Arnold, son of Thomas Arnold, the famous headmaster of Rugby school. Matthew Arnold disliked the pastor of the Metropolitan Tabernacle intensely. This was partly because they inhabited different cultural worlds.[50] But, again, there was something more. Spurgeon was one of those Arnold derided in print for asserting the "essentialness of their own supposed scriptural order."[51] We might say that Spurgeon was too biblical for Arnold. To an extent, then, his commitment to the biblical text led to criticism.

Nevertheless, he believed that his biblical emphases did make his ministry attractive, for the reason he highlighted in the final sentence of the extract cited from "The Sacred Love-Token." Yes, some might take "offense" at his approach, but it brought out the "fundamental truth of the power of God unto salvation." Through his faithful preaching of the gospel, God was at work in power and lives were changed as a result. He could point to many individuals in his own congregation who were living examples of this dynamic at work, for, even though there was some transfer growth helping to account for the burgeoning numbers at the Tabernacle, there was much conversion growth too. Indeed, there were a significant number of people who Spurgeon could point to who had lived wild and dissolute lives before coming to Christ through his ministry. Moreover, the vast majority of these were now pressing on in holiness, glorifying "Christ daily by their walk and conversation."[52] In short, he believed his own church was evidence enough that the biblical gospel, clearly and unashamedly preached, would win and transform many, even while others rejected it.

---

49. Cited by Munson, *The Nonconformists,* 99. Cf. Fullerton, *Spurgeon,* 222.

50. Bebbington, "Spurgeon and the Common Man," 63–64.

51. Arnold, *Culture and Anarchy,* 31.

52. Spurgeon, "General and Yet Particular," 237.

"Indwelling" the Biblical Text

I want to make one final point about Spurgeon's ministry, an appreciation of which is, I believe, crucial if the power and appeal of his preaching are to rightly understood. The point concerns the way he "indwelt" the Scriptures, seeking to inhabit them and live in the light of them. If they were authoritative for others then they were authoritative for him too.[53] Any other attitude would have smacked of hypocrisy, which he hated. He wanted to be shaped, in the inner and outer dimensions of his life, by the Bible. This commitment was deep and lifelong. As can be imagined, he read the Bible avidly; indeed, the one he used in his study from 1856 onwards was worn to pieces by 1870 when it was sent for rebinding.[54] But what needs to be underlined is the fact that, despite his love for preaching, his primary commitment was to read the Bible formationally, so that its message molded him personally. In a sermon entitled "How to Read the Bible" he set out a step-by-step process by which his hearers could engage with the Scriptures, a process which reflected his own method.

First of all, he emphasized the importance of reading with "understanding." The "benefit" of reading had to come to the "soul" by way of the mind. And, for a real depth of understanding to develop, it was crucial that time was given to the act of reading. He declared, "Do not many of you read your Bible in a hurried way—just a little bit, and off you go? Do you not soon forget what you have read, and lose what effect it seemed to have? How few of you are resolved to get at its soul, its juice, its life, its essence, and to drink in its meaning."[55]

Thus the encouragement was to a diligent, prayerful, slow reading of the Bible with the mind fully engaged in the activity. This might mean careful study of a passage and for this all "means and helps" such as biblical commentaries (Spurgeon himself had a vast stock of these) should be used to aid understanding. But his fundamental aim was to encourage meditation on the text of Scripture itself.[56] Through such careful wrestling with the Scriptures their essential meaning could be grasped.

---

53. See, e.g. Spurgeon, "The Word A Sword," Heb 4:12, 109.

54. Spurgeon, *Autobiography*, 4. 66.

55. Spurgeon, "How to Read the Bible," Matt 12:3–7, 627–31, esp. 631. For another sermon on this theme, see "Understandest Thou What Thou Readest?" Acts 8:30–33, 409–20.

56. Spurgeon, "How to Read the Bible," 630, cf. 626.

This was a vital first step to engaging with the biblical text but, as Spurgeon warmed to his theme in "How to Read the Bible," there was much more he wanted to say. Having reached a measure of understanding with regard to a particular passage, he insisted that its message must be appropriated yet more deeply. Understanding was good, but it was possible to have this and for the Bible to remain a "dead book" and the reader a "dead soul." Consequently, he emphasized the importance of believers knowing the Bible "experimentally," that is, in their own experience. A sound creed was all very well, but that creed needed to be written on the "tablets of [the] heart."[57] It was vital that meditation did not stop once a good level of understanding had been reached. In his commentary on Matthew's Gospel, the *Gospel of the Kingdom*, he echoed an Anglican collect when he encouraged his readers not only to "read," "mark," and "learn" the Scriptures but also to "inwardly digest" them, turning them over repeatedly in the mind so that the "soul" grew strong.[58] Elsewhere in the same commentary he made a similar point with the help of language derived from Bunyan's *Holy War*, "Do not be content merely to open ear-Gate; but rest not satisfied until the King himself comes riding through that gate right up to the very citadel of the town of Mansoul, and takes possession of the castle of your heart."[59]

In "How to Read the Bible" Spurgeon gave an example to illustrate his general point. "The doctrine of election is one thing," he said, "but to know that God has predestined you, and to have the fruit of it in the good works to which you are ordained, is quite another thing."[60] An understanding of the doctrine needed to be followed by the personal knowledge that one was the recipient of God's electing grace, followed in turn by fruitful Christian living. The power of the doctrine needed to be felt and a changed life needed to result. If these experiential steps were missed then the doctrine of election had not been properly appropriated by the Bible reader. Throughout his message, he stressed that, for the Bible to be imbibed spiritually, Jesus had to be present and working by the Holy Spirit. Prayer was vital at every stage. At one point in his message he broke off from addressing his hearers directly and cried out, "O living Christ, make this a living word to me. Thy word is life, but not without

57. Spurgeon, "How to Read the Bible," 633–34.

58. Spurgeon, *Gospel of the Kingdom*, 497. The words are from a Collect for the second Sunday in Advent.

59. Spurgeon, *Gospel of the Kingdom*, 493.

60. Spurgeon, "How to Read the Bible," 631–33.

the Holy Spirit."[61] What he was advocating for others was something he constantly desired for himself, and sought to practice.

This personal appropriation of the Bible's message clearly shaped his preaching, so that often Spurgeon was not only proclaiming its stories and truths but his own experience of them. His preaching on the atonement can again be taken as an example. In one of his Communion meditations, published posthumously in the book *Till He Come*, he declared,

> Beloved friends, we very calmly and coolly talk about this thing [the atonement], but it is the greatest marvel in the universe; it is the miracle of earth, the mystery of heaven, the terror of hell. Could we fully realize the guilt of sin, the punishment due to it, and the literal substitution of Christ, it would work in us an intense enthusiasm of gratitude, love, and praise. I do not wonder our Methodist friends shout, "Hallelujah!" This is enough to make us all shout and sing, as long as we live, "Glory, glory to the Son of God!"[62]

The "literal substitution of Christ" was not an abstract concept to be debated but something living and vital, to be believed in ever more deeply. If the atonement were truly appreciated it would "work in" the believer intense feelings of "gratitude" and "love" to God, feelings which could not help being expressed in praise. To Spurgeon's mind, for someone to discuss the atonement in a detached way was a sure sign that they had not really understood it. In point of fact, to speak "coolly and calmly" about the cross was quite beyond him, and statements about its "preciousness" for the believer were never far away from any of his expositions of the atonement.[63] He did not just believe in the work of Christ on the cross, he "rested" in it. At one point in the aforementioned "The Sacred Love-Token," he declared, "We dwell beneath the blood mark, and rejoice that Jesus for us poured out his soul unto death when he bore the sins of many." Phrases such as "we dwell," "rejoice," and "for us" bring out the extent to which his theology of atonement was deeply a part of him. It is little surprise that once again he stated that for him, these truths were "precious."[64]

61. Spurgeon, "How to Read the Bible," 633–34.

62. Spurgeon, "The Sin Bearer," 338. Spurgeon was converted among the "Primitive Methodists" who were known for their outbursts of fervent praise. For his conversion, see Spurgeon, *Autobiography*, 1.97–115.

63. See, e.g., "The Well Beloved," 104–5.

64. Spurgeon, "The Sacred Love-Token," 483–84.

Undoubtedly Spurgeon's theology of the atonement was, in Eugene Peterson's terms, a *spiritual* theology, that is one that is "lived," the antithesis of a theology "depersonalized into information about God."[65] This was true of his engagement with the Bible more generally. To sum up, his commitment to the Bible was not merely cerebral, neither was it "professional," a necessary commitment given that he was a preacher of its message. Indeed, such approaches would have been anathema to him. Certainly, he studied the Scriptures rigorously in order to understand them, and his commitment to preaching well was strong (even if his approach to sermon preparation was somewhat unorthodox). But he studied the Bible not primarily in order to preach but in order to live, and having made progress in understanding it he sought to appropriate its message in a way that encompassed both "head" and "heart." In short, his overriding desire was to indwell the Bible's message—a message he believed was focused on Christ and his gospel[66]—and then to live it out.

This commitment to "live out of" the text of Scripture was noticed by Spurgeon's contemporaries, a number of whom located his effectiveness in preaching and writing in his own personal appropriation of the message he proclaimed. The "chief secret" of his power, said one observer, was "his faith in the living God, and in the power of his gospel. He had a real belief in the gospel . . ."[67] This faith, according to another commentator, led to "genuine fervor of conviction" when he was in the pulpit.[68] He was regularly described as "earnest." Tabernacle elder Thomas Cox remembered his pastor as being "intensely earnest/at times terribly so."[69] This "earnestness" was alleviated by regular flashes of humor which further helped make his preaching attractive.[70] But his unshakable conviction that what he was preaching was true and vital, a conviction forged in his own experience of the message, was

---

65. Peterson, *Christ Plays in Ten Thousand Places,* 1. Elsewhere Peterson speaks of "Spiritual Theology" as to do with "prayer" and "spiritual formation," linked with reading the Bible "formationally, not just intellectually." See *Subversive Spirituality,* 259.

66. See the section "The Bible and Christ" in chapter 5 of Morden, *"Communion with Christ and His People,"* 121–27.

67. As cited by Fullerton, *Spurgeon,* 328.

68. As cited by ibid., 324.

69. Cox, "Notes on C. H. Spurgeon," 2. These handwritten notes are not bound but the pages are numbered. See Fullerton, *Spurgeon,* 322, for further descriptions of Spurgeon as "earnest."

70. See Morden, "Spurgeon and Humour," 20–22.

fundamental. People knew he believed and lived what he preached (he was, by common consent, a man of "transparent honesty").[71] Spurgeon did not parade this integrity, but people could not help noticing it. Of course he was a flawed individual,[72] yet he loved Christ, loved the Bible, and lived its message. And—whether in Rothesay or London or indeed around the world—people responded to Spurgeon's preaching, not just because of what he said but also because of who he was.

Conclusion

Preaching in 1888, just a few years before the end of his ministry (although, of course, Spurgeon did not know this), he declared,

> If we had common themes to speak about, we might leave the pulpit as a weary pleader quits the forum; but as, "The mouth of the Lord hath spoken it," we feel his Word to be as fire in our bones, and we grow more weary with refraining than with testifying. O my brethren, the Word of the Lord is so precious that we must in the morning sow this blessed seed, and in the evening we must not withhold our hands. It is a living seed and the seed of life, and therefore we must diligently scatter it.[73]

The preacher's words form a fitting conclusion to this study. Spurgeon was not—as I have sought to show—somehow isolated from the cultural currents which flowed through Victorian life. He was embedded in various aspects of Victorian culture both consciously and unconsciously. But while this in part helps us appreciate his popular appeal, on its own it is in an insufficient explanation. He cannot be understood unless his avowed commitment to proclaim the "text message" of the Bible without fear or favor is taken seriously. Moreover, for him the Bible was "living" and "precious." He had experienced its live-giving power personally through study and meditation and as he sought to live a life conformed to the contours of the gospel story. In other words, his commitment to proclaim the message of the Bible was so strong because he himself had been molded in significant degree by its truth

---

71. As cited by Fullerton, *Spurgeon*, 328.

72. For one example of his imperfections, see his mature account of his conversion, which I have argued was significantly embroidered. Morden, *"Communion with Christ and his People,"* 48–53.

73. Spurgeon, "The Infallibility of Scripture," Isa 1:20, 149.

and power. An appreciation of this is vital if we are to grasp both his appeal and the way he divided opinion. Having personally encountered full and rich life in Christ through the gospel "seed," he was determined to scatter that seed "diligently," with a real measure of cultural sensitivity but without smoothing out the challenging features of the message. Spurgeon's overall approach gives those of us who preach and teach today much to reflect on.

8

Homiletics and Biblical Fidelity
An Ecclesial Approach to Orthodox Preaching[1]
Andrew Walker

Introduction

IT IS DIFFICULT TO know how best to characterize Orthodox preaching: to call it public discourse is to tell us nothing of its content and to add the prefix "theological" suggests some kind of specialized academic treatment which is neither helpful nor accurate and misses the essential biblical nature of Orthodox preaching. As the New Testament was written in everyday Greek perhaps it would be helpful to look at some of the common usages that emerged in the mainly Greek-speaking Eastern Church.

The word preach does not exist in Greek but there are several terms that we translate in English as preaching. Preaching can be an announcement of good news, "good tidings of great joy" (Luke 2:10, NKJ), though we usually think of announcing good news as the gospel (*euangelion*). The most common Greek term translated in English as preaching in the New Testament is *kerusso* (used sixty-one times); this word is associated with *kerygma* because the kerygma centres on the message of salvation (though it only appears in the Greek text nine times). *Kerusso* is stronger than announce even more so than *diangello* (widely announce) and *katangello* (publicly announce). *Kerusso* is stronger because it is a proclamation, or

1. I shall use transliterations throughout this chapter.

117

the sort of important message associated with a herald. It has a town crier, "hear ye, hear ye," feel about it. Another example would be a Royal proclamation of pardon; perhaps even something more intimate like the annunciation to Mary by the Angel Gabriel[2] that although she is a virgin she will become the bearer of God (*theotokos*). In the words of St. Athanasius of Alexandria,

> Today is the beginning of our salvation,
> And the revelation of the eternal mystery!
> The Son of God becomes the Son of the Virgin
> As Gabriel announces the coming of Grace.
> Together with him let us cry to the Theotokos:
> Rejoice, O Full of Grace, the Lord is with you"![3]

There are two more NT Greek words that I want to include in this chapter (though there are others) to highlight an Orthodox understanding of preaching and they are *dialegomai,* which means discuss or converse, and *didache,* which means teaching (pedagogy). Although, like Catholics and Protestants, Orthodox have a history of missions and evangelization there is not usually a special mode or style that characterizes preaching for such special tasks; modern theological writers like Alexander Schmemann have stressed that missiology needs to be rooted in ecclesiology[4] and my aim in this chapter, with deep indebtedness to Schmemann, is to look at preaching "in the round" as an expression of the life and teachings of the Orthodox Church.

A perennial temptation for all Orthodox writers is to confuse the empirical church with the eschatological church, idealize it and then historicize it. This amounts to hagiography more often than not—as if every word of the Desert Fathers were worth re-iterating; or we conveniently forget that the downside to having your village priest as one of your own class (nineteenth-century Russian rural priests, for example, were usually from the peasantry) is that they were often ignorant of their own tradition and illiterate. The approach I am going to take is not to rubbish this idealization for this chapter is not essentially one of historiography nor an exercise in chest beating or confession of empirical in-exactitude (though we could do with a more balanced appraisal of our past). What I plan to do is to identify the key components of Orthodox preaching by taking an

2. Angels are usually heralds from God in the New Testament.

3. From the Troparion of the Feast of the Annunciation, Orthodox liturgy.

4. Schememann, *Church World Mission.*

historical approach that I believe identifies what is most distinctive about the practice.

Having said that, there is, in fact, no identifiable unique way of preaching in the Orthodox Church,[5] but I think there are three historical factors that have shaped its development. The first is that Orthodoxy sees itself as a biblical Church or to be more precise an apostolic one. In order to explain this I will endeavor to show that to drive a wedge between Bible and Tradition is alien to Orthodox sensibilities. The second historical factor is to highlight that the ancient Sees of Alexandria and Antioch developed distinct styles of biblical hermeneutics, which polarized the ancient church to a limited degree, although eventually both methods became absorbed in the Orthodox Tradition. Alexandria with its strong Platonic and Stoic influences on both Jewish and Gentile populations favored allegorical approaches to the Bible (as did the Alexandrian Jewish philosopher Philo [20 BC–30 AD] before Clement [c 150–215 AD] and Origen [185 AD–254] adopted the method for the church). In simple terms the Bible was read on three levels—the literal meaning, the moral meaning, and the spiritual meaning. Origen stressed both the need for divine guidance and intellectual rigor.

By contrast Antiochean hermeneutics did not go beyond the literal meaning and paid great attention to historical context. Antioch Christians thought allegorical interpretations were fanciful and rejected any notion of hidden meanings in the text. Conversely Alexandrian Christians thought Antiochean hermeneutics were pedestrian and lacked spiritual insight.[6] I am going to concentrate on the person and ministry of St. John Chrysostom, an Antiochean,[7] as my third key historical factor in

---

5. There are, however, different ways of looking at things. John 20, for example, is most famous in the Western churches for the story of "Doubting Thomas," but in the Orthodox Church he is hailed as a hero of the faith, a Confessor, for he is the only person in the new Testament to call Jesus God, *ho kyrios mou kai ho theos mou*, literally translated as "the lord and the God of me."

6. These hermeneutical differences have been influential on the Christian church from the patristic era to the present day (though like the Orthodox, Roman Catholics, and Protestants have freely borrowed from both schools). C. S. Lewis, I would say, was more Alexandrian in his interpretation of the Bible than a follower of the Antiochean school (see my article Walker, "Scripture, Revelation, and Platonism," 19–35) and I would say the preacher who exhibited the purest example of Antiochean hermeneutics I ever heard was Dr. Martin Lloyd Jones of Westminster chapel. His expository style is seen at its best in six published expositions of the epistle to the Romans by Banner of Truth.

7. I am aware that Chrysostom is deeply offensive to many Jews and Christians

the development of Orthodox homiletics, because he was a rhetorician, a charismatic preacher without peer in the early church, and originator of the most widely used Eucharistic liturgy in Orthodox worship. My belief is that it is this liturgy—that bears his name—which is the main repository and vehicle of Orthodox preaching.[8]

Preaching, therefore, is typically ecclesial and expository rather than rhetorical or rhapsodic. Ironically Chrysostom's preaching style is replete with rhetorical flourishes but his approach has been so influential that he will be the main focus of this chapter. Typically he favored the sort of homily that BBC Radio 4 used to call "Lift up your hearts" before they gave us the anodyne "Thought for the Day." There is no better way in showing what he brings to the Orthodox table than to point to his Easter homily, used universally in the Orthodox Church today (and placed at the end of this chapter, by way of reference). When it is read everybody stands. This demonstrates his extraordinary influence on the Orthodox Church for this is an honor usually restricted to the reading of the Gospel.

Scripture and Tradition

Before we pay due homage to the role of Chrysostom in the development of preaching in the Orthodox Church it will be helpful to say something about how the Eastern half of Christendom believe that Scripture and tradition cohere rather than live in dialectical tension as seems to be the case in many Western Churches.[9] I wrote at some length about this some years ago[10] but there are a number of points I wish to reprise here.

---

alike and rather than excuse his anti-Semitism by pointing to his Arab parenting and culture I prefer to take the view that even saints are sinners under grace; they are advanced spiritually in many areas of their lives but they are also retarded in others. Chrysostom uses a particular rhetorical form known as *psogos* when he attacks Judaism and Jews. This rhetorical style is designed to attach blame to a person or group and also pour opprobrium on them. The quote that follows demonstrates why Chrysostom attracted so much criticism: "Are you Jews still disputing the question? Do you not see that you are condemned by the testimony of what Christ and the prophets predicted and which the facts have proved? But why should this surprise me? That is the kind of people you are. From the beginning you have been shameless and obstinate, ready to fight at all times against obvious facts." *Adversus Judaeos*, Homily V, XII.1.

8. I will not go into details here but preaching in Orthodox churches is not only a function of the word—architecture and icons also tell the story. See Trubetskoi, *Icons*.

9. Though things are improving, see Williams, *Evangelicals and Tradition*.

10. Walker, "Deep church as *Paradosis*: Relating Scripture to Tradition," 59–80.

Perhaps the most important is to recognize that Orthodox believers, like Evangelicals among others, think of themselves as people of "The Book." Preaching, therefore, is essentially *biblical*, and fidelity to the gospel is its hallmark. In order to understand this primordial fact it would be helpful if Protestants do not read the history of biblical canonicity through the eyes of the Reformation and Counter Reformation. Events such as Luther's nailing his ninety-five theses to the Wittenburg door in 1517 and the Council of Trent (AD 1545–63) are historically contingent on the fact that the West had already divided from the Eastern churches in the Great Schism of the eleventh century. Strictly speaking the early church was not Roman Catholic or Orthodox, and Protestants did not exist (though heretics were legion). There was the *one undivided church*.

There were of course local customs that we could think of as traditions if we wish but to assume that these customs had anything in common with the theology of Papal infallibility, indulgences, "works righteousness," etc., against which the Reformation doctrines of *sola fidei, sola scriptura* were opposed, is to miss the mark. When the Orthodox use the word Tradition spelled with a capital T (and sometimes there is a prefix attached such as "Holy" or "Sacred") they mean the apostolic (deposit of) faith of the New Testament, as handed down from generation to generation and accumulating dogmatic and universal canonical form along the way (Scripture, creeds, conciliar councils, for example) and the authoritative but not binding sayings and writings of saints and savants of the church.

From at least the time of Irenaeus (c. AD 130–200) the issue of doctrinal authority in the church was never exclusively confined to written biblical texts. This was a pragmatic decision based on common-sense, not an ideological platform to launch polemical assaults on enemies of the church. In what was essentially an oral culture Christian faith was handed on by word of mouth and religious practices sanctioned by time as well as texts enshrined in canonical certainty. St. Basil of Caesarea writing in approximately AD 380 said, "Of the beliefs and practices preserved in the church . . . we have some derived from written teaching; others delivered to us 'in a mystery' from the tradition of the Apostles; and both classes have the same force for true piety. No one will dispute these; no one, at any rate, who has the slightest experience of the institutions of the church . . ."[11] Culturally, we need to remind ourselves, the early church

---

11. Quoted in Battenson, *Later Christian Fathers*, 59.

belongs in antiquity, where in contradistinction to modernity it was *de rigueur* to look to the past for legitimating new arguments.

The honor given to ancient authorities was both appealing to the Early Church and compelling. It was appealing because until late in the second century there were still people alive who could remember people who "knew the Lord." Irenaeus was himself one such person; he was a disciple of the martyr Polycarp, who in turn was a disciple of the Apostle John, "the disciple whom Jesus loved" (John 21:20, NRV). But honoring the past was also compelling because the great problem heretics had to overcome in order to overturn orthodoxy in the early church—however philosophically sophisticated their arguments were—was that of demonstrating that the apostles and their acknowledged successors also favored the same arguments—and this they could not do. So, for example, Marcion (expelled from the church in AD 144) failed in his project to exclude the Old Testament from Christianity because he could find no apostolic witness to support him; there was also the embarrassing fact that Jesus quoted copiously from the Torah.

In the modern era the German theologian, Adolf Harnack has done much to promulgate the idea that the Orthodox Church was a Hellenistic hijacking of the primitive Jewish church.[12] It is certainly the case that the "way of negation," which is often thought to mirror Greek mysticism (*apophasis,* to give it its Patristic form), lends itself to a contemplative spirituality in which silence is valued more than words. Such mysticism, however, is not a function of the *apophatic* logic of the Greek Athenaeum. As Jaraslov Pelikan has shown, such logic was a feature of Greek language itself,[13] and in classical culture trying to know who God is by telling us who and what he is not was thought to be a superior way of coming to know God while admitting there was an unknowingness in this method (*agnosia*), and that meant that all positive statements about God (the *cataphatic*) were provisional and subject to re-formulation. If the strong *apophatic* side to Orthodox Tradition—which affords it some modesty and leaves room for wonder and surprise—is put into abeyance the Orthodox are capable of slipping into self-righteous fundamentalism and becoming unbearably smug.

It has been necessary to demonstrate Orthodox commitment to the Bible and creed as an antidote to the erroneous view that Orthodoxy is

12. Nowak, et al., eds., *Adolf Harnack.*

13. Pelikan, *Christianity And Classical Culture,* chapter 3.

some sort of traditionalism in which biblical faith is fragile and tangential. When the Bible is carried into the nave of the church it is carried aloft in a celebration of the word of God that would warm the heart of a Scottish Presbyterian. Before the Gospel is read by the priest the deacon intones "Wisdom: let us attend," and during the reading of the passage it is the only time you can be certain that all chattering will cease for the faithful know that in a very special way God is speaking to them directly.[14]

But, as I said at the beginning of this section, the Orthodox do not believe that true faith comes in unwrapped biblical form; there is a great deal of Tradition that comes from being a member of the Body of Christ living in the commonwealth of the ecclesia and learning from received religious practices handed down. Jesus, of course, left no written gospel of his own (the only writing attributed to him in the New Testament was writing with his finger on the ground in the Temple when the Pharisees brought to him a woman "caught in adultery" (John 8:6)).[15] And while we clearly have written accounts of his life and those of his disciples they are by no means exhaustive. The final verse in John's Gospel reads, "But there are also many other things that Jesus did; if every one of them were written down, I suppose that the world itself could not contain the books that would be written" (John 21:25, NRV).

It is time to draw this preliminary discussion of Scripture and Tradition to a close. Dr. William Abraham—Professor of Wesleyan Studies at Southern Methodist University, Texas, and author of *Canon and Criterion in Christian Theology* (Clarendon, 1998)—reminded the audience at a recent conference at King's College London that the Bible is the book of the church, the church is not a product of the Bible. This really is the bullet Protestants have to bite on if they are going to be loyal to the apostolic tradition and follow the main road, as Lewis called it.[16] It took several centuries before a canon of Scripture was established,[17] but it is

14. During Holy Week at the end of Great Lent all four Gospels are read consecutively in one sitting—or more appropriately one standing.

15. John's Gospel neither tells us what language he wrote in or what he wrote—it might have been a doodle in his native Aramaic for all we know.

16. See his preface to the 3rd edition of the *Pilgrim's Regress* (1943). First published in London by J. M. Dent & Sons Ltd. (1933).

17. This is because there were several disputed books of apostolic origin (*antilegomena*). Jude, for example, was suspect because he quotes from the apocrypha; 2 Peter, because it appears so late in the tradition, church authorities were not certain whether it was written by the Apostle Peter or not. There were others but by far the most contentious was John's Revelation. Indeed although the Roman Catholic Church

not really possible when considering the patristic era to isolate Scripture from canons of creeds, liturgical norms, and the writings of the Fathers (though this is not to say that there is no hierarchy in canonical criteria). The late Fr. Lev Gillet, who always signed his writings as "a monk of the Eastern Church," put Scripture first, followed by the definitions of the ecumenical councils, next are the liturgical texts, and bringing up the rear the writings of the Fathers.

St John Chrysostom:
From Pagan Rhetorician to Christian Preacher

Unless you are a person who has been influenced by the cult book *Zen and the Art of Motor Cycle Maintenance,*[18] there is a strong chance that you have never come under the spell of rhetoric and certainly not as it was conjured up by Greek Antiquity. And yet while rhetoric has a chequered career in Greek philosophy[19] it was one of the most prestigious courses to study at the Athenaeum during the classical period of Greek

---

seemed happy with it from the Council of Ephesus (AD 431), probably because it was on Athanasius' (the hero of Nicaea) list of New Testament books, the Orthodox Church kept it at arms length. In the fourth century St. John Chrysostom argued fiercely against its inclusion—mainly on grounds of contentious interpretations and the Syrian Church did not include it until the fifth century. Remarkably it was not accepted as canonical by Constantinople until the ninth century. Possibly because an ecumenical council never ratified Revelation, it is the only canonical book of the New Testament never to be read in Church and is absent from the lectionary. Protestants also have their own *antilegomena* and this calls into serious question the reliance on *sola scriptura*. To be fair Calvin never denied the authenticity of John's Apocalypse (though it was the only book of the Bible for which he never wrote a commentary). Luther, on the other hand, initially excluded it, as he did Hebrews, James, and Jude. When he published his version of the New Testament in 1522 he placed them at the end of the main text with a preface, which declared mischievously that these books were not as authentic as the rest of Scripture, as they were disputed in the early church. A more plausible explanation is that Luther could find nothing of worth in them concerning his primary conviction of "justification by faith." The suspicion that Luther operated "a canon within the canon"—as if he were the sole arbiter of truth—is supported by his famous comment on James that it was an "epistle of straw," and on his unwarranted translation of Romans 1:17 as "justification by faith *alone*."

18. Pirsig, *Zen and the Art of Motor Cycle Maintenance*.

19. Not every philosopher was a fan. Plato had no time for it, but Aristotle believed that rhetoric was an art of persuasion and should be studied in its own right. Even Aristotle, however, realized that rhetoric could be used for evil purposes so that in itself rhetoric was neutral; see the very good entry on Aristotle's Rhetoric in the revised *Stanford University Encyclopaedia*.

philosophy. But rhetoric lost its glitter in Greece by the beginning of the Common Era (it was always more popular with the *polis* anyway than the philosophers partly because it had an egalitarian appeal to the baker and barber, etc.—for all citizens could become rhetoricians—and its role in early forms of democracy in Athens was significant).

Rhetoric, however, had a second coming not in Greece but in Rome[20] and pagan cultures outside the Greek mainland. And it played a major role in Christianity both in the West under Augustine[21] and in the East with Origen and Chrysostom. It was in Egyptian Alexandria where the most brilliant theologian of the first two centuries, Origen, put rhetoric firmly on the Christian map. But even then, with its association with pagan thought, dissimulation, and potential for evil, it was considered suspect by many Christians. Consider this extract from an oration of thanks to Origen from one of his greatest disciples,[22]

> For a mighty and energetic thing is the discourse of man, and subtle with its sophisms and quick to find its way in to the ears and mold the mind and impress us with what it conveys; and when once it has taken possession of us, it can win us over to love it as truth though it be false and deceitful, overmastering us like some enchanter and retaining as its champion the very man it has persuaded (*deluded*).

150 years later, however, it was John Chrysostom of Antioch who emerged within the Orthodox Tradition as the pre-eminent Christian orator. Renowned in his lifetime as the greatest living preacher, some 150 years after his death he received the accolade of "golden mouthed"— Chrysostom in Greek—which is more of a fond nickname than a formal title of honor. In fact we don't know his family name only that his father was Greek and his mother Syrian. There is not space to go into the details of his life here but there are aspects of his training and personality, which explain why, like his friend Basil of Caesarea, he is a hierarch of

---

20. Cicero is probably the most influential Roman thinker on rhetoric and makes his mark before the common era begins (d. BC 43).

21. His defense of Christian rhetoric is masterly. See *De doctrina christiana*.

22. St. Gregory the Wonderworker quoted by the Dean of St. Vladimir's Theological Seminary, Fr. John Behr, on the 1600 anniversary of St. John Chrysostom's death. Orthodox Church of America, parish of St. John Chrysostom, Home Springs, Missouri, September 29th 2007. Original source, *Origen the Teacher; Being the Address of Gregory the Wonderworker* (but no direct reference given).

the church.[23] Unlike Basil, however, he plays no serious role in conciliar councils or doctrinal disputes; indeed as an original thinker he cannot hold a candle to any of the three Cappadocians.[24]

To keep it simple, if we translate these theologians into modern categories we would call the Cappadocians dogmatic theologians and Chrysostom a pastoral/practical theologian. What is fascinating is that he and Basil become friends before they became committed Christians and both studied philosophy under the brilliant pagan rhetorician Libanius, who was in Antioch. Coincidentally, Antioch was the city in which Chrysostom lived where he was "home-schooled," as the Americans say, by his widowed young Christian mother. Chrysostom became a monk but at his mother's request did not enter a monastery for some years. After being ordained "Reader" he became a monk at Mt. Silipios under the spiritual direction of Diodore of Tarsus. John never did anything half-heartedly and after a thorough grounding in church history and doctrine he went into seclusion. His ascetic feats were as legendary as his preaching.[25] He fasted so severely that his health never really recovered and he did sleep very occasionally but did so, allegedly, standing up.[26] In AD 378 his ill health forced him back to Antioch where he was ordained deacon in AD 381 and priest in 386. Only priests were allowed to preach in the Syrian Church. From the time of his

23. Basil, *De Spiritus Sancta*, 66. Quoted in Bateson, *Later Christian Fathers*, 59. One of the Fathers from Cappadocia (which is in present day Turkey), St. Basil is one of only three authorities in the Orthodox Church to be given the title hierarch. The other two are his friend Gregory of Nazianzus who we have already seen was also honored with the title of Theologian. The third hierarch is St. John Chrysostom who is the main subject of this section.

24. Personally I would name four Cappadocians not three, for the Grandmother of Basil of Caesarea, Macrina, was both saintly and intellectually her grandsons' equal. The two grandchildren in question, Basil and Gregory of Nyssa, and their friend Gregory of Nazianzus were never as influential in the East as Augustine in the West but they were nevertheless outstanding thinkers. Nyssa, for example, is without doubt the greatest thinker of the three, and yet is the least honored; my own theory about that is that Nyssa was the most Hellenistic of the three. Basil, on the other hand, while almost Nyssa's intellectual equal, was pastorally more sensitive and, along with John Chrysostom, becomes one of the only three named hierarchs in the Orthodox Church. Gregory Nazianzus, however, outguns them both for he is the only person recognized in the Tradition to be named both hierarch and theologian.

25. He apparently knew the whole of the Bible by heart.

26. A feat of endurance popularized by the desert father St. Symeon the Stylite a Syrian contemporary of Chrysostom.

ordination, to the end of his life in AD 407, John's reputation as the greatest preacher in the Byzantine Empire was unquestioned.[27]

His reputation was already established by AD 387 before he left Antioch. Statues of the Emperor Theodosius were attacked by mobs in the streets of the ancient city when they heard that they had to pay more taxes. When word reached Constantinople that the Emperor had been insulted the imperial troops were dispatched with orders to destroy the city. The local bishop and senior clergy were thrown into a panic but Chrysostom, fearless and displaying his astonishing grasp of Scripture and rhetorical technique, delivered a series of brave, defiant, yet optimistic sermons to mixed crowds of pagans and Christians. The erudition of Chrysostom's *Homilies of the Statues* may have persuaded the Emperor to spare Antioch; whether this is true or not, news of the local boy's oratory and personal holiness spread rapidly throughout the whole Byzantine Empire.

Chrysostom, in addition to being a trained rhetorician, who could adapt his style to any audience regardless of high rank or lowly status, was also a master of *dialegomai* (conversational or ad lib preaching). He could break off from his homily and addresses his congregation with exhortations or admonitions.[28] Here is a much quoted example, "Please listen to me; you are not paying attention. I am talking to you about the Holy Scriptures and you are looking at the lamps and the people who are lighting them. It is very frivolous to be more interested in what the lamplighters are doing than in what the preacher is saying. After all I, too, am lighting a lamp, the lamp of God's Word."[29]

To use a modern term usually enunciated by followers of the social gospel, John clearly had a bias towards the poor. The rich and powerful constantly plotted against him because he was so overtly against wealth and privilege. He did not pull his punches. He would not absolve the wealthy of their sins unless they gave alms to the poor.

---

27. The middle part of his life was spent in Constantinople where he became Archbishop in AD 398. His life as a bishop was steeped in controversy mainly because of his uncompromising attack on the wealthy but also because he had a difficult relationship with the empress Eudoxia who was a Christian but capricious; she seemed to spend an inordinate amount of her time either playing a major hand in banishing John or bringing him back to Constantinople.

28. The English word for sermon is taken from the Latin *sermo*, which literally means talk or conversation.

29. Quoted in Kerr, *Preaching in the Early Church*, 62.

When he became the Archbishop of Constantinople, Chrysostom was the recipient of bad feeling by a number of senior bishops within Eastern Christendom because, unlike Rome, Jerusalem, Antioch, and Alexandria, Constantinople had no traditional tie with the era of The New Testament. It derived its status exclusively from being the seat of the Roman Empire since the Barbarian tribes had rent the Rome of the early Caesars from its Empire leaving the city subject to siege and periodic assaults.

St. John Chrysostom also made bitter enemies, notably Bishop Theophilos of Alexandria. They were totally opposed over biblical interpretation: Theopholis followed Origen's allegorical/spiritual tradition, Chrysostom believed that the Antiochean approach of letting the text speak for itself was the better way; he personally favored a more demotic delivery than the scholarly style of the Egyptians and was a pioneer in what we might call the triangulation method of preaching: a sound exegesis of the biblical text, the charisma of the preacher, and the specificity of the congregation/audience. Chrysostom remained formally opposed to the Origenistic method of interpretation until the day he died (though his own extreme and sometimes disingenuous rhetoric strays un-bidden into Alexandrian linguistic territory).

John's Christianized pagan rhetoric led to a homiletic standardization for several centuries after his death so that, along with fellow hierarch, Gregory of Nazienzus, their sermons were collected (and printed in later centuries) and used either as a model for preaching or were read out aloud in church. But it is not John's rhetorical influence on homiletics that is his major contribution to preaching—it is his liturgy. By this statement I do not mean to play down John's panegyric skills. His commentaries on Acts and Paul are masterly and not florid or over-embellished. You can tell what the nineteenth-century Caledonian preacher Edward Irving's preaching style is like from his writings, for all his sermons were written out in long hand in high Puritan style: to read Irving is to hear him. The same cannot be said of John because while his preaching style was rich in rhetorical detail he writes for the church in an exemplary expository manner. There are givens: Acts and the four Gospels are treated like history, and the Apostle Paul as a divinely inspired fount of knowledge and wisdom. With some confidence we can say that reading John is to read the Tradition handed down from the apostles.

Since John Williams Bugeon's research on the ancient Greek texts it is well established that in the Byzantine texts (as Bugeon calls them)[30] a lectionary was in use from at least the second century CE. The main Christian service of worship, the synaxis, was based on the Synagogue tradition: this included two readings from the Bible (the difference being, unlike the Rabbinical tradition, the Torah would be complemented by readings from the growing corpus of New Testament material). The synaxis in short was Bible readings plus prayers and the Eucharist.

The genius of Chrysostom's liturgy is that it contained not only the early synaxis, and a complete biblical lectionary (remembering that Revelation was excluded) but also a Christian calendar with feasts and fasts, saints' days and themed hymns (the *kontakion*). 70 percent of the liturgy was directly taken from Scripture or paraphrases from the Bible. In addition to oral traditions (see first section), other texts known in Greek as *Anagignoskomena* were used; these are not biblical but are considered venerable (these texts would be from the apocrypha, for example,[31] but also from the Fathers).

Sermons in the Orthodox churches since the fall of Constantinople in the sixteenth century have mainly been exhortations and homilies. There is no place for personal aggrandizement, hobbyhorses, or joy rides. The sermon itself is a moveable feast: it is sometimes available before the Eucharist, sometimes at the end of the liturgy. There may be no sermon at all. I once heard Metropolitan Anthony of Sourozh say to an ecumenical gathering, "a sermon is an important part of the liturgy but it is not essential, for the liturgy itself is the breath of the Holy Spirit bringing the words (*logoi*) of God to life." To be an inspired preacher (as he was) is a charism not a result of professional training; gifted teachers like Bishop Kallistos Ware also stand out as a preacher/teacher but what determines the minimum standard—the lowest common denominator in Orthodox preaching—is fidelity to the biblical text. A priest follows the lectionary not the dictates of his personal predilections.

---

30. Bugeon, *Byzantine texts, Revision Revised.*

31. Though the New Testament is not without direct apocryphal sources; notably the epistle of Jude.

Conclusion

St. John Chrysostom's personal ascetic life, his dedication to pastoral theology, and above all his liturgical instincts, has left the church with an extraordinary legacy: in homiletics he is an exemplar *par excellence* but his liturgy has provided an environment in which, from cradle to grave, Christians who are initiated into the body of Christ through baptism learn to become committed Christians. This transformations comes primarily by attending the divine liturgy of St. John Chrysostom. At Easter, the author of the liturgy we celebrate all year speaks to us directly. We can note something of the rhetorician here for this homily has certainly been handed down orally. More importantly we should notice St. John's generosity.

> If any man be devout and loveth God,
> Let him enjoy this fair and radiant triumphal feast!
> If any man be a wise servant,
> Let him rejoicing enter into the joy of his Lord.
> If any have laboured long in fasting,
> Let him now receive his recompense.
> If any have wrought from the first hour,
> Let him today receive his just reward.
> If any have come at the third hour,
> Let him with thankfulness keep the feast.
> If any have arrived at the sixth hour,
> Let him have no misgivings;
> Because he shall in nowise be deprived therefore.
> If any have delayed until the ninth hour,
> Let him draw near, fearing nothing.
> And if any have tarried even until the eleventh hour,
> Let him, also, be not alarmed at his tardiness.
> For the Lord, who is jealous of his honor,
> Will accept the last even as the first.
> He giveth rest unto him who cometh at the eleventh hour,
> Even as unto him who hath wrought from the first hour.
> And He showeth mercy upon the last,
> And careth for the first;
> And He both accepteth the deeds
> And welcometh the intention . . .

PART THREE

TEXTUAL

Living with the Text

Ian Stackhouse

Opening the Text

I HAVE THE BEST job in town. Every Tuesday morning, I arrive at my study, open my Bible at the passage for this week's sermon, and begin to read the text. Sometimes I am looking for the passage almost as soon as I have finished last Sunday's sermon—an admission that I guess shows how "sad" I am. And if not Sunday, then certainly by Tuesday morning, I am in the text once again, ready to practice again the ancient craft of preparing a sermon for the congregation. American homiletician Thomas Long describes this activity as witness: the congregation sending the preacher out week after week to listen to the word of God, and then bringing back a message to the congregation. It is an arresting image.[1] And having done this for nearly twenty years now, and being thoroughly convinced that it is both essential as well as historic, I am truly happy to do this work. It is one of the great boons of pastoral ministry.

The beauty of a text, of course, is that it is given to you. Preaching from the lectionary, or working one's way through a Bible book, as I do, means that we don't have to go scratching around on a Tuesday morning for a text, trying to decide prophetically what the Spirit is saying to the church. Instead, we ask what the Spirit is saying to the church through

---

1. See Long, *Witness of Preaching.*

the passage of Scripture that has been given to us this week. My own
view about this practice is that such respect of the given text is potentially
every bit as prophetic as a charismatic utterance, since the Scripture itself
is a prophetic challenge to the powers of this age. Our familiarity with
the Scriptures means we tend to forget that.[2] In fact, one could argue
that a commitment to routinized preaching through the Scriptures is
more prophetic, for instead of the congregation wondering why it is the
preacher that is having a go at them about a particular subject, or why
it is that he has chosen a particular passage this week (a decision that is
often quite subjective), in this scenario both congregation and preacher
find themselves gathering around the objectivity of a given word, having
to submit to both its demands as well as its promises. As early as Tuesday
morning the preacher is aware that they are the first person to hear the
gospel summons as a word external to them.[3]

In that sense, I have never quite understood the distinction between
study that is for a sermon and study that is more devotional (just as I have
not really understood the negativity that surrounds theology, as if intellectual enquiry is antithetic to the life of faith), for in reality (and every
preacher knows this, if they are honest), it is almost impossible to detach
the reading of the Bible from the preaching of the Bible. Preaching the Bible
in a congregational setting is the Bible's natural habitat.[4] And though one
needs to be careful that preparation for preaching doesn't become the sole
reason why we preachers open our Bibles, nevertheless pouring over the
Scriptures week after week in order to discover a message is just about the
most wonderful way of encountering Scripture as well as growing in a life
of faith. It is what Eugene Peterson calls "vocational holiness," and it is one
of the reasons why pastors who preach every week have a sporting chance
of godliness.[5] Indeed, if we were to describe things more existentially, I often wonder if that is all preaching is: one person wrestling with the text and
with their soul before God and before this congregation.

2. Brueggemann, *Finally Comes the Poet.*

3. See Willimon, *Conversations with Barth on Preaching,* for an elaboration on this
point. Like Willimon, I have a number of problems with Barth's anti-rhetoric, as well
as his strange inability, despite all he says about the importance of exegesis, to preach
the actual text. What I do love about Barth, however, is his insistence that the gospel
cannot be read off from nature but is always in the first instance a word external to
ourselves—not simply intratextual but extratextual.

4. Willimon, *Shaped by the Bible,* 47.

5. See Peterson, *Under the Unpredictable Plant.*

Which brings us onto another preliminary point: the question of the inspiration of Scripture. Is the Bible inerrant? Is it infallible? Personally, I have never really been switched on by the word "inerrant." If the matter came to a head and I had to deny inerrancy or face the execution squad, I reckon I could defend the word. But to me inerrancy is a nineteenth-century word; a utilitarian word that fails to do justice to the beauty of Scripture. Arguing the case for inerrancy is akin to taking down a Rembrandt off the wall and putting up a flow chart in its place. It just doesn't have the same appeal somehow. Apart from which, it is unnecessary. As any preacher will tell you: handling the Scriptures each week in the form that we have them, delighting in the artistry of the text, the subtleties of language and, above all, the consistency of the narrative, carries its own authentication. As J. B. Philips said, apparently, having finished his translations of the New Testament, the thing is alive. We are handling mysteries. When I open my Bible on a Tuesday morning in order to find the text for this week's sermon, I really ought to be putting on gloves. It's like a precious jewel.

Text Work

And so begins the process of working with the text, letting the text speak for itself rather than imposing my own grid upon it. And this requires time—more time than most of us are prepared to give it. Given our propensity to jump to conclusions, or to want to make something relevant of the Bible, it is likely we will find a word, before the word finds us. So urgent has the need for application become in our day, the Bible ends up as nothing more than a manual for the congregation. As it says on a wayside pulpit that I passed the other day: BIBLE: Basic Instructions Before Leaving Earth.

But if we have the courage, we must at this point simply be in the text. As Dietrich Bonhoeffer remarked in his little known lectures on preaching with reference to the task of exegesis: "The torment of waiting for fresh ideas disappears under serious textual work. The text has more than enough thoughts. One really only needs to say what is in it."[6] In other words, we do not need to bring to the text our preconceived jokes, our already determined theological grid, or a recently read illustration just waiting for a sermon to fit it. All these can wait. Rather, we need to

6. Bonhoeffer, *Worldly Preaching*, 25.

simply listen to the text, letting the text itself suggest the form as well as the content of our message.[7] This is especially the case if we have been preaching a long time, but is just as important if we have only just started out. Some texts are so well-known to us that there is every chance we won't even read them, let alone hear them. Add to that the tendency for preachers to grind their theological axes and the result is often bad news for the congregation. But by listening to the text, there is every chance that we will avoid this, and enter instead into what Barth famously referred to as "the strange new world" of the Scriptures.

Commentaries are wonderful in this regard. They are one of the lost treasures of the church that urgently need to be retrieved. For sure, most commentaries don't tell us anything new. They go over old ground, and oftentimes simply repeat what others have said. Furthermore, there is always the issue of how quickly one jumps to the commentaries. Darrell Johnson advocates leaving the commentaries until we have had a chance ourselves to write out, listen to, and even memorize the text.[8] But that aside (and my own view is that we need not be too prescriptive on this), what commentaries insist on, as Dominican preacher Timothy Radcliffe points out, is that we slow down, linger with the words and phrases, and take seriously the context in which the word of God is presented to us. We live in a Christian culture that is desperate to be relevant, quick to apply, and anxious to be topical. But what a commentary helps us to do is put aside for a moment the important task of application and simply immerse ourselves in the immediacy of the narrative: in a sense defamiliarizing ourselves with this Bible we think we know in order that we might hear it afresh, as if for the first time. Of commentaries Radcliffe notes that "a vast amount of erudition produces only a little light, but they slow down one's eye. . . . If one follows the text slowly with the help of an exegete, then one may recapture a sense of its foreignness. The spell of over-familiarity may be broken and we will be puzzled."[9]

Just so. The heart of all great communication is defamilarization.[10] Jesus did it, Paul did it, and if one thinks about it, all great preaching that we have ever heard has at its core the element of surprise. We think we know this story, we may even know what we think about this story, but

---

7. Lischer, *The End of Words,* 49–87.

8. Johnson, *The Glory of Preaching,* 110.

9. Radcliffe, *Why Go to Church?* 49.

10. See K. Case-Green, "Text and Defamiliarization" in this volume.

the preacher comes along and purges us of clichés and platitudes by telling the text as it really is, often with scandalous results. By staying with the text long enough we realize that David is not the idealized king, so beloved of pietistic preaching, but a somewhat ambiguous character;[11] that Paul's letter to the Romans is not a Reformation tract against Romish corruption, but a pastoral appeal for unity around the cross in the face ethnic pride;[12] and that even a cursory reading of the Gospels reveals Jesus not so much "meek and mild" but, as Mark Galli puts it, "mean and wild."[13] In other words, lingering with the text lights up the message.

Pastor as Exegete

All of this listening presupposes, of course, the need for time and silence. Given the demands of modern church life, and the need for the pastor to double up as CEO, not to mention the noise of the church office, this is more easily said than done. As T. S. Eliot says in the poem *Ash Wednesday*: "Where shall the word be found, where will the word/ Resound? Not here, there is not enough silence."[14] At which point I propose, somewhat romantically I admit, that we change the title "office" into "study," and "church leader" into "church theologian," hoping in some way to protest against the awful trivialization of the preacher's call in our day. How can we expect our sermons to be worth listening to, if we ourselves have not had the time to eat the word? Because this is what preaching is: digesting the word so that instead of just a set of notes, we carry something internal—a kind of pregnancy. If we are rushing around our congregations trying to be Messiah, or, more specifically, if we commit too early to paper for the sake of having at least something to say on Sunday, this conception cannot take place.

11. See Peterson, *Leap Over a Wall,* for an example of how to let the text speak. Not only are these sermons object lessons in narrative preaching, they are also a great rejoinder to so much pious nonsense about David as the ideal king. As Peterson says, what we have with David is not an ideal life but an actual life, which is why, in my opinion, David is so compelling, for in the end it is with God that we have to deal with in the David stories, and not some moral paragon.

12. See Wright, *Fresh Perspectives,* for an explanation of this new approach to Pauline theology, although quite why he is so dismissive of Lutheran hermeneutics is strange to me. It is not anachronistic, in my opinion, or an example of eisegesis, to read a law/grace tension in Paul's letters.

13. Galli, *Jesus Mean and Wild.*

14. "Ash Wednesday," in Eliot, *Collected Poems,* 102.

Of course, sometimes a sermon can come to us in one hour. Other weeks we are fighting for each sentence. But always, whether it takes an hour or eight hours, we are looking for the fresh angle, a way of saying it, that is not necessarily original—the sermon doesn't need to be original—but does justice to the originality of the text. Once this angle has been located, the rest is easy. As Craig Barnes puts it, in describing the preacher's search for this primal word: "I never begin to write that sermon without that line from above. It is the little miracle that wins me over and convinces me that this sermon is exactly what the congregation, and I, most need to hear."[15]

People don't see this work, which is perhaps why we feel uneasy about it. It cannot be accounted for. Much of this work takes place other than in the church: out walking, driving in the car, lying in the bath. The conception can happen almost anywhere. But happen it must if our sermons are to carry the day, and not fall to the ground. The very center of the preaching vocation is getting into the text, feeling the burden of the word, letting the Scripture act prophetically so that there is a burden to our song. Expository preaching is not line-by-line exegesis of a text. It is a mistake to portray it this way. Rather, it is uncovering the burden of the text, so that what the preacher does is do to the congregation what the text did to its original hearers. And of course depending on what that text is, our sermon may range from being cryptic parable to outright exhortation. It just depends. As Richard Lischer puts it, if the text is a song, then our sermon will need to sing; if it is a parable, then we will need to be parabolic; if it is a narrative, then we will need to become storytellers—or at least observe the *spirit* of the genre.[16] In other words, the text determines not just what is said, but how it is said; not just the content but the form also. We do an injustice to the text if we try to make John for instance sound like Paul; or if we make of the Israelites marching round the walls of Jericho a three-point sermon, every point beginning with "p." It seems, to me at least, that to do justice to the text we must have our congregations, in their imaginations, marching around the walls also, noticing the battlements, and wondering what on earth the Lord is up to.

And thus begins the process of committing to paper—a dangerous thing, to be sure, since preaching is an oral event. So when we say committing to paper, it is always with a view to hearing one's voice. And of

15. Barnes, *Pastor as Minor Poet*, 125.

16. Lischer, *End of Words*, 82. See also D. Ridder's chapter, "Genre-Sensitive Preaching," in this volume.

course writing down a sermon can in itself release a certain creativity in this regard. Depending on one's creative impulse, sometimes it is only as we begin the write that the word comes to us. Again, how late we leave this is a moot point. I know preachers who say that we ought to have our sermon finished by Wednesday—Thursday at the latest. And for years I felt guilty about that. Thursday, and I am only just beginning to get a feel of what is going on. Indeed, it may not be until Friday that we begin to commit to paper. The gestation is only just beginning. To circumvent that by needing to have everything down by Wednesday is the homiletical equivalent of a premature birth. In fact, it may be as late as the early hours of Sunday morning that we put our final full stop, print out our sermon, and go off for a shower. This is not lack of preparation (although if it is, then it is inexcusable) but if anything, over preparation, and is related as well to the not unusual practice of wanting to preach one's sermon out, or at least parts of it, just prior to the event of preaching. The last thing we want to be in the pulpit is reliant on our notes. We want to be free.[17] So by preaching the sermon out before hand, whether in an empty church, or in a field, or driving in the car, we learn to feed the sermon on to the bobbin of our consciousness.

And here is the wonderful thing: it is often only then that we understand what the Lord wants to say in our message: only by preaching it out that we get to feel internally the weight of the word for that day. Numerous times, it is only when I finally get to preach the sermon out, internalizing some of the images, familiarizing myself with the flow of my own thought, that I understand what I have been doing all week. It is a dangerous occupation, to be sure. One more than one occasion I have startled an early morning dog walker, minding their own business; and in the days before hands-free mobile phones, I guess the sight of a man driving along, speaking into an empty car, must have been an odd sight indeed. It still is, in fact. But risks aside, what these times achieve for the preacher is critical for the immediacy of the sermon: not so much memorizing the sermon (to remember a sermon word for word could very much stifle the creativity of the Spirit), but internalizing the message for that day.

And then comes the final discipline of preparation, and perhaps the most difficult of all, which is waiting to stand up and deliver the sermon. Preachers are notoriously bad at this. They chomp at the bit, waiting for that moment when it is their turn to climb into the pulpit, thus rendering

---

17. Ellsworth, *Power of Speaking God's Word*. See also R. May, "Preaching without Notes" in this volume.

the rest of the service redundant, or rendering themselves an irritation to the person leading the service. Is there anything worse than trying to converse with a preacher who is waiting to preach? So a bit of advice from Episcopalian Robert Capon: having got one's sermon notes together, arrived at the church, and said hello to a few people, forget the sermon altogether, trusting that God will resurrect it in the pulpit at the appropriate time.[18] Indeed, we must relinquish everything so that we might truly inhabit the rest of the liturgy. After all, preaching is not the only thing that constitutes worship. Apart from those few ultra-Reformed Christians, who see the sermon as the only good reason for gathering the saints, there are hymns to sing, confessions to make, intercessions to pray, bread to be broken and offerings to give. By being present to these also and not just the sermon, and maybe even according them the same amount of time, it may well be that the sermon ends up more powerful not less, because instead of being detached from the liturgy it now derives power and legitimacy from it.

Preaching as Theater

I guess for those who have not grown up in churches with a preaching tradition, all of the above confirms their worst fears about preaching: namely, that it is overly dramatic. But that is the point. For all our fears of performance, and for all our disdain for mere pulpiteering, that is what preaching is, or should be: pure theater. Preaching is not simply a talk, or a lecture, but an event, utterly unique and unrepeatable. It is the unique coming together of congregation, preacher, and Holy Spirit, so that on *this* day, in *this* actual place, we might hear the gospel summons again. The word is the deed. Anything less than this, and I want my money back. Those who complain that they didn't get anything out of the sermon, or that they cannot remember after five minutes what the sermon was about, miss the point. We don't learn anything much in the sermon. We save learning for the catechetical processes of the church. Rather in preaching we expose our congregations to the great drama of salvation, hoping that somewhere in the retelling, our congregations will live for another week. "Tell me the old, old story lest I forget so soon."[19]

18. Capon, *The Foolishness of Preaching*, 26.

19. I love what Richard Lischer says about this. We need not worry about people remembering our sermons, he says, "for the words are needed only as long as it takes

No wonder our notes seem unusable after the event. In fact, as I look over my old sermons, I wonder how on earth I managed to inspire anyone with them. They look so paltry; because actually, they we conceived in the vortex of a moment utterly unique in the journey of this one congregation. I may try to use them again; there are some that live in other contexts. But at their best, the scribbled dog-eared notes in my draw are testimony, as the old preacher muses in Marilynne Robinson's stunning novel *Gilead*, to a passionate love that is now spent.[20]

From what I have said earlier about preparation, one may infer that I think we need to be increasingly wary of illustrations. Whole books are devoted to illustrations for this or that theme, many of which are powerful and useful. But the danger of an illustration is that it can so easily obscure or substitute for the Bible's own vivid imagery. And then what happens is that the congregation lauds the preacher's humor, or even his family, without ever inhabiting the world of the Bible. Instead of books of jokes, illustrations, we should in preaching plunder the imagery we have been given, working as much to bring our listeners into the world of the Scripture, as bringing the world of Scripture to our listeners.[21] Who needs illustrations to embellish the story of the prodigal son, so-called? The narrative is replete with images—an old man running, a disheveled son, an angry brother—each one capable of carrying a whole sermon in itself.[22] To illustrate other than from the story itself is not only unnecessary but unbelieving, for by so doing the preacher betrays a distinct lack of trust in the ability of the Bible to carve out its own hearing. Yes, there is the work of contextualization. Every generation must read the words of Scripture afresh in its own language. I have found Brueggemann's homiletical anachronisms very helpful here: a quick and often humorous way

---

for them to form Christ in the hearers." Lischer, *A Theology of Preaching,* 79.

20. Robinson, *Gilead,* 46: "There's not a word in any of those sermons I didn't mean when I wrote it."

21. Note the work of George Lindbeck in this regard: Lindbeck, *The Nature of Doctrine.* A great deal of preaching conforms in my opinion to what Lindbeck describes as the *Experiential-Expressive* model of religion, where the listener is king. However, instead of trying to get something *out of* Scripture, our task as preachers ought to be that of immersing our congregations *in* the world of Scripture. Lindbeck would describe this as a *Cultural-Linguistic* alternative.

22. See Bailey, *Poet and Peasant and through Peasant Eyes,* 158–206, as evidence of the dexterity of the narrative. I plundered heavily from this book in my very earliest days of preaching and was repeatedly overwhelmed by the way Bailey brings out the richness and artistry of the narrative.

of connecting up the world of the Bible with our world. But the point about his anachronisms, and the point of good contextualization, is that it pays respect to the power of scriptural imagery to deliver Christ to the congregation. In fact, as Craig Barnes points out, "the Bible has very few illustrations. But it is filled with powerful images. When the first psalm claims that those who delight in the law of the Lord are like trees planted by streams of water, it is providing not an illustration but an image. A preacher can spend the whole sermon on this text, peeling this image like an onion, and never make it to the eternal core."[23]

What I am trying to argue is this: the strangeness and inaccessibility of Scripture is no excuse to abandon the text. That the congregation doesn't get it first time around should not dissuade us from doing it again. It may well be that they have just encountered something bigger than themselves. In fact, whereas I used to feel a failure when someone didn't understand what I was on about, these days I take it as a sign of hope: there is more here than meets the eye, more than can possibly be shown on powerpoint with neatly arranged points. Actually, there is a growing consensus among preachers (not to mention a similar consensus in the business community about the use of screens), that for preaching to be truly preaching powerpoint needs to be abandoned. It just doesn't do justice to what preaching is. Preaching is an *oral* event. For all the complaints of educationalists who talk about different learning styles, preaching is *sui generis*. For preaching to be truly preaching, the preacher must be unfettered by the fear of the congregation and delight simply in doing the text. This is our sole authority. Instead of flying off to either side of the pulpit, thus betraying our disdain for the text, we would better serve our congregations if we stayed put, preaching through the text, not around it. The text is our only authority. Having immersed ourselves in it for most of the week, we would do well to hide behind it in the pulpit. I know one pastor who from time to time would turn on his congregation in the middle of a sermon and say to those taking notes, with some sternness it might be added, to put their pens down. "Just listen," he would say. "Listen to the words." In a culture where the word has been systematically humiliated, to use Jacque Ellul's term, this is a brave step.[24] It is not every preacher who can do this. I imagine most of us would take it as a compliment if someone in our congregation took notes from our

23. Barnes, *Pastor as Minor Poet*, 130.
24. Ellul, *Humiliation of the Word*.

sermon. We would conclude that they were taking the word seriously. On the contrary, argues Peterson, preaching is an audio event. Faith comes by hearing, and hearing by the word of Christ.

Post-Text Blues

And so we come to the most challenging part of the sermon: the aftermath. If preaching can be likened to a birth, then not only is there conception, gestation, labor, and birth, but also the possibility of post-natal depression. I don't know a preacher in all of Christendom who doesn't suffer from it. In fact, on more than one occasion I have come away from church determined in my heart that I am never going to do this thing called preaching ever again. Not only does it seem the most ridiculous arrogance to stand in front of an audience and talk monologue for thirty or forty minutes, it is also a lot of work for seemingly little return.

But it is just here, precisely at this point of utter dejection about what we preachers do, that faith must be exercised: faith not in our abilities as communicators, nor in our exegetical competence—for it is often these things that we doubt—but faith in the Holy Spirit to take what we have just offered and work it by ways only he knows into the hearts of our congregation. After all, the whole project that we call preaching is from start to finish, from conception to delivery, a work of the Holy Spirit. As Lesslie Newbigin points out, the Holy Spirit is not there to assist, but rather the one who co-opted us from the very beginning of our task, to bear witness.[25] And so it makes sense, at this most vulnerable point that the preacher arrives at, immediately after the sermon, to relinquish control once again, trusting what Jesus said that "the wind blows where it wills."

What this means, of course, is that we can never really second-guess what God is up to. Those sermons of ours that even we think were better than average often elicit nothing more than a conversation in the coffee lounge after the service about the weather; whereas those sermons that even we the preacher did not understand, are the very same messages that seem to inspire life transforming decisions. Indeed, I can vividly

25. Newbigin, *Light Has Come,* 208: "It is in this sense that the disciples will be witnesses . . . Their life, their words, their deeds, their sufferings will thus be the occasion, the place, where the mighty Spirit bears his own witness in the hearts and consciences of men and women so that they are brought to look again at the hated, rejected, humiliated, crucified man and confess 'Jesus is Lord.'"

recall sitting in my study one Tuesday morning, lamenting last Sunday's sermon and wondering if I could go through it all once again, when I heard a light knock at the door. "About Sunday's sermon," said the person whose head peered round the door. "You have no idea what how powerful it was. God really spoke to me." At which point, we need to stop worrying about what impact we are making with our sermons, do as best we can in working the text, and simply trust that the Holy Spirit can adopt our most fallible words and let Christ move among the congregation.

10

Defamiliarization

Purging our Preaching of Platitudes

Karen Case-Green

There was an awful rainbow once in heaven:
We know her woof, her texture; she is given
In the dull catalogue of common things.
Philosophy will clip an Angel's wings,
Conquer all mysteries by rule and line,
Empty the haunted air and gnoméd mine-
Unweave a rainbow[1]

When first the Fox saw the Lion he was terribly frightened, and ran away and hid himself in the wood. Next time however he came near the King of Beasts he stopped at a safe distance and watched him pass by. The third time they came near one another the Fox went straight up to the Lion and passed the time of day with him, asking him how his family were, and when he should have the pleasure of seeing him again; then turning his tail, he parted from the Lion without much ceremony. Familiarity breeds contempt.[2]

IN 1998 MY HUSBAND and I travelled to Tunisa. It was our first experience of North Africa, and the day we arrived in Tunis we were eager to visit a traditional souk. The market was a riot of the senses: smells, colors, and

---

1. Keats, "Lamia," 193.
2. "The Fox and the Lion," *An Aesop's Fable*, www.aesops-fables.org.uk.

noise jostled for our attention, and the bustle was increased by a number of sheep being led through the tiny, crowded streets into what looked like people's homes. In my naiveté, I thought that these might be family pets. However, the next morning, the bleating in the streets ceased and the eerie silence was followed by the acrid smell of singed wool. It was only then we discovered that the sheep had been slaughtered for *Aid el Kebir*, a festival which commemorates Abraham's sacrifice of a lamb instead of his son. I will never forget wandering through the quiet streets that day and my shock at seeing blood on the steps of the buildings. The familiar words "the lamb of God" took on a much grittier, more concrete meaning for me.

Familiarity Breeds Contempt

Those of us who have spent much time in church inevitably become very familiar with the images and stories in Scripture. While we may not like to admit it, the conclusion to Aesop's fable—"familiarity breeds contempt"—may well be true of us. The thrill of the gospel can fade, even at a young age, as words and stories from Scripture are heard so frequently. They lose their edge and cease to unsettle us.

How is this played out for a preacher on a Sunday morning? As I will explore later, many of the rich metaphors in the Bible become worn down. They are reduced to clichés. Metaphors such as "the lamb of God," which for most of us were never part of everyday reality anyway, quickly lose their concrete meaning. While we may not doubt Scripture, we may well be dulled to its touch. NIV-weary, story-familiar, psalm-numb, we need to hear it fresh. As Walter Brueggemann puts it "The biblical text needs to be rediscovered each week in its angular scandal,"[3] and I believe the preacher is in the wonderful position of aiding such a rediscovery.

Our Problem or Theirs?

Some might argue that if churchgoers are weary of hearing the same biblical truths being spoken out, surely this is their problem, not the preacher's? The seventeenth-century clergyman and writer, Thomas Fuller, suggests that "with base and sordid natures familiarity breeds contempt."[4] Therefore, the problem may well lie in the heart of the listener, not the

3. Brueggemann, *Finally Comes the Poet*, 7.
4. Fuller, *Comment on Ruth*.

speaker. In his book, *The Soul of Prince Caspian*, Gene Veith argues that in a media-sated world, many listeners are guilty of sloth and a failure of the imagination.[5] Hyperstimulated by constant media bombardment, he claims that people require a larger dose of stimulation each time if they are to perceive anything at all. The repercussions for preachers are clear, states Veith: "when the bombardment slows—when we have to endure silence, when we have to do something that is not fun but necessary, when we have to attend to someone other than ourselves—we can hardly handle that at all."[6] He challenges the notion that such a thing as an "uninteresting subject" even exists and, quoting Chesterton, suggests that "The only thing that can exist is an uninterested person."[7] This idea is illustrated in the film *American Beauty*,[8] when perhaps the moment of true "beauty" in a film smeared with cynicism emerges during a scene in which two teenagers stand in silence, watching a videotape of a plastic bag being blown by the breeze in an ordinary suburban street for minutes on end. It is a "gradual instant"[9] of the most spellbinding kind. The suburban street is transformed into a thing of extraordinary beauty simply because the teenagers pay attention.

If we have grown tired and immune to the impact of Christianity's most treasured words and symbols then perhaps we should heed G. K. Chesterton's words:

> A child kicks its legs rhythmically through excess, not absence, of life. Because children have abounding vitality, because they are in spirit fierce and free, therefore they want things repeated and unchanged. They always say, "Do it again;" and the grown-up person does it again until he is nearly dead. For grown-up people are not strong enough to exult in monotony. But perhaps God is strong enough. . . . It is possible that God says every morning, "Do it again," to the sun; and every evening, "Do it again," to the moon. It may not be automatic necessity that makes all daisies alike: it may be that God makes every daisy separately, but has never got tired of making them. It may be

5. Veith, *The Soul of Prince Caspian*, 27.

6. Ibid.

7. Chesterton, *Heretics,* as cited in Veith, *The Soul of Prince Caspian*, 28.

8. *American Beauty*, directed by Sam Mendes.

9. Michaels, *Fugitive Pieces*, 171.

that He has the eternal appetite of infancy; for we have sinned
and grown old, and our Father is younger than we.[10]

Let me preface, therefore, what I am about to write. I believe that we
come to a God who rejoices in the routine gathering of his church with
the delight of an infant, and who does not tire of the weekly preaching
of the ancient story.[11] Instead he says, "Do it again," for we have a story
that does not fade or wear out. So I am certainly not suggesting that we
pander to those people who wish to depart from God's word for the sake
of mere homiletical relevance. Rather, I believe that it is *because* Scripture
holds such ancient living truth and because that truth is conveyed with
great literary creativity and care by the biblical writers that it is *worth*
telling well by the preacher. The aim then is not to create something new;
rather, it is to lead us back, more deeply than before, into the old story.

Unfortunately, some preachers "unweave a rainbow" when they
preach. With the cold stare of Keats's philosopher in "Lamia," they reduce
all the mystery and wonder of Scripture—both the judgements and the
promises—to "the dull catalogue of common things."[12] They dissect the
text, forgetting Balthasar's warning that "Anatomy can be practiced only
on a dead body."[13] The word is living, and the preacher would do well
to employ the artist's skill in approaching it. By this I do not mean em-
ploying the clever techniques and tricks that Bonhoeffer warns preachers
against.[14] Richard Lischer is helpful in determining what this artistic skill
might and might not involve for the preacher:

> If one's notion of art is limited to what is new, preaching the
> old story is not art. If the idea of art is restricted to poetic self-
> expression, then preaching the church's gospel in public does
> not qualify . . .
>
> But if your idea of art is something the creature, who
> knows she is a creature, sings back to the Creator with some-
> thing of the Creator's own pizzazz (as Annie Dillard put it), then
> preaching has the potential, at least, to be more like art and less
> like an endowed lecture series.[15]

10. Chesterton, *Orthodoxy*, 58.

11. Lischer, "Stick with the Story," *The Christian Century*.

12. Keats, "Lamia."

13. Balthasar, *The Glory of the Lord: A Theological Aesthetics*, 1.31.

14. Bonhoeffer, "The Causality and Finality of Preaching," 138.

15. Lischer, "Stick with the Story," *The Christian Century*.

Art protects biblical truths from spiritual atrophy. It can feed the "eternal appetite for infancy," an appetite that I believe we share with our Creator. Art has the ability to bring to a jaded world familiar objects and concepts, and to help us to see them with fresh eyes. The preacher employs the skill of an artist, not to draw attention to himself or to create something new, but in order to "sing back to the Creator" his own word, in all its dazzling glory.

Worn New Again

The artistic medium of any preacher is words, and a good preacher will take familiar, ancient words and make them new. The nineteenth-century prose writer and literary critic Edward Thomas suggests in his poem "Words" that, however old they may be, words can be

> Worn new
> Again and again;
> Young as our streams
> After rain[16]

This chapter will therefore explore how a preacher can take the familiar words of Scripture and help them to become "worn new." To do this I will first explore the concept of "defamiliarization."

Ostrananie: Making Strange the Familiar

In the first half of the twentieth century, a group of Russian literary theorists who became known as the "Russian Formalists" turned their attention to the problem of overfamiliarity. One of the Formalist leaders, Victor Shklovsky, concluded that perception becomes automatic when it is part of habitual routine, and that, in this process of "over-automatization," the object which one perceives "fades and does not leave even a first impression; ultimately even the essence of what it was is forgotten."[17] One needs only to think of driving a car or riding a bicycle to see the truth behind this: while a great amount of perceptive effort is used when we *first* learn such a skill, as time progresses the effort employed to perform the skill decreases until it is automatic—almost unconscious. It is natural that we

16. Thomas, "Words."
17. Shklovsky, "Art as Technique," 48.

economize in this way: human beings inevitably want to save themselves effort, be it physical or perceptive.[18] However, by going on "autopilot" we fail to notice things before our very eyes. The Russian Formalists were partly inspired to address this problem by Leo Tolstoy, who had drawn attention to it in his diary on February 29th, 1897:

> I was cleaning a room and, meandering about, approached the divan and couldn't remember whether or not I had dusted it. Since these movements are habitual and unconscious I could not remember and felt that it was impossible to remember—so that if I had dusted it and forgot—then it was the same as if I had not. If some conscious person had been watching, then the fact could be established. If, however, no one was looking, . . . if the whole complex lives of many people go on unconsciously, then such lives are as if they had never been.[19]

There are a number of people who attend church quite happily each week but later on cannot, if they are honest, remember what the sermon was about. Tolstoy's conclusion would imply that, for that half hour at least, their lives are lived as if they had never been. While such amnesia might be considered a blessing by some members of a congregation, it is questionable how much glory it brings to God. The Russian Formalists set out to address the problem of habitualization by exploring the ability of art to make the over-familiar things *strange* once more, so that a person might see with renewed perception that to which he had grown numb. Shklovsky wrote: "Art increases our perception, our ability to see something, whereas habitualisation devours work, clothes, furniture, one's wife, and the fear of war. . . . Art exists that one may recover the sensation of life, it exists to make one feel things, to make the stone stony."[20]

This technique of making "the stone stony" became known as "*ostrananie*," or "defamiliarization." Tolstoy's writing is full of examples of this technique. He made familiar objects or concepts seem "strange" once again by omitting to name them or by describing them as if for the first time. In one story, Tolstoy defamiliarizes the concept of private property by narrating it from the perspective of a horse. He overhears people discussing their property and muses: "What's the meaning of 'his own,' 'his

18. Ibid.

19. Tolstoy, as cited in Shklovsky, "Art as Technique," 48

20. Ibid, 49.

colt?' . . . The words 'my horse' seemed as strange to me as the words 'my land,' 'my air,' 'my water.'" He goes on:

> They agree that only one may say "mine" about this, that or the other thing. And the one who says "mine" about the greatest number of things is, according to the game which they've agreed the rules to among themselves, the one they consider the most happy. . . . There are people who call a tract of land their own, but they never set eyes on it and never take a stroll on it. There are people who call others their own, yet they never see them . . .[21]

Here Tolstoy gives a perfect example of a notion voiced in an Emily Dickinson poem: "Tell all the truth but tell it slant/ Success in circuit lies."[22] How much more effective Tolstoy's "slanted" rebuke than one given head-on! Later we shall examine how this circuitous truth-telling can be applied to the sermon.

At this point some people may be thinking, "But a preacher should just get straight to the point. There's no time for all this artistic rambling!" Then I would direct them to the seventeenth-century priest and poet, George Herbert. Despite being a formidable rhetorician himself, Herbert was also acutely aware of the dangers of what he called "trim invention."[23] He believed that what should characterize a sermon was not eloquence or wit, but rather "holiness."[24] In one poem, "The Windows," Herbert warns that speech alone, if not lived out in actions, "Doth vanish like a flaring thing/ And in the eare, not conscience ring."[25] However, in this same poem he acknowledges that the preacher can become a "window" through which God can tell his story:

> Lord, how can man preach thy eternall word?
> He is a brittle crazie glasse:
> Yet in thy temple thou dost him afford
> This glorious and transcendent place,
> To be a window, through thy grace.[26]

The last line presents a beautifully simple but apt image for the preacher today. Most preachers would agree that language matters, and

21. Tolstoy, *Kholstomer: The Story of a Horse*, as cited in "Art as Technique," 50.

22. Dickinson, Poem 1129, *The Collected Poems of Emily Dickinson*.

23. Herbert, "Jordan (II)," *The Complete English Poems*.

24. Herbert, "A Priest to the Temple," *The Complete English Poems*, 209.

25. Herbert, "The Windows," *The Complete English Poems*.

26. Ibid.

should not be used to obscure our view of God but rather to bring it into sharper focus. C. S. Lewis shared this view. It was Lewis' discovery on a train ride one day of George MacDonald's *Phantastes* that served to sanctify his love of language, an encounter that led later to his conversion. He describes it in *Surprised by Joy*: "I met there all that had already charmed me in Malory, Spenser, Morris, and Yeats. But in another sense all was changed. . . . It was Holiness. . . . That night my imagination was, in a certain sense, baptized; the rest of me, not unnaturally, took longer. I had not the faintest notion what I had let myself in for by buying *Phantastes*."[27]

It is in Lewis' writing that we find some of the best examples of defamiliarization. Within *The Chronicles of Narnia* we discover ancient and familiar biblical metaphors and stories "made strange" once again. After years of Easter celebrations, many of which merged into one other, I will never forget the first time I read the chapter entitled "The Triumph of the Witch" in *The Lion, the Witch and the Wardrobe* and the subsequent chapter in which Aslan returns from the dead. The power and wonder of Jesus' death and resurrection crept up on me afresh as I read this familiar story, "worn new" through Lewis' telling of it.

This has happened with my own children too, who could easily grow inured to wonderful Christian truths. For example, *The Horse and his Boy* contains a scene in which Bree, a Narnian horse, is being asked by his travelling companions (who have never set foot in Narnia) what Aslan is like. Like any good gnostic, Bree is quick to distance Aslan from humanity and he dismisses the idea that Narnia's great deliverer would ever manifest himself as a *real* lion; indeed he argues that it is disrespectful to even suggest such a thing:

> "If he was a lion he'd have to be a beast just like the rest of us. Why!" (and here Bree began to laugh) "If he was a lion he'd have four paws, and a tail, and Whiskers! . . . Aie, ooh, hoo-hoo! Help!"
>
> For just as he said the word Whiskers one of Aslan's had actually tickled his ear. Bree shot away like an arrow to the other side of the enclosure and there turned; the wall was too high for him to jump and he could fly no further. Aravis and Hwin both started back. There was about a second of intense silence.
>
> Then Hwin, though shaking all over, gave a strange little neigh, and trotted across to the Lion.

27. Lewis, *Surprised by Joy*, 144–46.

"Please," she said, "you're so beautiful. You may eat me if you like. I'd sooner be eaten by you than fed by anyone else."[28]

The Word made flesh; the fear of the Lord; the beauty of Christ: it is all here, "worn new." This passage leads us towards Scripture rather than away from it, and the images may nudge away at us long after we have closed the book.

Preacher as Poet

So how can this technique of defamiliarization be applied to the art of preaching? For this, we can learn from the poet. But first, let me put any fears to rest. The last thing a congregation needs is a prima donna preacher with a Byron-complex! I am not advocating that we begin our sermons with long, incomprehensible quotations of poetry, or that we stop mid-sentence to gaze rapturously into space, or that we wash our preaching in purple prose. I *am*, however, advocating a closer attention to the richness of the biblical language which does justice to our Creator God and to his word. For this, the preacher allows God to use her poetic creativity, much like the psalmist in Psalm 45:1 who announces, "My tongue is the pen of a ready writer."[29] In doing so, she becomes like Herbert's window. According to Richard Lischer, the preacher "makes" (*poiein*) words, an average of 1,500 of them on a Sunday morning, and three million in a career.[30] So let them be good words! Words which reflect the glory of the King and which create a vivid picture for the congregation of what it means to live in his kingdom here on earth.

Poetic language has the power both to unsettle our relationship with this worldly kingdom and to help us see God's own counter-kingdom, even right in our midst. Walter Brueggemann has written widely about the need to harness the gift of poetic language for this purpose, and his own writing is a very good example of this. In his book *Finally Comes the Poet* he states, "Reduced speech leads to reduced lives. Sunday morning

---

28. Lewis, *The Horse and His Boy*, 641–42.

29. Alter translates it "as the pen of a rapid scribe," and notes that "rapid" meant "skilled." *The Book of Psalms*, 158. However, he also comments that it is unusual to find a psalmist drawing attention to his own art. Again, we return to the point about our artistic skill being directed to the glory of God and God alone.

30. Lischer, "Stick with the Story," *The Christian Century*.

is the practice of counter life through counter speech."[31] When Brueggemann goes on to suggest how this counter speech might take place there are many resonances with the defamiliarization outlined above in this chapter. He reminds us that the preacher does not preach a new text but an old one, to which everybody knows the ending already:

> But it is a script to be played afresh, so that in this moment of drama the players render the play as a surprise to permit a fresh hearing, a second opinion. . . . At the end, there is a breathless waiting: stunned, not sure we have reached the end. Then there is a powerful sense that a world has been rendered in which I may live, a world that is truly home but from which I have been alienated.[32]

The poet-preacher cuts the sword of the word more deeply through what T. S. Elliot called "this twittering world"[33] into its word-weary inhabitants. This counter-speech is a gift of God's Spirit, and it is one we should perhaps be asking for a little more often. Therefore, the aim behind the following section is to apply the art of the poet to preaching, so that our congregations, along with their preachers, might see the Scriptures with "baptized" imaginations.

1. Let Your Imagination Roam the Text

Why are some evangelicals so twitchy about the imagination? It has been instilled in many of us that the imagination is self-indulgent at best and self-deceptive at worst. This suspicion of the imagination may result from the way that certain Bible translations have used the term *imagination* pejoratively to translate a wide range of Hebrew and Greek words. For example, the KJV translates Genesis 6:5 as "God saw that the wickedness of man was great in the earth, and that every *imagination* of the thoughts of his heart was only evil continually" (italics mine). Yet the NRSV renders the Hebrew word *yetser* as "inclination" and the NIV also uses "inclination": this is by no means an isolated example of the negative use of the word "imagination" when alternatives have been used by other translators, and some scholars believe that it has contributed to a suspicion of the imagination amongst Christians today.[34]

31. Brueggemann, *Finally Comes the Poet*, 3.

32. Ibid., 10.

33. Elliot, "Burnt Norton," *The Four Quartets*.

34. In "A Suspicion Observed: Christian Responses to the Imagination," Trevor Hart illustrates that some translations have used the word *imagination* in a rather

Our fear of the imagination may also be attributed to the connection drawn after the Reformation between the power of the imagination and men and women's tendency to create idols. This is a very valid concern, and may go some way to explaining why some preachers treat the imagination like an embarrassing relative whom they wish to put discreetly in a corner. We should remember that the making of any graven image was clearly forbidden in the Old Testament (Exod 20:4). Moreover, we witness the terrible pull that these images exerted on God's people when they were made, and the tragic downfall that resulted from this. However, as the Scottish theologian and minister John McIntyre points out, the parables, poetry, and apocalypses in the Bible *depend on the imagination and on images.*[35] What are we to make of this tension?

Put simply, it would seem that the imagination, along with many other God-given gifts, can be used to point us towards God or to lead us away from him. For, as Calvin reminds us, human nature is something of an idol factory.[36] And we need not look far today to find examples of the way that people create their own gods through the grave misuse of the imagination. However, the issue at stake here is what we *do* with the imagination. If we believe that the imagination is a God-given gift to us, then we need to use it to reflect glory back to him. Banishing it to a corner does not do this. When surrendered to God, the imagination can become a glorious means for his revelation,[37] just as it was for the Old Testament prophets and for Jesus himself.

So, when opening the Bible to prepare a sermon, the preacher can let her imagination roam the text, fully surrendering it to God. No matter how familiar the passage, look twice, with the humility and absorption of a child. I am saddened when I hear preachers sound familiar and tired with Scripture, as if nothing of the word cuts them anymore. Little wonder if their congregation follows suit and treats Scripture with a familiarity verging on contempt. Instead, under the guidance of the Spirit, preachers should expect to be surprised by the text—the discoveries that they pass on to their congregation are the ones that *they* have stumbled across and been humbled by.

---

general and derogatory sense when other words have been preferred by different translators. Further examples include Jer 3:17; Lam 3:60; Rom 1:21; Luke 1:51; 2 Cor 10:5.

35. McIntyre, *Faith, Theology and Imagination*, 3.

36. Calvin, *Institutes of the Christian Religion*, 1.1.

37. Taylor, *The Preaching Life*, 45–48.

In order to do this, they engage their imaginations to explore the text. Barbara Brown Taylor likens our imagination to a child who "has no point to make, no ax to grind," but rather roams the neighborhood one afternoon, picking up bits and pieces along the way that catch the eye:

> When imagination comes home and empties its pockets, of course there will be some sorting to do. Keep the cat's eye marble, the Japanese beetle wing, the red feather. . . . Jettison the bottle cap, the broken glass, the melted chocolate stuck with lint. But do not scold the imagination for bringing it all home, or for collecting it in the first place. There are no treasures without some trash, and the Holy Spirit can be trusted to go with us when we wander and to lead us back home again, with eyes far wiser for all they have seen.[38]

2. Piecemeal and Accumulation

As we have seen, the best treasures are often stumbled upon when we have freedom to roam. They cannot be rushed. When commenting on the search for truth, John Henry Newman stated: "We know, not by a direct and simple vision, not at a glance, but, as it were, by piecemeal and accumulation, by a mental process . . . by the comparison, the combination, the mutual correction, the continual adaptation of many partial notions . . ."[39]

It may be tempting to try and nail the sermon points as soon as we have read the text, but we should remember that God's word is a living "thou." It is a subject, not an object. Getting to know the text "by piecemeal and accumulation" allows it time to breathe. Treat God's word as subject and you will naturally want to give God time to speak to you as you prepare. More often than not, this speech will be in God's timing, not ours. God's truth may come to us circuitously, as Dickinson's line, "Success in circuit lies," suggests; and in doing so, it may also turn up some "superb surprise"[40] that simply cannot be corralled into our tightly-structured sermon plan. As Timothy Radcliffe points out, the truth often eludes us if we try to "grab it by the forelock."[41]

38. Taylor, *The Preaching Life*, 51.

39. Newman, 'The Idea of a University,' *Discourse VIL* as quoted in Radcliffe, *Sing a New Song*, 239.

40. Dickinson, Poem 1129, *Emily Dickinson: The Complete Poems*.

41. Radcliffe, *Sing a New Song*, 239.

Some preachers rush the sermon straight into a neatly pre-conceived polemic. Eager to step into the role of apologist, they anticipate all the arguments that people might throw at Scripture and attempt to beat down each and every one of them. This leaves the congregation with a headful of clever rhetoric—and they may even be dazzled by the preacher's verbal acrobatics. However, all this can be a noisy distraction from the word of God, and it is God whom, after all, the congregation needs to see and hear. At the end of the sermon, the preacher is not interested in what impression has been left of himself; the only question is, has the sermon created in my congregation a desire to venture more deeply into this text and to allow the "thou" behind it greater access to their lives? The preacher trusts the word to accomplish God's purpose; his role is to disclose what is already there and to bring the congregation to a place of "beholding" it. In his book *The Pastor as Minor Poet*, Craig Barnes suggests that "when preachers think of their sermons less as polemics and more as art, they are allowing the congregation to behold Jesus. . . . Poets don't make arguments; they reveal mysteries."[42] One way of doing this is to bring the congregation more closely into the particular world of the biblical text.

3. Pay Attention to the Particular

Reading more literal translations of the Bible may de-familiarize passages we know well and help us to pay greater attention to their grittiness and particularity. Bible translators perform a balancing act, weighing, on the one hand, the concern for readability in the target language against the need to stay faithful and accurate to what the biblical writers wrote.[43] It is significant that, when translating the Bible c.1380, John Wycliffe's translators produced not one version of the Bible but two: a "domesticated" translation which was sensitive to the receptor language (English) and a more literal translation which was much closer to the Latin Vulgate and was not written in fluent English.[44]

Many of us are in the privileged position to have access to a wide range of Bible translations, and part of the "knowing by piecemeal and accumulation" comes about by exposure to a variety of them. At times, in our desire to pave the way to understanding, we may choose dynamic equivalent translations that smooth over any linguistic and cultural

42. Barnes, *The Pastor as Minor Poet*, 127–31.

43. Ryken, *The ESV and the English Bible Legacy*, 41–42.

44. Ibid., 18.

differences with the source text. While I think that such translations can serve a useful purpose sometimes, the danger is that we forget that the biblical text is essentially a foreign one. The French translator and theorist, Antoine Berman, argued that a foreign text should be received for exactly what it is, and that the destruction of expressions or idioms in the source text effaces or deforms it.[45] Translations which "foreignize" the source text rather than "domesticate" it, as Venuti would later point out, sacrifice the standard target language in order to render the linguistic and cultural differences between the source text and the translation.[46] They move the reader *towards* the source text, rather than away from it,[47] thus maintaining the sharpness of the original images and preventing them from being blandly absorbed by the target culture. Lelan Ryken believes that, until the mid-twentieth century, while their concern with clarity left English Bible translators quite prepared to smooth out the text at times, they were equally concerned with their fidelity to the words of the original text.[48] In fact, William Tyndale is believed to have contributed 1,700 "first instances" of a word in English, which seems proof of his determination to render faithfully the biblical texts, even if it meant creating new words.[49]

In sermon preparation at least, we need a sharp awareness of the "otherness" of the biblical text and the particularity of its language if we are to avoid the trap of over-familiarity. The Hebrew scholar and translator, Robert Alter, has written translations of several Old Testament texts which can jolt the preacher from his complacency and "make the stone stony" during our sermon preparation.[50] Alter's *The Book of Psalms* is a good example of this. Although not always uncritical of the King James Version, Alter *is* prepared to subordinate his translation's fluency to the desire to pay attention to the concrete language of the Hebrew Psalms. While pointing out that some Psalms seem clearly to be liturgical texts

45. Berman, *L'épreuve de l'étranger: Culture et traduction dans l'Allemagne romantique.*

46. Venuti as cited in Hodges, "Cultural Approach to Translation Theory."

47. Schleiermacher as cited in Hodges, "Cultural Approach to Translation Theory."

48. Ryken, *The ESV and the English Bible Legacy*, 38–42.

49. Clark, "Hidden Tyndale in *OED's* First Instances from Mike Coverdale's 1535 Bible," 289–93, as cited in Ryken, *The ESV and the English Bible Legacy*, 38.

50. See Alter's *The David Story*, 1999; *The Five Books of Moses*, 2004; *The Book of Psalms*, 2007; *The Book of Genesis*, 2009; *The Wisdom Books*, 2010.

and therefore follow certain literary conventions,[51] Alter suggests that the biblical poets themselves often "rework" familiar stock images, putting a "fresh spin" on them.[52] This suggests that the concept of defamiliarization was at work even amongst the writers of the Psalms!

Therefore, Alter seeks to do justice to the concrete, physical nature of the psalmist's imagery and resists abstractions wherever possible, even at the expense of an easy read. For example, he rejects the King James Version of "soul" in Psalm 63:2, arguing that the Hebrew word *nefesh* means "life breath" and is associated with the throat. His translation reads:

> "God, my God, for You I search.
> My throat thirsts for You,
> my flesh yearns for You
> in a land waste and parched, with no water."[53]

For "salvation" (with its associations of eschatological redemption), Alter uses the word "rescue" because this comes closest to the original Hebrew meaning "to get somebody out of a tight fix."[54] Such literal translations may slow us down at first because we are not used to them, but I believe that this is precisely why they are useful in the early stages of sermon-preparation. We have to pay attention to the text, and they help us to recover the concrete grittiness of the original images.

Interestingly, C. S. Lewis claims that his inspiration for writing *The Chronicles of Narnia* started with particular images rather than abstract ideas. He was quick to dispel the myth that he had written *The Lion, the Witch and the Wardrobe* in order to impart a clearly-defined theological "truth":

> Some people seem to think that I began by asking myself how I could say something about Christianity to children; then fixed on the fairy tale as an instrument; then collected information about child psychology and decided what age group I'd write for; then drew up a list of basic Christian truths and hammered out "allegories" to embody them. This is all pure moonshine. I

---

51. In *The Art of Biblical Poetry*, Alter argues that such conventions are necessary if the text is to be familiar enough for liturgical use. For example, if pilgrims are to chant it as they ascend the Temple mount, "you don't want a lot of fancy footwork in the imagery and syntax; you want, in fact, an eloquent rehearsal of traditional materials and even traditional ways of ordering those materials in a certain sequence," 140.

52. Alter, *The Book of Psalms*, xxiv.

53. Ibid, xxvii.

54. Ibid, xxxiv.

couldn't write in that way. It all began with images; a fawn carrying an umbrella, a queen on a sledge; a magnificent lion. At
first there wasn't anything Christian about them; that element
pushed itself in of its own accord.[55]

The preacher can learn something here. Rather than jumping
straight into an abstract sermon point, we would do well to pay attention to the particular images we see before us in the biblical text. Barbara
Brown Taylor remembers how her understanding of Jesus's humanity
grew when she learned that his having "compassion" for the crowds who
were like sheperd-less sheep meant that "his very bowels turned over inside of him."[56] Rob Bell pays attention to particular images in the Bible
through his NOOMA films.[57] In many ways the films are good examples
of someone who allows the Holy Spirit to breathe life into ancient stories
and metaphors so that the truth may be "worn new." In one of the films,
Bell takes the image of the trees found at the start and end of Scripture:
the tree of the knowledge of good and evil in the Garden of Eden (Gen
2:9) and the tree of life found in Revelation 22:2. While planting two
large trees by the side of a road, he muses over what it means for us to
be "living between the trees."[58] The concrete images spin out to explore
how Adam and Eve's story is mirrored today, what God teaches us about
living in the here and now, and how we can take part in God's redeeming
purposes for this broken world. Like Lewis, he starts with the concrete
image and then the Truth pushes forward of its own accord.

4. Roughen the Text

Easily heard is easily forgotten. Personally, I believe it a fallacy to
think that our job is to render the text as accessible as possible to the
congregation. If the Russian Formalists were right and an experience
becomes more memorable in relation to the *slowness*—rather than the
speed—of perception, then perhaps the preacher should start considering ways to throw obstacles across their listeners' path instead of clearing
them! After all, when he quoted from the book of Isaiah to explain his
use of parables, Jesus drew a sharp distinction between "hearing" and

55. Lewis, *On Stories*, 46.

56. Taylor, *The Preaching Life*, 60.

57. Author and founding pastor of Mars Hill Bible Church in Michigan, Bell is the
featured speaker in these short films, the title of which is based on the Greek word
pneuma, meaning wind or spirit.

58. Bell, *Trees*.

"understanding,"[59] and seemed remarkably unconcerned with how accessible (and palatable) his words were.

So familiar texts may need to be "roughened," not just for a preacher during sermon preparation, but sometimes for the congregation too. One application of this concerns the public reading of Scripture, which I believe should be given a much higher priority in many churches. The auditory form of the passage was an integral part of its original design, and attention should be given to the way it *sounds*. A biblical text can be flattened or brought to life according to the way in which it is read. I have heard many passages of Scripture so reduced through an over-familiar reading that the only question left for the preacher is: "How do you recover the text from here?" The reading of Scripture should create a sense of anticipation in the congregation before the sermon begins.

One way to roughen the text is to use different translations. As has been suggested, using more literal or "foreignized" translations, like Robert Alter's, can increase the grittiness or roughness of Scripture. This can be useful when reading well-known biblical passages with which a congregation may be overly-familiar. For example, even the phrase "familiarity breeds contempt" has become a cliché in itself over the years and has fallen foul of its own moral. It fails to cut. However, hear exactly the same concept expressed in Middle English—"Men seyn that 'over-greet hoomlynesse engendreth dispreisynge'"[60]—and you will probably have to work a little harder to figure it out! As a result, you may stumble upon new nuances, nuances that will stick. While I am not advocating that Scripture should be read in Middle English, my point is that the more important a passage or phrase, the more it may need to be "roughened" during the reading.

Hearing Scripture read in a different language can be another way to roughen the text and to heighten the congregation's perception of it. One of the most memorable Bible readings at our church for me was carried out by two of our Chinese members, first in Mandarin and then in English. Apart from allowing me a small window into their linguistic world and deepening our fellowship through this, it made me pay attention to the familiar English text far more closely. If I hadn't been following the passage closely in my own Bible, I would have been lost. Similarly, the Lord's Prayer took on a whole new meaning for me when I had to

59. Mark 4:11–12.
60. Chaucer, "Tale of Melibee," from *The Canterbury Tales*.

stumble through it in Spanish each week at our local church in Peru. This idea of "roughening the text" raises the question of whether projecting the Scripture reading onto a large screen every week with the aim of making the text more "accessible" is always a good idea. It can leave the listener with little inclination to pick up the text and engage with it further during the sermon. Once the slide changes the text may quickly be forgotten, although this may be combated if the preacher incorporates the text into a powerpoint presentation during the sermon.

Another way of making the biblical text "strange" once again is to play a professional reading of it. This may be more appropriate with some books of the Bible than others. For example, one church embarked on a preaching series of Song of Songs, and in the first service the congregation was asked to read the text aloud, the men reading the part of the Lover and the women the part of the Beloved. Our British reserve reduced the reading to a sort of dirge, interrupted occasionally by a fit of giggles. I cannot remember a single line or image from that reading, only the pressure of my toes curling inside my shoes. For the second sermon in the series, the preacher wisely ditched his congregation's live reading and played a recording of the passage instead. It brought the dialogue to life beautifully, and hearing a disembodied voice reading a passage so full of yearning and desire created the necessary distance between the text and the congregation, allowing the latter to put aside their self-consciousness and to listen to the text's meaning from a position of safety. Recorded readings could also be used with very familiar poetic or narrative texts in order to defamiliarize them. The question the preacher must ask is, "Will this reading bring my congregation closer to the reality of this text—will it "make the stone stonier" for them—or will it just distract them from it?"

5. Avoid Clichés

One thing that preachers can be guilty of indulging in is the use of platitudes and clichés. The word "platitude" comes from the French word *plat* meaning "flat," and is defined as "a trite or commonplace remark, especially one solemnly delivered."[61] A cliché is a hackneyed expression or figure of speech that has lost its edge. The words are worn out through over-use and so the listener experiences a numbness akin to that of Tolstoy cleaning his room. For example, in the UK at least, many evangelical Christians will be very familiar with the following passage from *Mere*

---

61. *The Concise Oxford Dictionary*, 912–13.

Christianity, in which C. S. Lewis ridicules the notion that Jesus could simply be a good "moral teacher." He makes the excellent point that a man who made the kind of claims that Jesus made "would not be a great moral teacher. He would either be a lunatic—on a level with the man who says he is a poached egg—or else he would be the Devil of Hell."[62] This may be a sharp, original figure of speech for those hearing it for the first time; but it has arguably been worn-down to cliché through over-use in many sermons and outreach courses in the UK. Clichés have such power because they are often true. However, the preacher needs to ask himself the question: will this expression *sharpen* my congregation's perception of what it represents, or will it flatten it? We need to allow the words of Scripture to be "worn new/ Again and again"—not worn out.

So how can a preacher avoid cliché and platitudes in his sermons? When approaching a familiar passage from Scripture, Craig Barnes finds that the first priority is to address the congregation's preconceptions about the text as soon as possible. He does this through asking probing questions about their assumptions and then showing that this sermon is not going to simply reiterate what they already know. The purpose of this is not to be novel, but to "be faithful to my own assumption . . . that there is more in this . . . poetry of the Bible than any of us have already discovered."[63] Thus, approaching the Bible with the anticipation of a child, and expecting to discover some "superb surprise," will rid our sermon notes of cliches.

This is not without its dangers. As Luke Bretherton points out in "Beyond the Emerging Church," the challenge is how to avoid being a mere "novelty act" or simply picking and choosing pieces of undigested material and ignoring the uncomfortable parts.[64] Similarly, in adopting a post-modern playfulness with the word, there is a danger that the preacher can throw the baby of truth out with the bathwater of cliché (now there's an expression that needs to be "worn new"!).

However, it would be wrong to be paralyzed by fear and resort to acceptable clichés. Jesus promised the disciples that the Holy Spirit "will guide you into all truth."[65] If, as Barbara Brown Taylor suggests, we be-lieve that our relationship with the Bible is "not a romance but a mar-

---

62. Lewis, C. S. *Mere Christianity*, 40–41.

63. Barnes, *The Pastor as Minor Poet: Texts and Subtexts in the Ministerial Life*, 132.

64. Bretherton, "Beyond the Emerging Church," 47.

65. John 16:13.

riage," and we are committed to living with the Scriptures day in, day out and accepting the parts that we do not like or understand as much as those we do,[66] then we can trust God's Spirit to guide us in truth. We needn't be afraid to use our God-breathed creativity to allow the words to be worn new. In *The Go-Between God,* John V. Taylor reminds us of the link between the Holy Spirit and inspiration. The latter has its etymological roots in the verb "to breathe" or "to blow":

> Psalm 33:6 in the Revised Standard Version states, "By the word of the Lord were the heavens made and all the host of them by the breath (*ruach*) of his mouth"; when describing the artists and craftsmen who were called to design and the tabernacle in the desert, Exodus 31:2–3 records the Lord saying, "See I have called by name Bezalel . . . and I have filled him with the Spirit (*ruach*) of God, in wisdom and in understanding and in knowledge and in all manner of workmanship"; the same word, *ruach,* is used later to refer to God's Spirit inspiring David's mind with the temple designs (1 Chron 28:11–12).[67]

We see this Spirit-breathed inspiration evident in the psalmist. Even when drawing from a familiar repertoire of images, the psalmist allowed those images to reverberate in his imagination, creating many innovative associations. For example, Psalm 104, which takes the stock image of "God as King," allows the image movement. Associations reverberate from the image until pictures of royal clothing and light fuse and we are left with this remarkable description of God the King: "Wrapped in light like a cloak, / stretching out the heavens like a tent-cloth."[68] This is poetic art at its best, signifying, while never defining, our Glorious God. It is this inventiveness, Alter argues, that has meant that the Psalms still speak with lively eloquence to people today, two and a half thousand years later.[69]

Conclusion

We worship a God who surely delights in creativity. Creation and the Bible reveal a God of infinite variety, who has imparted this desire to "make" (*poiein*) to the hearts of men and women. Those who preach the

---

66. Taylor, *The Preaching Life,* 60.

67. J. V. Taylor, *The Go-Between God,* 25.

68. Robert Alter's translation of Psalm 104:2. *The Book of Psalms,* xxviii.

69. Ibid.

word can employ this God-given gift of creativity in the reading and the preaching of Scripture, not to create novelty, but rather, as the Russian Formalists did, to "make the stone stony." Defamiliarization can be used to render that which has been flattened through over-familiarity, wonderfully sharp and strange and true once again. In this way, world-weary imaginations can be breathed upon by the Spirit—and God's word is given a fresh hearing.

11

Preaching without Notes

Robert May

PREACHING WITHOUT NOTES SOUNDS a bit like a trapeze artist without a safety net or sky diving without a reserve chute or finding someone's house in the dark on a windswept moor without a map or SatNav. What if it all goes wrong or I lose my way and I have no back-up plan? What if, in the middle of the most important point of the sermon, my mind goes blank and I have nothing more to say to an expectant congregation? How can I ever recover my credibility for the following week let alone my self-confidence? There was an unfortunate incident recently in a US Republican presidential candidate debate where one of the early front runners, Rick Perry, forgot the name of the third government department he would close. For fifty-three excruciating seconds we watched with a mixture of fascination, sinister delight, concern and shared pain (those who engage in public speaking anyway) as he fumbled and mumbled and tried to drag from some dark recess of his memory that third department, but he failed, possibly ending his bid for the Republican nomination. If only he had it written down in front of him on a small piece of paper all would be well.

For others their concern about the possibility of note-less preaching is less about the possibility of looking stupid and more about probability of looking flashy. More of a self-indulgent "Hey, look at me! I am doing this without a safety net or back-up plan!" What if all the congregation talks about after the service is how the sermon was delivered and talk little of what the sermon was about? Delivery before content? Style over substance? This surely cannot be our goal.

Moreover there will be those who would see this as a capitulation to cultural trends and driven by an anxiety to engage (or impress) those currently outside the life of the local church. It was noticeable in recent times how much attention was given in the UK national press to David Cameron's speeches, which he delivers from time to time without notes.[1] It is one thing using this as a technique for political gain; it is quite another thing to use it in the context of worship within the household of God. This is not where we parade our ability to memorize our lines as though we are on the stage or worse. We are in an age where we are told that there are few places where anyone will go and listen to a monologue of any length. However we are also in a time where the stand-up comedian has achieved the status of "rock-god." In the UK in particular stand-up comedians like Michael McIntyre and Eddie Izzard are on sell-out arena-sized tours speaking for over an hour without notes and with little or no visual aids except their capacity to create images of surreal curiosity and side-splitting humor equipped only with their culturally cultivated and trained imaginations, high-performance memory and a deep passion for what they do. But we must note that their "congregations" are utterly absorbed. There is a legitimate concern that too many preachers will draw too much their inspiration from the world of stand-up comedy. Sermons may become engaging, creative, culturally aware and, of course, funny, but before long it will become all too evident that the content is thin, any theological rationale is all but absent and the glorious wonder, seriousness and power of preaching is emptied of its very soul. However, to ignore the cultural significance of this phenomenon and to fail to discern and to learn lessons that might allow the gospel a more culturally-relevant hearing seems foolish and short-sighted.

For others, they simply don't see the need for this kind of note-free delivery. It's not that they are concerned about looking stupid—they have done that often enough anyway—and it's not that they are concerned about appearing to show off—all good preaching requires a fairly healthy ego and an element of theater[2]—they simply don't see what is to be gained from tried and trusted methods that involve well-structured notes and

---

1. http://www.spectator.co.uk/coffeehouse/5806383/the-no-notes-speech-does-the-trick-for-cameron-again.thtml accessed 26th October 2011, 08:30. Cameron's first significant speech "without notes" was delivered at the Conservative Party Conference in 2005 from where he went on to gain the leadership of the Conservative Party.

2. See Childers, *Performing the Word* for a helpful study along this theme.

carefully crafted manuscripts that have served them well over many years of faithful and fruitful preaching. Why take the risk?

So, first we must be very clear what preaching without notes is not. It is not "preaching without preparation,"[3] or a stand-up and just "wing-it" approach to preaching. This kind of approach can claim to have too high a view of the presence and inspiring role of the Spirit to deliver the goods when asked for "in faith" but little or no time for the true and honest perspiration of the preacher laboring in their study with Holy Scripture and the insights from two thousand years of faithful witness on behalf of the cause of Christ. This represents a "just me and the Spirit" arrogance that is normally all too obvious and disturbing to some but sadly impressive and enticing to the vulnerable and naively susceptible. To preach without notes is to preach from thorough and rounded preparation even if one aspect of the goal of that preparation has a slight twist: this must be delivered without notes on Sunday so I had better start paying attention now.

Nor is "preaching without notes" preaching a memorized text. It is not the work of an actor delivering their lines word perfect or the child nervously repeating a poem at a school event. To preach without notes does involve memory and requires the confidence that memory remains a God-given gift. Memory may therefore be submitted, in faith, to the active presence of God as much as any other aspect of the human person. "Preaching without notes" requires careful, systematic preparation and rehearsal but it is better to think of the "internalization" of a message rather than simply the memorization of the message. To preach without notes well requires the preacher to "feel" or "internalize" the message that goes beyond simply remembering a series of points arranged in a logical and helpful order. In other words, to preach without notes is indeed to engage our memory in the service of God but only as we submit all of our being to the presence and service of God. To preach without notes is to preach out of a life immersed in the life of God, authentic and compelling. It is not the use of some technique of memory to merely bring about some desired outcome in the behavior of those who listen. This sermon, as with all good sermons, will indeed have a structure (even if it is only clear, at times, in the mind of the preacher) and this structure will form the framework from which ideas and illustrations and information and stories and exhortations and applications and introductions and conclusions and so on can be attached and then skillfully and faithfully

---

3. Although there are, of course, times when preachers are called upon to deliver a sermon or address with little or no preparation but this is not our subject here.

delivered. But it will be delivered from the mouth of one whose entire being, including her memory, has been laid before the throne of Christ in the service of the church and the world.

You may not be surprised to know that preaching without notes is not a modern fad; I hope so. In light of its history it is clear that it will not pass like other fads nor is it the preserve of some preaching elite who through constant and rigorous mind training exercises have achieved some higher state of preaching ability. Preaching without notes or, as it has sometimes been called historically "extempore preaching," has its roots in the earliest days of the Christian church. Classical Greek and Roman oratory[4] was often delivered without notes and many of the early church fathers were committed to or adopted this practice. Chrysostom and Augustine both delivered sermons without notes[5] and Augustine was particularly concerned about the inability of the preacher to react to a congregation "in the moment" because their delivery was from a prepared or memorized speech.[6] Historically, to speak without notes was seen as the most effective way both to communicate content and also to motivate a response. The speaker engaged with the hearer in the most direct way—eye to eye—in order to maximize the drama and desired impact of the event.

It seems that during the times of the Puritans, finely written sermons with full manuscripts that were tightly argued were more frequent, driven by a fear of departing from the Puritan view of the Christian life while still being delivered with finesse and not a little somberness. These sermons were often (but not always) written more to be published than preached by weak clergy more concerned to keep their job and move up in the life of the church. However, all was not lost and, in Wesley and Whitfield in particular, there was a recovery of the glory of sermons delivered extemporaneously with a rawness and passion that was less about the political and ecclesiastical correctness of the day and more about a genuine yearning to see the lost redeemed and the saints matured.

In recent times, preaching without notes has found its place in more scholarly works. John Broadus[7] wrote in his book, *On the Preparation and*

4. There is a very helpful study of the place of memory in ancient rhetoric in Leith, *You Talkin' to Me*, 143–57.

5. Webb, "Without Notes," 429.

6. Saint Augustine, *On Christian Teaching*, R. P. H. Green (translator), 4.10.25.

7. Broadus, *On the Preparation and Delivery of Sermons*, 273–79. This book was first published in 1870.

Delivery of Sermons, about "Free Delivery" being one of four legitimate methods of delivery (the other three being "Reading," "Recitation," and "Extemporaneous Preaching" which he defined as preaching with limited preparation as opposed to preaching without notes). For Broadus there were three essential elements involved with "free delivery:" careful preparation; notes of any form must definitely not be taken into the pulpit; and no attempt should be made to memorize the sermon. The preacher must focus on the sharing of thoughts and ideas rather than concentrating on the words themselves.[8] In turn there were six advantages: the development of the memory; the creation of written work in preparation that can be reviewed; the oratorical freedom to engage with and react to the congregation; it's the most popular and effective way to be spoken to; it fits best the ministry of a "herald" called to proclaim the gospel; and it is the most satisfying and joyful experience for the preacher.[9]

Charles W. Koller's *Expository Preaching without Notes* in many ways speaks for itself.[10] In chapter 4, Koller argues that "note-free preaching" is preferred by most congregations and is the most effective way to deliver a sermon.[11] He argues that this can be supported from "antiquity," citing Cicero and Quintillian; from the "consensus of modern observers"; from "experience" citing many notable preachers and homileticians of his day; and finally from "the laboratory" where psychological research supports the notion that "Retention increases to sixty-seven per cent when the thought is expressed, not by reading, but by direct address. We want our message to be remembered."[12] Koller argues forcefully for the importance of eye contact and direct engagement with the congregation as the most important aspect of delivery if you want to make an impact.

More recently, Fred Craddock's *Preaching*,[13] which has become a standard text in many homiletics departments, urges that whatever use is made of notes in the delivery of a sermon, the preacher must seek to do that which "aids most effectively in the free, unhindered release of the message."[14] It should be noted that Craddock goes on to caution

8. Ibid., 273.

9. Ibid., 274.

10. Koller, *Expository Preaching without Notes* although originally published in 1962.

11. Ibid., 34–40.

12. Here Koller quotes from Booth, *The Quest for Preaching Power*, 222.

13. Craddock, *Preaching*.

14. Ibid., 215.

against a perceived hierarchy in delivery that places "full manuscript" delivery at the bottom of the pile and "without manuscript" delivery at the top. He is right to state that "an excessive appetite for preaching without notes can cause a sacrifice in content in favor of the accolade."[15] But this is more about a justifiable concern about a preacher's self-interest rather than one driven by a desire for the most effective and authentic form of delivery. Tom Long constructs a similar argument in *The Witness of Preaching*[16] where he weighs the strengths and weaknesses of full manuscripts, edited notes or outlines, and no notes at all. In the end he leaves it to the preacher to decide which one works best for him or herself both in terms of personal preference and also context but recognizes that "there is an undeniable sense of authenticity and immediacy involved when the preacher speaks directly to the listeners with no written 'screen' between them."[17]

Michael Quicke is one of the more forceful advocates of preaching without notes today. In his blog,[18] Quicke, having recently read O. C. Edwards, *A History of Preaching*, quotes one of the few sweeping generalizations that Edwards can make from his magisterial analysis of preaching which is that, "with rare exceptions, the most effective preachers have not preached from manuscripts."[19] While acknowledging that in his preparation he writes extensively, revising and editing his script continuously, his ultimate goal is to deliver the sermon without notes. Interestingly this is not just because of his belief in its effectiveness to engage the listeners but also because "much is left open, giving preachers flexibility to respond to the Spirit's prompting."[20] For Quicke, preaching without notes moves from merely the realms of effective communication cautiously into a world of Spirit-empowered event, the character and integrity of the preacher, and the openness to encounter and new insight, even while in the moment of preaching.

15. Ibid., 215.

16. Long, *The Witness of Preaching*.

17. Ibid., 183. See also Graves, *The Fully Alive Preacher*, 141–49 for another helpful discussion about the exhilaration and possibilities of preaching without notes.

18. See http://michaelquicke.blogspot.com/2011/07/history-of-preaching-3.html accessed 25th November 2011.

19. See also Edwards Jr., *A History of Preaching*, 836.

20. Quicke, *360 Degree Preaching*, 185–86.

Joseph Webb's short but very helpful and practical book, *Preaching without Notes*, gives three reasons why we should preach without notes.[21] First, preaching without notes maximizes the connectedness between preacher and congregation. Webb does not deny that other styles of delivery have a measure of connectedness but for him it is a matter of degree and "without notes" creates the strongest bond by freeing the passion of the preacher from the constraints of notes to their fullest, unhindered by text. Second, preaching without notes maximizes participation with the congregation. For Webb, this is achieved by understanding the difference between deductive and inductive speech modes. In the deductive speech mode the audience is given the impression that every word is pre-planned and, therefore, instills a certain measure of passivity in the hearer. However, in an inductive speech mode the audience senses that the words are not planned in advance and that things remain up in the air and are unfolding as the speaker continues. This encourages a greater degree of active listening in the congregation.[22] Third, to preach without notes is to reflect an authentic witness. Webb boldly states that "To give one's most powerful witness, at least for the majority of people, it is necessary to stop reading, stop following notes, set the paper aside, and just stand up and talk. . . . Tell us from your heart, and we will know that what you say is true—if not true for all of us, at least true for you. And that, in itself, will mean a great deal."[23]

Preaching is at its very core an oral form of communication. Whether full manuscripts are used or none, oral style must take precedence over a literary or written style. For the preacher, the object of delivery is the ear and not the eye. Language used when speaking is different to language that is used in written forms and the best preaching does not just acknowledge this but seeks at every point to be delivered as an oral form with all the messiness and awkwardness this brings.[24] Even the most staunch proponents of full manuscript preaching would never consider simply handing out copies of their full manuscripts to their congregants, give them fifteen minutes (or fifty minutes?) to read them quietly to

21. Webb, *Preaching Without Notes*, 25–30. Another recent book making the case for preaching without notes is Lybrand, *Preaching on Your Feet*.

22. Ibid., 29.

23. Ibid., 30.

24. Fant, *Preaching for Today*, has some very helpful things to say in this area. See especially chapters 8, 10, and 11.

themselves and then offer to take any questions. Sermons are not to be read but preached and they must be preached in an oral form.

But the voice of the preacher is not a disembodied voice. Despite the proliferation in recent decades of tape (now CD/mp3/online and so on) ministries, no preacher would ever seriously consider recording his message in advance, entering the pulpit on Sunday with a CD player and hitting the "play" button while then retiring to their chair in the corner to catch-up on some letter writing. A voice but no body! "Does anybody want a copy to take home with them?" Preaching has always been embodied and experienced live in the realm of heartfelt worship with the preacher on fire for the sake of the church and the world.

However, this embodied voice cannot be a distant, cold, and detached voice. This embodied voice comes with eyes and hands and feet and a body. It comes with a personality and a sense of humor (hopefully) and love and compassion and understanding. But it comes first and foremost as one who is also a follower and disciple of Jesus Christ. One who is deeply aware that she is a worshipper long before she is a preacher.[25] It is a voice that weeps with those who weep and rejoices with those who rejoice; serves and encourages and loves deeply the community that we know as the church. It is a human person that engages a congregation in the sermon, not as an itinerant celestial being paying some mystical visit, but real flesh and blood. This person believes something passionately, feels something deeply and has been overwhelmed with this message in a way that—well, quite honestly they should be prepared to die for. They have emerged from within the life of the community of faith and stand and speak on behalf of the community of faith.[26] They take the Scriptures as seriously as anyone, recognize that they stand as just one in a great line of glorious saints who have wrestled with these same Scriptures and many of whose works are available to converse with and to be enriched by or enraged by. They walk to the pulpit fearful of the task that they are called to but hopeful of the God that once again will meet them in their moment of delivery. And they stand with compelling gaze, making eye contact with one and then another, as they search the congregation and sense the expectation, and the words now flow, spilling out in language that invites and arouses engagement and imagination and the anticipation of truth and proclamation and conviction and comfort. From presidents and prime ministers with their autocue to

25. See Quicke, *Preaching as Worship*.

26. Long's idea of "the preacher as witness" is very helpful here. See Long, *The Witness of Preaching*, 42–47.

teachers and the leaders of armies and the captains of sports teams, there remains nothing quite as compelling as the eye to eye engagement of a real and gifted speaker with deep conviction trying to change the world![27] But unlike most others, this is done in the name of the creator, sustainer and redeemer of all things: God himself.

Preaching, therefore, needs to move from something textual to something oral; it also needs to move from something oral to something truly embodied, truly human. However it also needs to move from that impassioned body towards the possibility that preaching is supremely incarnational in nature and flirts dangerously with the boundaries of a truly sacramental act. In other words, and as Michael Quicke alluded to earlier, preaching needs to recognize that the work and voice of the Spirit does not remain behind in the study while the preacher enters the pulpit alone except for his notes or highly trained memory. Rather the renewing voice of the Spirit remains an active possibility even in the midst of delivering a finely crafted, theologically robust and engaging sermon. Just as bushes and donkeys can occasionally be the means by which God speaks in an awkward and unplanned moment, how much more should those called and equipped anticipate that in their fleshly frailty God remains an active source of grace and inspiration?

In this sense, therefore, to preach without notes goes beyond all that we understand about public speech and direct engagement with a congregation and, as with any act of preaching, it is also an act of faith and obedience embodied in one who is both "faith-full" and obedient. The preacher, I would suggest through this particular kind of prophetic act, states in this particular way that he or she remains open to the possibility that the Spirit may well bring fresh inspiration even as they speak.[28] But this is not the behavior of one who once again puts "The Lord her God to the test" in some manipulative kind of way. It should not be understood as the rash act of faith of the preacher who sees no point in disciplined study and exegesis, or the preacher who too easily dismisses the beauty of

27. The speech of Colonel Tim Collins of the Royal Irish Regiment on the eve of battle in Iraq in March 2003 was delivered without notes but was extraordinarily crafted and achieved world-wide recognition. Go to http://www.telegraph.co.uk/comment/3562917/Colonel-Tim-Collins-Iraq-war-speech-in-full.html for a full copy of the speech. I suspect that much careful preparation went on beforehand and he had spoken much of the speech in his head many times before he finally delivered it.

28. By this I am not saying that other forms of preaching are closed to this possibility but I am saying that in the act of preaching without notes, this aspect of the preaching event is embodied by the preacher in this particular way.

the homiletical craft and the construction of sermons that work; nor the act of one who seeks to disguise his empty spiritual state in impressive technique. It is the act of one who has stewarded their call well and has set an example to those who believe; who has done their preparation as much as the week has allowed and has carefully and wisely crafted this sermon; and now, still, remains open to the very present reality of the unseen God in the gathering of the people of God and in the act of preaching. God remains free to intervene, or not, but should he choose to the preacher will not be bound to his or her notes. I have experienced, more often than I had expected to when I first decided to preach without notes, the odd experience of both forgetting things that I had thought I would say and suddenly remembering something mid-flow that had never entered entered into my preparation that turned out to be both timely and relevant. This experience was not unfamiliar to me when I preached with notes and I know many preachers who would be conscious of the Spirit's prompting while preaching and share thoughts and ideas that may have been absent in the preparation and planning. However, in the decision to preach without notes I have felt that in some way I have opened myself up to a greater awareness of this possibility and that my level of expectation and freedom to respond to these promptings has increased.

But whether or not an occurrence of divine intervention or convenient recall takes place in the moment of preaching, the goal of the preacher must be to have so internalized the message of the text and to have become so gripped by its, in the language of Long, "focus and function," that the need for notes at the point of delivery evaporates and all that is left is to deliver this message in the most effective way possible: out of a life fully submitted to and immersed in the life of the triune God.

So How Do You Go About Preaching without Notes?

You may be pleased to know that the tried and trusted methods of sermon preparation remain thoroughly intact. For many it is helpful to separate sermon preparation into two broadly distinctive phases: the work of exegesis with the biblical text followed by the homiletical task of sermon construction. Finding something to say first and then finding the best way to say it. However, to preach without notes is to enter into this process of preparation with an underlying anticipation and focus on a delivery that will be without notes. Therefore, at its simplest, I have found that I concentrate a lot more and I pray a lot more. I need to learn the text and seek to be grabbed by the text more deeply.[29] For me, I need to come to a place where I have moved beyond the essential place of satisfying myself at an intellectual level that this sermon will work; a place where, in the language of Tom Long, the sermon will at least "say" and "do" something.[30] Rather, I also need to come to a place where I have "felt" the sermon, recognizing and submitting myself to its implications; where I have somehow embodied the sermon. In the language of Greek rhetoric, I do not have a grasp of just the logos, but also a feel for the *pathos* and the *ethos* too. Once again this should be part of any good preaching but, as with Webb earlier, it is a matter of degree. To prepare to preach without notes increases for me the need to feel and to experience the sermon at an emotional level in my preparation as much as I need to do this at an intellectual level. It is this "experiencing" of the sermon in the preparation that enables me to become increasingly less reliant on the need for notes and will eventually enable me to discard them altogether. In other words, I have become sufficiently compelled once again to share and proclaim the ideas and thoughts of the text without being too concerned about the words that I will use. I know that they will be there.

I spend more time, therefore, with the text, prayerfully reading it over and over, analyzing its genre[31] and rhetorical structure, its context, exploring it in different versions, dipping into the Greek and Hebrew texts as much as my limited knowledge will allow me to. I have created for myself a framework of questions mostly drawn from Long[32] and Brueggemann[33] that provide some measure of focus to the exegetical work. I am not enslaved to these questions and find that from time to time different passages, occasions and experiences with the text changes the way that the sermon begins to emerge but I would not want to start without a framework.

The repeated questioning and analysis of the text generates pages and pages of notes and ideas. At some point in this process, sometimes

29. I have greatly benefitted from the insights of Walter Brueggemann in the area of rhetorical criticism and the rhetorical analysis of the text. See especially Brueggemann, "That the World May be Redescribed," 359–67.

30. Long, *The Witness of Preaching*, 78–91.

31. See especially Long, *Preaching the Literary Forms of the Bible*.

32. Long has a very helpful set of questions and a helpful framework that can be used to explore the text more creatively in Long, *The Witness of Preaching*, 68–77.

33. Brueggemann, "That the World may be Redescribed," 359–67.

sooner and other times later, I will engage with commentaries and other reference books to interact with the scholars and writers who have wrestled with the same passage and had the same questions that I have. From time to time a useful story or illustration or quote will pop into my head which I quickly write down long before I have begun the homiletical phase. Similarly, I try to remain open to exploring a particular sermon form that will serve the sermon's purpose best although I do not make decisions about form early—in fact it's usually one of the last things I do but more about sermon forms shortly.

My goal at the end of this phase is to have somewhere between three and nine chunks "chunks" of ideas or, in the language of Buttrick, "moves." These "moves" or "building blocks" should be able to be written as a simple sentence or idea. For example, in a recent sermon from *1 Corinthians 11:17–34* where Paul addresses concerns about the way that the Lord's Supper was being administered at Corinth, my "moves" included: give some examples of inclusive and exclusive meals in modern culture; give some examples that illustrate the power of taking communion; some examples from church life where one group can humiliate another group (or rub their noses in it) even unintentionally; re-tell and re-imagine how communion was probably being taken at Corinth; contrast a communion service at Corinth with what happens in our church; outline how and why Paul tackles the issue from the gospel text. I try and write these sentences in an oral form as far as that is possible. In fact, I try and write as much down in my preparation as I imagine myself saying it from the pulpit. This helps to maintain the oral focus of the sermon.

Once again I turn to Long and ask myself what the "focus" and "function" of the sermon is: what is the passage "saying" and what is the passage "doing?" I do not always formally write these down but they do provide a way of trimming down the ideas that I have generated so that the sermon can become more focused and I am once again free from the burden of trying to say everything that can be said from the text. The next question for me is critical if I am going to deliver the sermon effectively without any notes: what is the best sermon form to use to preach the message that has emerged from this passage?

One of the great sadnesses of so much preaching is that texts can be forced into sermon forms that they do not fit—I will find three points beginning with "P" from this passage in Haggai even if it kills me, and the sermon. Or that congregations are asked to endure another predictable sermon form that over time can increasingly obscure some, hopefully, excellent content: here we go again, two stories from the preacher's week (the first one trying to be funny), a thesis statement about the passage, some clever stuff from the commentaries, three uninspiring or impossible things that I am supposed to do this week, and a heart-tugging story about a small boy and a puppy to round things off![34] The greater sadness is that both of these forms (the "Three Point Sermon" and a form of the more traditional deductive sermon) are perfectly good sermon forms and have their place among the many sermon forms that exist, but when all passages and every congregation are forced to fit a single sermon form, too much over time is lost. Further, we now know much more about individual learning styles and left and right-brain thinkers, so we must give serious consideration to the need for variety in the way that sermons are delivered. More predictable three-pointers readily engage one part of the congregation while boring another part; tension building narrative preaching excites the anticipation of some while leaving others bemused and confused. If you have ever listened to Fred Craddock preach, you either get it or you don't! So we need to mix it up appropriately.

But the temptation to stick to one familiar form each week when deciding to speak without notes is a real issue to be faced. If I know that there will always be three points each week and I just have to remember what this week's letter is; and the three points that start with the magic letter then I am less concerned about forgetting something. If my road map is so familiar I know it like the back of my hand, how am I ever likely to get lost? There is a genuine dilemma here but help is at hand.

There are indeed many different sermon forms but the best ones tend to be simple and easy to remember. Once again Tom Long provides an excellent list of these forms in *The Witness of Preaching*[35] and the creative and willing preacher would do well to look through them and learn some of them.[36] The choice of form should take into account the genre of the passage: some forms work better with narrative passages than others and so on. The key thing is that the sermon form provides a scaffold on which the "moves" or "chunks" or "ideas" can be hung in an order that works and is memorable. In fact the test as to whether the order works

---

34. No sooner have I written this than I want to apologize. This is a perfectly valid sermon form (including the puppy reference!) but when it becomes too predictable over time we do both the text and the congregation a disfavor.

35. Long, *The Witness of Preaching*, 126–32.

36. Another source of inspiration to explore different styles of preaching is Stone, *Refining Your Style*.

is the extent to which one idea flows naturally into the next in a way that makes sense and, importantly, is easily remembered and generates a sense of momentum and passion. You know either the form or the order is wrong when you cannot find a way to remember how you get from one part of the sermon to the next part without the feel of a very clumsy link; something is wrong somewhere and if you cannot follow it, how can you be sure your congregation will?

Once a suitable form has been identified and the various parts of the sermon have been attached to it, including inserting any illustrations or quotes or clips from films and so on, a steady and ongoing process of prayerfully recalling the structure and occasionally refining it continues up to the moment of delivery. My sermon from 1 *Corinthians* ended up being of this simple form: This is our experience today—This is what the Bible teaches—This is the application. I talked about experiences of inclusive and exclusive meals and also situations where we can humiliate one another intentionally or not in the first part. In the second part I re-imagined and re-told the way that communion was happening at Corinth drawing out relevant points and then moved onto describe how Paul used the gospel to make his point. In the third and shortest part of the sermon I made some points of application moving the message from communion to other aspects of the Christian life. The simple three-stage shape made it easy to recall and to locate the individual parts in sequence.

So on the morning of the service, whatever each preacher does should be done as usual and when the time comes to speak, simply enter the pulpit, make eye contact with the congregation, trust your preparation, your memory, your passion in the faithful presence of God, say a silent prayer, and then go for it! You will rarely forget anything significant although you may from time to time miss or forget a quote or an illustration but the heart of the message will be there. You will be the only one who will know. And this for me was very liberating. The congregation only hear what you say; they do not have a copy of the sermon in front of them checking off whether you have remembered everything or not. It remains a whole sermon to those who hear it even if you are aware that you missed something that during your preparation seemed to be of some importance. Trust that this omission will not be of any great significance. Similarly you may recall in the middle of the sermon something that just seems so apt and before you know it you are speaking it out, surprised how well it fits. Give thanks to God for this serendipitous moment and then move on; nobody else need know anymore. I found that when I started to preach without notes my preaching was less likely to wander, became more focussed and was often slightly shorter. With notes in front of me I was always battling the temptation to run off in some fanciful direction of thought knowing that I could look at my notes when it was over and carry on from where I had left off. This is less likely to happen now. From time to time I may have a quote written down on a small card—I do not feel obliged to memorize everything. Similarly I may print off an illustration from a website or read from a newspaper clipping or magazine article. This is simply because they have been written better than I am likely to be able to memorize them and it just seems more natural to me. Other times this is not necessary. At the moment of conclusion, and there are many times that I am not sure exactly how I will conclude, again trust that you will know what to say and your work will be done and that the promise of God's faithfulness to bless the preaching of his word will happen again. And now all that is left is for the unseen presence of God to take this sermon and work it out in the coming week in the lives of those who heard it while you get a cup of tea and greet people at the door.[37]

To preach without notes is to be in a place of full engagement with the text, its message and the congregation. It is truly to be fully alive to God in the pulpit, raw and unguarded by notes, eye to eye with those loved by God and loved by you; free to speak with passion and conviction to those hungry for a word from heaven from one who speaks on behalf of God himself. But it is the act of one who has submitted all of their being in the confident knowledge of the active and faithful presence and purposes of God, a disciple and a worshipper first, now called to speak on behalf of God and his church.

---

37. Webb's final chapter here was tremendously helpful in understanding the moment and process of delivery. He has twelve helpful pieces of advice: 1. Plan to be nervous. 2. Speak naturally and conversationally. 3. Do not hide or disguise emotion. 4. Try not to think ahead. 5. If you forget something move on to where your memory takes you. 6. View the whole sermon as drama. 7. If you need to read something out, say what you are doing, do it and then move on. 8. Interact with the congregation. 9. Be open to unexpected insights. 10. Have fun. 11. But maintain your dignity. 12. Allow yourself time to come down from the sermon. Webb, *Preaching Without Notes*, 108–18.

1 2

Genre Sensitive Preaching

David Ridder

THERE ARE MANY WAYS to structure a sermon. Some preachers shape their sermons according to time-honored principles of classical rhetorical discourse.[1] Others advocate that a sermon should take the structure that will best achieve the purpose of the sermon.[2] Still others argue that the sermon's shape should be driven by sociological considerations that militate against speaking authoritatively from today's pulpit.[3] The idea I would like to advance is that while the above considerations must be taken into account in the shaping of the sermon, the single most important factor when determining the shape of the sermon is the text itself. My conviction is that faithful preaching of the text requires that the sermon reflect the form of the text as well as the meaning of the text. Genre is an important consideration when interpreting a text. It also ought to be considered when preaching a text.

I like to challenge my students to think about how to make a sermon on a narrative text sound like it is telling a story. A sermon on a psalm should feel poetic rather than didactic. A sermon from the prophets may need to convey the thunder of the voice of God. This is more than just an argument for homiletical variety in preaching. It comes from the conviction that the medium and the message are inextricably intertwined. Meaning is best preserved if it is delivered in a manner consistent with

1. Broadus, *On the Preparation and Delivery of Sermons*, 85.

2. Robinson, *Biblical Preaching*, 116.

3. Lewis and Lewis, *Inductive Preaching*, 54.

how we receive it in the text. I believe a biblical and theological case can be made for genre sensitive preaching.

Making the Case Biblically

The single text which speaks most directly to the subject of how the Scriptures should be handled by the preacher or teacher is 2 Timothy 2:15: "Do your best to present yourself to God as one approved, a work-man who does not need to be ashamed and who correctly handles the word of truth." This implies that there is a correct way and an incorrect way to handle the Scriptures. One may not handle them any way one chooses. It does not mean that every expositor will necessarily choose to preach a given text the same way or with the same sermonic structure. It does mean that the "word of truth" bears a sacred meaning which the workman must be careful to convey. As will be argued below, getting at this meaning requires giving careful attention to the form of the text in one's study. It normally also requires reflecting the form of the text in the preaching of the sermon, since it is doubtful that the text's meaning can be adequately conveyed if it is divorced from its form.

The compound word *orthotomounta*, which is at the heart of the verse, is translated variously by English versions. The New International Version has "correctly handles." The New American Standard translates it "handling accurately." The Revised Standard Version has "rightly han-dling." The King James Version translates it "rightly dividing." This word is significant for understanding exactly what Paul is saying to Timothy about how one should deal with the word of truth. The difficulty is that the exact meaning of the word is uncertain, because the verb *orthotomeo* occurs only twice in the LXX (Prov 3:6 and 11:5) where it appears to mean "to cut a straight road." Commentators weigh in on the meaning of the word in 2 Timothy 2:15 in a variety of ways as will be seen below.

Donald Guthrie wrestles with whether the straight road image is the best way to understand *orthotomounta*. While it is used to describe a road in the two places it occurs in Proverbs, the word by itself cannot naturally be understood of a road. Guthrie is drawn to the notion that the word should be taken quite generally as an exhortation to straight-forward exegesis: "The idea of cutting which is inherent in the verb is thought to mean the correct analysis of the word of truth, either in its separate parts or in its whole. . . . In this context . . . the main idea seems to be that Timothy must be scrupulously straightforward in dealing with the word of truth, in strong contrast to the crooked methods of the false teachers."[4]

William Hendriksen is somewhat more adamant that the literal notion of "straight-cutting" probably has not been retained in the use of *orthotomounta* in 2 Timothy 2:15. He argues that in a composite verb the meaning-emphasis may shift to the prefix, until in the semantic process the literal sense of the base is lost. In this case, the meaning should be understood as "handling aright." It speaks of handling the word of God in a proper, straightforward manner. With this understanding of the word Hendriksen applies the verse as follows:

> The man who handles the word of truth properly does not change, pervert, mutilate, or distort it, neither does he use it with a wrong purpose in mind. On the contrary, he prayerfully interprets Scripture in the light of Scripture. He courageously, yet lovingly, applies its glorious meaning to concrete conditions and circumstances, doing this for the glory of God, the conversion of sinners, and the edification of believers.[5]

Ralph Earle is more inclined to think the straight road image has been retained in the use *orthotomounta* in 2 Timothy 2:15:

> BAG says "Found elsewhere independently of the NT only in Prov 3:6, 11:5, where it is used with *hodous* and plainly means cut a road across country (that is forested or otherwise difficult to pass through) in a straight direction, so that the traveler might go directly to his destination. Then *orthotomein ton logon tes aletheias* would perhaps mean guide the word of truth along a straight path (like a road that goes straight to its goal), without being turned aside by wordy debates or impious talk" (p. 584). The context suggests that Paul is warning against taking the devious paths of deceiving interpretations in the Scriptures.[6]

John Stott is also inclined to the viewpoint that *orthotomounta* means to "cut a path in a straight direction" or "cut a road across country in a straight direction."[7] He comments that such straight teaching of the truth is meant to stand in evident contrast to the false teachers who

---

4. Guthrie, *The Pastoral Epistles*, 148.

5. Hendricksen, *Thessalonians, Timothy, and Titus*, 263.

6. Earle, *The Expositor's Bible Commentary, vol. 11, 1 and 2 Timothy*, 402.

7. Stott, *Between Two Worlds*, 136.

were swerving from it. Paul is emphasizing the need for such loyalty and simplicity in our exposition that our hearers can understand and follow it with ease.

Stephen and David Olford are in essential agreement with Stott's interpretation of 2 Timothy 2:15: "While difficult to translate into English, it essentially means 'handling aright the word of truth; declaring the word of truth without distortion; rightly administering the word of truth; giving the truth a right of way.'"[8]

The main point of agreement among all these commentators is that the "word of truth" is to govern the message. The thoughts of the preacher or teacher are to be shaped by it, and that requires handling it correctly. For us, it requires handling the sacred text correctly, which is the "word of truth" handed down to us.

While there may not be unanimity among commentators regarding how *orthotomounta* should be understood, it is clear that there is considerable agreement about what 2 Timothy 2:15 means. It calls for the preacher or teacher to make a correct analysis of the word of truth in the part and in the whole. It demands that one be scrupulously straightforward in dealing with it, never changing, perverting, or distorting it. One who handles the word of truth must respectfully let the text govern the message, going straight to the destination without turning aside. It calls for loyalty to the text and such simplicity in our exposition that our hearers can understand and follow with ease.

Accurately Handling the Word of Truth

All of these perspectives on 2 Timothy 2:15 certainly argue for a high view of the text, and encourage the preacher to be careful in handling it. But does all of this demonstrate a need for genre sensitive preaching? That is to say, does "accurately handling the word of truth" necessarily require that the shape of the sermon should be determined primarily by the structure and flow of the text itself? Such a case would be difficult to make from this lone text. On the other hand, a compelling argument may be made that the surest way to handle accurately the word of truth is to convey the truth in a manner similar to the way the text itself does.

---

8. Olford and Olford., *Anointed Expository Preaching*, 72.

It is only reasonable to suggest that "handling accurately" or "rightly dividing" the word of truth means paying attention to the form of the text as well as to its meaning. James Cox argues:

> Get as much of the form of the sermon as you can from the form of the text. The poet John Ciardi was right, I believe when he gave the title to a collection of his poems How Does a Poem Mean? Not What Does a Poem Mean? For the very "how"—the form, the style—of a poem is often a part of its meaning. So it may be with your sermon. The closer the sermon sticks to the text, the closer it may be to God's intention for its use in a particular situation.[9]

This understanding that part of the meaning of a passage is carried in its form is critically important for "rightly dividing the word of truth." It means that one cannot dissect a passage to find its meaning, discard the original form like a worn out carcass, and then find some flashy new form to communicate the meaning. One cannot accurately convey the meaning of the text apart from its form. Walter Liefeld goes so far as to suggest that out of respect for the inspiration of Scripture, one must pay attention not only to the meaning of the text, but also to the way the text is presented:

> What I am suggesting then is that we study the text carefully before we begin to write down our points, to see what parts of the text will contribute toward the opening "statement," and what parts lend themselves, by their very nature, to a sense of progression in the sermon. If we would like our sermon to include an introduction, a climax, and to have a final impact, we will be wise to see if we can find such in the text itself. The great probability is that these goals will be achieved simply by following the text in its biblical sequence. That should always be our first approach. . . . Remember that the Holy Spirit has inspired Scripture in the form in which it exists. There is a reason why the elements of a passage stand in the sequence in which we find them.[10]

Following Liefeld's logic, Paul's encouragement to Timothy is seen to be all the more weighty. If "all Scripture is inspired by God" (2 Tim 3:16, NIV), then one must be all the more careful in the handling of it. To disregard the form of the text is to give short shrift to the way the Spirit

9. Cox, *A Guide to Biblical Preaching,* 22.
10. Liefeld, *New Testament Exposition,* 118.

intended to get the meaning across. It is no wonder, then, that the one who fails to handle the word of truth accurately has cause to be ashamed.

It is ironic that those of us who hold the highest view of Scripture have sometimes not held such a high view of the text. As Evangelicals, we are quite rigorous in our dissection of the text to get at its meaning. We are generally not as astute at appreciating the form of the text and understanding how the form of the text contributes to its meaning. Thomas Long's perspective is particularly insightful on this point:

> It is particularly crucial that preachers give attention to biblical literary form and dynamics because these are precisely the aspects of biblical text commonly washed out in the typical text-to-sermon process. It is ironic that preachers often disregard these dimensions of a text since attention to these "textual poetics" brings us into contact with what resonates most harmoniously with a key ingredient in the homiletical task: deciding how to preach so that the sermon embodies in its language, form, and style the gospel it seeks to proclaim. . . . An unfortunate result of overlooking the literary properties of biblical texts is the tendency to view those texts by default as inert containers for theological concepts. The preacher's task then becomes simply throwing the text into the winepress, squeezing out the ideational matter, and then figuring out homiletical ways to make those ideas attractive to contemporary listeners. The literary and rhetorical shape of the text matters not at all; it is discarded as ornament. The mistake in this, of course, is that the literary dimensions of texts are not merely decorative. Texts are not packages containing ideas; they are means of communication.[11]

I agree with Long's conviction that everything about the text works to create its meaning. That is why in order to be accurate the sermon must be faithful to the form, function, tone and content of the text. Sidney Greidanus is one who advocates such a careful approach to the text:

> If the text seeks to evoke a "wow!" or a "hallelujah!" from the hearers while the sermon manages to evoke merely intellectual assent or a yawn, the problem may well lie in the form of the sermon: a wrong form can undercut the message of the text and thus distort it, while, conversely, an appropriate form can help the message get across as originally intended. . . . The significance of the sermon form becomes evident when one realizes

11. Long, *Preaching and the Literary Forms of the Bible,* 12.

that this reshaping will distort the text's message unless it is done with sensitivity to the text's form.[12]

Greidanus advocates that even the tone and the mood of the sermon need to be respectful of the text:

> If the text is a narrative, then the sermon ought to exhibit the characteristics of narrative; if the text is a lament, then the sermon ought to set the tone and mood conveyed by the lament; if it is teaching, then the sermon ought to be didactic in character. The point here is not, of course, slavish imitation of the form of the text, but such respect for the textual form that its spirit is not violated by the sermonic form; such respect for the textual form that its characteristic way of conveying its message becomes a mark of the sermon.[13]

The point being reinforced here is that one cannot accurately handle the word of truth while being inattentive in the sermon to the form, tone, and mood of the text.

Fred Craddock is in essential agreement with Greidanus on this point. The form of the text must not be ignored in designing the sermon, because its form often reveals what a text is doing. For the sermon to do what the text does, the preacher must hold on to the form. The form captures and conveys function, not only during the interpretation of the text, but during the designing of the sermon as well. To ignore the form of the text and merely preach the propositions and themes in the passage is like boiling off all the water and preaching the stain in the bottom of the cup.[14] In other words, the fullest effect and experience of the text upon the listener is lost when the form of the text is ignored in the sermon. But Craddock asserts that it is not just a matter of how the listener experiences the sermon. The sermon's accuracy and integrity are at stake: "The values of permitting the biblical text to instruct the sermon on form as well as content are evident. . . . There is more assurance of integrity in the sermon if both design and substance come from the same source rather than having a message from one source and the form for its delivery from another."[15] Craddock helps to make the case that the best way to ensure the accurate handling of the word of truth is for the preacher to let the

12. Griedanus, *The Modern Preacher and the Ancient Text*, 141.
13. Ibid.
14. Craddock, *Preaching*, 123.
15. Ibid., 178.

form of text drive the structure of the sermon. Not to do so would be to jeopardize the sermon's accuracy and integrity.

The Variety of Scriptural Forms

It would seem obvious that the great variety of genres found in Scripture suggests the need for variety in our preaching. In Peter Adam's practical theology of expository preaching he makes the point that the varied forms of Scripture require varied forms of sermons. He says the Bible contains "a great variety of styles of communication, including propositions, parables, history, sayings, apocalyptic, warnings, and narrative."[16] If this is the style of Scripture, he insists that it must also be the style of our preaching. Adam is trying to find a way forward in the debate between propositionalists and non-propositionalists. He claims that any adequate view of revelation must allow both that the Bible includes propositions, but also that the revelation is not given exclusively in terms of propositions. Adam then makes the following application of his view of revelation to our preaching:

> If this is true of the Bible, it will also necessarily be true of our preaching, which should exhibit the same variety and pluriformity. If the Bible is God preaching, then our preaching should echo and resonate with his preaching. The consequence of this is that if our preaching contains no intellectual, conceptual or propositional content, it is not true to the Bible. Conversely, if all our preaching does is convey intellectual, conceptual content, we may equally well claim that it is not being true to the Bible. Our preaching should convey, not reduce, the intellectual and emotional impact of the text.[17]

The implication of this for our discussion is that the great variety of Scripture texts demands great variety in preaching. Our preaching must echo and resonate with all that is going on in the text. The preacher cannot capture all the richness of varied biblical texts by always relying on the same handful of sermon forms. The preacher needs an approach to preaching that is capable of embracing all the variety that the Scriptures have to offer. Walter Liefeld agrees with this perspective when he writes of the "variety inherent in the text itself," and suggests the need for great

16. Adam, *Speaking God's Words*, 94.
17. Ibid., 97.

variety in the way sermons are structured.[18] Harold Freeman makes a similar point when he states: "In addition, the different types of literature found in the Bible call for variation of homiletical forms. Scripture is comprised of legal, historical, narrative, poetic, didactic, dramatic, prophetic, and apocalyptic literature; yet sermons tend to take on the same form regardless of the form of the biblical literature of the text."[19]

Freeman decries the tendency of preachers to produce cookie-cutter sermons, regardless of the fact that the text does not want to go into their homiletical forms. The result is that the text is inevitably tortured to say things it was never intended to say.

Fred Craddock has a good example of what Freeman is talking about. He advocates paying careful attention to form both in the text and in the sermon. He warns how a change of form from text to sermon may alter the meaning of the text for listeners: "For example, a sermon on 'blessed are the poor in spirit' (a blessing) which comes across as 'we must be poor in spirit' (an exhortation) represents a shift not only in form but also in meaning. A sermon on a blessing should pronounce the blessing."[20]

If our homiletical procedure is not flexible enough to accommodate the varied nuances of the text, we are likely to misrepresent what it is saying. Craddock's example argues again for the need for our preaching to be as varied as the texts we preach. Craddock is quite emphatic in the way he states the point:

> The Scriptures continually remind pulpit and pew not only what but also how to preach. The rich variety of its passages constantly objects to the boredom of imported outlines that ill-fit the contours of the text and creates a stir among preachers and listeners who had settled for monotony as somehow the way it is. . . . A stirring text well read creates an expectation in listeners which the sermon should not disappoint.[21]

I was weaned on the sermons of Lloyd Perry and other modification (or keyword) method preachers. I came out of seminary convinced that the great majority of scriptural texts should be preached by following that method. While extremely grateful to have learned from Lloyd Perry and his disciples the valuable discipline of the modification method (as well

18. Liefeld, *New Testament Exposition*, 12.

19. Freeman, *Variety in Biblical Preaching*, 21.

20. Craddock, *Preaching*, 179.

21. Ibid., 27.

as its variations—clarification and investigation), it wasn't long before I began to experience in my preaching the sameness of which Craddock complains. Whether preaching from the Gospels, the Psalms, or the Epistles of Paul, all of my sermons began to sound the same. Along with that realization came a gnawing suspicion that one sermon structure could not do justice to the great variety of texts to be preached. In this regard, I strongly identify with the observation made by Thomas Long:

> Preachers who have sought to be open and attentive to biblical texts in their preaching have long sensed that a sermon based upon a psalm, for example, ought somehow to be different from one that grows out of a miracle story, not only because of what the two texts say but also because of how the texts say what they say. A psalm is poetry, a miracle story is narrative; and because they are two distinct literary and rhetorical forms, they "come at" the reader in different ways and create contrasting effects. What is needed, then, is a process of sermon development sufficiently nuanced to recognize and employ these differences in the creation of the sermon itself.[22]

A Proposal for Genre-Sensitive Preaching

Having argued that sermons should adequately reflect the genre of the text that is being preached, I venture to offer a proposal for how this may be done. I readily admit that this is not necessarily ground-breaking work. It is, rather, an attempt to synthesize the good work done by many others in an attempt to help preachers do a better job of being faithful to both the form and meaning of the text. I suggest that the preparation of a genre-sensitive sermon involves six steps.

Step One: Study the Sermon Text
Until You Arrive at the Main Preaching Idea

The assumption being made here is that the reader is already proficient in biblical exegesis. The preacher's first responsibility is to study the text well, following sound hermeneutical principles. The objective is to discover the author's intent in writing to the original readers of the scriptural text. It is important that the preacher have an accurate understanding of what

22. Long, *Preaching and the Literary Forms of the Bible*, 11.

the text meant in its original context. The preacher then seeks to understand ways that message cuts across the centuries and speaks to us today. It takes the main idea of the passage and applies it to our own situation. The statement of this application becomes the central idea of the sermon.

Step Two: Divide the Text into Its Primary Movements, Being Mindful of How a Text of a Particular Genre is Likely to "Move"

It is likely that the preacher will have done some of this work already in attempting to discover the original meaning of the text. In fact, it is hard to imagine how one can arrive at a valid preaching idea without some analysis of how the parts contribute to the meaning of the whole. This may have involved the use of syntactical block diagrams, or some other method of diagramming the passage.

Even if the preacher already has done some of this work, it is now time to be very deliberate about dividing the preaching text into its primary movements. This work is critical to understanding how the text is best preached. As we have already seen, many homileticians argue that the form of the sermon is best supplied by the text itself. In other words, the structure with which the text was originally written is likely the best structure to convey the text's intended meaning in the preaching of the sermon.

Each genre of Scripture has its own patterns of structural development. If one ignores these patterns and treats every kind of text the same way, an important dimension of the text will be lost. To understand the development of the text in a genre-sensitive way is not only essential for grasping the meaning of the text, but also yields valuable clues as to how the text may best be presented in the sermon.

Step Three: Analyze How the Movements of the Text Support Its Main Idea

Having divided the text into its primary movements, the next thing to ask is how the parts relate to the message of the whole. If the primary movements of the text lead up to the main preaching idea, it is likely that the sermon should be structured inductively. In this case, what the text is about is not entirely clear at the outset. It is as one considers the various movements of the text that the truth dawns on the listener. It all "adds up" to the sermon's "bottom line." The scenes of a narrative may lead one to a particular life principle. The strophes of the psalm may lead one on an emotional journey that ultimately results in a choice to trust in God. An epistolary passage may raise a question, explore and reject several possible answers, and finally arrive at the right one. All of these should suggest to the preacher that the sermon is best preached as the passage unfolds, namely in an inductive manner.

On the other hand, many passages beg to be preached in a deductive manner. Such a treatment of a text is suggested when the main preaching idea lies near the surface, and the primary movements of the text flow out of that main idea. Paul's epistles, for instance, tend to be very deductive in their development. Often a clear thesis is stated toward the beginning of the passage. The balance of the passage goes on to explain, prove, or apply the thesis. It makes sense to preach such a text deductively. State the main preaching idea at the beginning of the sermon and show how the movements of the text support it.

How did you discover the main idea of the passage? Let your own discovery process help determine how the text is preached. The general idea is a simple one. If the primary movements of the text lead one toward the main idea of the text, one should probably preach the text inductively. If, on the other hand, the primary movements of the text flow out of the main idea of the text, explaining, proving, or applying it, one should probably preach the text deductively.

Step Four: Following the Main Movements of the Text as They Support or Develop the Main Idea of the Text, Create Corresponding Movements of the Sermon to Support or Develop the Main Idea of the Sermon

Up to this point, I have encouraged that all the attention be given to the structure of the text. How does the text divide into movements? How do the movements of the text support the main idea of the text? It is only when these questions are answered that we are ready to move from the text to the sermon. Having done this work will go a long way in helping us develop a sermon that is true to both the form and meaning of the text.

The preacher is often wise to take the modern listener down a path similar to the one down which the ancient writer took the original readers of the text. The basic idea is that the first place to look for the main movements of the sermon is in the main movements of the text itself.

Most often, though not always, the preacher will be wise to divide the sermon in a way that parallels the divisions of the text. As the divisions of the text move toward the central meaning of the text, the preacher may have complementary divisions of the sermon that move toward the central idea of the sermon.

Having divided the text into its primary movements, whether scenes, strophes, or paragraphs, we analyze how the movements of the text support the main idea of the text. Do the movements draw us toward the main idea of the text? Such a text is best preached in a more inductive fashion. Is the main idea of the text stated early on, and then explained, proved or applied by the movements of the text? That text begs to be preached deductively. Following the main movements of the text as they support or develop the main idea of the text, create corresponding movements of the sermon to support or develop the main idea of the sermon. Let the sermon move toward its big idea similar to the way the text moves to its climax. The result will be a sermon that is true to both the form and meaning of the text. A sermon based on a narrative text will tell a story. A sermon from the Psalms will sound poetic. A sermon from the epistles may come across as quite didactic. Your sermons will not all sound the same, but will take on the varied textures of the Scriptures themselves.

Step Five: When It Can Be Done with Faithfulness to the Text, Consider Adapting a Stock Sermon Form

Some would question whether stock sermon forms have any usefulness at all. By stock sermon forms I mean those traditional ways of developing sermons that have been catalogued by Donald Hamilton[23] and others. These may include the Keyword method, the Analytical method, various textual methods, or sermons built around a problem-solving pattern, to name a few. There clearly is value in being a student of time-honored sermon forms. With some regularity the preacher is likely to recognize that a text develops in a manner that resembles one of these traditional sermon structures. In such a case it may be beneficial to borrow the stock form to help you structure your sermon.

It is important to make sure that there is sufficient correspondence between the stock sermon form and the structure of the text itself. Where there is such a correspondence, one may safely borrow the form without

23. See Hamilton's *Homiletical Handbook*.

doing damage to the text. When the form doesn't quite fit the text, borrow what is useful in the form. Amend the form to fit the text, instead of bending the text to fit the form.

On the one hand, it is clear that too heavy a reliance on stock sermon forms can result in lazy preaching that distorts the message of the text. On the other hand, it is wise for the preacher to be a student of sermon forms. At times a standard sermon form will serve very well to put on display what is happening in the text. A preacher who is astute enough to recognize this when studying a text will not only be saved a great deal of work, but will benefit from centuries of rhetorical wisdom. At other times the preacher will have to amend substantially a stock form or reject the use of stock forms altogether. In any case, the preacher is being made to wrestle with how best to communicate the message of the text. It is a good thing for a preacher to be able to articulate why one form was chosen over all others. A preacher who understands the "why" of a sermon's structure as it relates to the text is much more likely to present the message of the text faithfully and clearly.

Step Six: Test Your Outline for Text Integrity

This step is born of my own experience with such things. I am embarrassed at how often I have gone back to reproach an old sermon, and have found it to violate just about every conviction of this chapter. Sometimes they are sermons of my early ministry, when I was forcing every text through the mill of the keyword method I had been taught in seminary. Others are sermons of later years that reflect times I was stuck in the rut of another sermon form I had been experimenting with, had become enamored of, and had begun to overuse. Sometimes we are too close to our own work to see that we are not handling the text as skillfully as we should.

As you come near to the end of your sermon preparation, take a step back and ask whether the sermon handles the text with integrity. Check to make sure that the structure you have chosen for the sermon really does justice to nature of the text. Have you chosen a sermon structure that is foreign to the nature of the text? Do the meaning and form of the sermon come from the same source, namely the text itself? Does the sermon move to its climax in a similar fashion to the way the text moves to its climax? If you are preaching a narrative text, does your sermon tell a story? If you are preaching a psalm, does your sermon sound poetic? If you are preaching from the prophets, does your sermon sound prophetic? If you have employed a stock sermon form, is that form really descriptive of the way the text moves, or are you trying to squeeze the text into an ill-fitting form? Lest you preach a sermon you later regret, you will be well advised to check your work before you step into the pulpit.

Summary

Rightly dividing the word of truth surely demands that we take the form of the text as seriously as we take the meaning of the text. Indeed, we cannot do the latter apart from the former. This is true not only in our study, but also in our preaching. Faithful preaching of the text requires that the sermon reflect the form of the text as well as the meaning of the text. If we are sensitive to the genres of texts in the sermons we preach, not only will our preaching take on the rich variety of the texts of Scripture, but our sermons will convey the truth in a manner more consistent with the way the Spirit delivered it to us.

13

From Text to Message—
The Text Living in the Preacher

"Talk less, say more"[1]

John Woods

"WHAT IS THE ISSUE with preaching? Decisively that the community, and with it the world, should remind itself or be reminded explicitly of the witness with which it is charged, that it should find reassurance as to its content, that reflected in it Jesus Christ Himself should speak afresh to it, that it should be summoned afresh to His service in the world."[2] Ian Stackhouse has helpfully written in this volume concerning the importance of "living in the text." Ian is not unaware of the obvious danger of this approach; a preacher living in an exegetical ghetto, a structure that has walls but no windows into the congregation or the wider world. Living in the text can lead to be lost in the text, dead to the world and oblivious to what if any connection there might be between the text and the hearers that will listen to this message. If the preacher is to live in the text in preparation then it is important to take the hearers and their situation there too. This is something I have appreciated in the work of Tom Long.[3] Tom seems to be able to inhabit a biblical text with such

---

1. McKenzie, "Homiletical Proverbs," 114–20; Carl, ed., *Best Advice*, 120.

2. Barth, *Church Dogmatics, Volume* 1:3:2, 867.

3. Thomas G. Long is the Bandy Professor of Preaching at Candler School of Theology in Atlanta Georgia. He is the subject of my D.Min thesis, submitted to the University of Wales in 2008.

skilful empathy that its characters, details, and plot line become part of his world. Yet he never forgets to take the congregation with him. Those who travel into the text of Scripture must take the return journey so that the text begins to live in the preacher, the congregation and the world. In this chapter I want to take a complementary approach to the one written by Ian Stackhouse, as I explore the journey a text must take through the preacher to the message.

I am reluctant to introduce the word "bore" in a book about preaching! Nevertheless, this all reminds me of the holiday in Nova Scotia when my family stopped off at the Bay of Fundy to observe the wonders of the tidal bore. This is an astonishing phenomenon that occurs twice a day. The river is flowing in one direction and then, almost by magic begins to flow in the opposite direction. Something similar happens when preachers prepare to preach. At first we are moving in the direction of the text, entering into its meaning as we live in the text; then the movement begins to work in the opposite direction as the text becomes a message, the text living in us. Is this something of what Paul has in mind when he makes the following exhortation? "Let the word of Christ dwell in you richly as you teach and admonish one another with all wisdom, and as you sing psalms, hymns and spiritual songs with gratitude in your hearts to God. And whatever you do, whether in word or deed, do it all in the name of the Lord Jesus, giving thanks to God the Father through him" (Col 3:16–17, NIV).

Of course, we know that Paul is not primarily talking about the preacher; he is addressing the whole congregation; when he urges the hearers to let the word dwell in "you," he is using a plural. Yet; "If the double reference of within you and among you is in view then this rich indwelling would occur when they came together, listened to the word of Christ as it was preached and expounded to them and bowed to its authority."[4] What Paul is saying is the word is to govern and shape the speech acts that take place in the congregation, whether these are words of instruction, exhortation or congregational praise. Is what is true for all speech in a congregation setting also true for one of the main forms of speech there: its preaching? In some ways these verses represent a vivid

Woods, *Bearing Witness*. On two visits to Atlanta over a two year period I was able to spend some time observing Long teaching preachers. He also graciously allowed me to interview him and pester him with countless emails. In addition, I was able to interview Long's predecessor at Candler, Fred Craddock, and other homileticians.

4. O'Brien, *Colossians and Philemon*, 207.

picture of what preaching is designed to do. This being the case, how in practice does the preacher let the word dwell in their lives?

We Welcome the Spoken Word: "Word of Christ"

We speak because someone has spoken; we use words because a word has already has come to us. The preacher's voice is always the echo of another voice. This is the voice of one who is eager to enter into conversation with us. William Willimon describes the Bible as "a long story of God's attempted conversation with humanity."[5] Preachers are people who have paid attention long enough to communicate what they have heard, as Fred Craddock puts it: "To preach . . . is to shout a whisper."[6] Tom Long describes this process as "witness":

> Before a preacher *says* something a preacher must *see* something. To be a preacher is to be called to be a witness, one who sees before speaking, one whose right to speak is created by what is seen. Sometimes pulpits are used as lecterns, but that is not what they really are. A pulpit is not a lectern or a podium; it is a witness stand, and the preacher's task is to tell the truth, the whole truth, and nothing but the truth about what is seen.[7]

To hear such a word we must learn to be attentive. In an average week a preacher will face many legitimate tasks and encounter a multitude of potential distractions.

Preparing to preach is not looking for a quick fix. "The danger in all reading is that words be twisted into propaganda or reduced to information, mere tools and data. We silence the living voice and reduce words to what we can use for convenience and profit."[8]

It requires faithful imaginative interaction with the text of Scripture if we are to hear the voice which shapes our own voice in preaching. There is a time to speak and there is a time to be silent; our ability to speak as preachers invariably flows out of the silence, when we are listening not to our own voice, opinions or expectations, but his voice. Ellen Davis points the way to how we can avoid distractions and pay attention: "If there is a

---

5. Willimon, *The Collected Sermons of William Willimon*, 200.

6. Craddock, *Preaching*, 64.

7. Long, *The Senses of Preaching*, 4.

8. Peterson, *Eat this Book*, 11.

secret to getting involved with God through the pages of Scripture, then perhaps it is this: *turn the pages slowly.*"[9]

Preachers need to be ready to listen—this of course is not unrelated to viewing homiletics as an integrated Christian practice. "Preaching flows from an interaction between the spirituality of Scripture and the spirituality of the preacher. . . . It is my resource for preaching, because it is my resource for living."[10] P. T. Forsyth boldly claims "The Bible is the preacher for preachers."[11] The preacher's best preparation for speaking is listening. "The Sovereign LORD has given me an instructed tongue, to know the word that sustains the weary. He wakens me morning by morning, wakens my ear to listen like one being taught. The Sovereign LORD has opened my ears, and I have not been rebellious; I have not drawn back" (Isa 50:4–5, NIV).

We Welcome the Gospel Word: "Word of Christ"

This is the only place in the New Testament where the phrase *"word of Christ"* occurs. This suggests the centrality of the gospel word as the foundation of congregation life and witness. This is the word that forms the church and shapes its response to God and one another. The language of these two verses is very similar to what Paul says earlier in this letter:

> This is the gospel that you heard and that has been proclaimed to every creature under heaven, and of which I, Paul, have become a servant. Now I rejoice in what was suffered for you, and I fill up in my flesh what is still lacking in regard to Christ's afflictions, for the sake of his body, which is the church. I have become its servant by the commission God gave me to present to you the word of God in its fullness—the mystery that has been kept hidden for ages and generations, but is now disclosed to the saints. To them God has chosen to make known among the Gentiles the glorious riches of this mystery, which is Christ in you, the hope of glory. We proclaim him, admonishing and teaching everyone with all wisdom, so that we may present everyone perfect in Christ" (Col 1:23b–28, NIV).

---

9. Davis, *Getting Involved with Go,* 3.

10. Goldingay, "The Pastor's Opportunities," 198.

11. Forsyth, *Positive Preaching and the Modern Mind,* 17.

This passage shares with Colossians 3:16–17 the idea of a word which brings the message and presence of Christ to us personally and inwardly. Colossians 1:28 also shares with Colossians 3:16 the words *"admonish,"* *"teach,"* and *"wisdom."* Therefore it is a reasonable assumption to link what Paul says in chapter 1 with what he says in chapter 3. Then the phrase "word of Christ" is a reminder of the importance of the testimony of the gospel that has its focus on Jesus. The church's worshipping life is shaped by this testimony. One of the main ways a church hears this testimony is through the preacher as a witness. As we have seen, the preacher as witness is a brilliant description of the two-way process of preaching described in this chapter. The witness takes a journey into the text to see what the Lord has said and done; then takes the return journey to tell what is seen.

If the preacher is going to preach this gospel word, it is important for the preacher to be gripped by the gospel. Preaching is more than passing on information, more than education; it is rather the living communication of experienced truth. Preaching is not talking about Jesus, it is preaching Jesus. Thinking about preaching in relation to Jesus reminds me of the importance of faith within the homiletic process. What an audacious thing it is to stand up in a pulpit and preach the gospel. How can we? How should we preach? As a younger preacher I was helped by the insights of a man called Jack Miller, founder of New Life Presbyterian Church in Philadelphia, who used to speak about "Preaching by faith." By this he did not mean, stepping into the pulpit "on a wing and a prayer," rather he meant with a conscious moment by moment dependence upon Christ to sustain his feeble thoughts and words. Paul speaks of this experience of what lies at the core of his life: "I have been crucified with Christ and I no longer live, but Christ lives in me. The life I live in the body, I live by faith in the Son of God, who loved me and gave himself for me" (Gal 2:20, NIV). A contemporary preacher who learned a great deal from Jack Miller is Tim Keller of Redeemer Presbyterian Church in New York. Keller has gained deserved attention for his preaching. Many things could be said about what makes that preaching effective, but perhaps the chief thing is that it is rooted in a heart set free by Christ. In reading a biography of the iconic seventeenth century preacher Jonathan Edwards, I stumbled upon a fascinating footnote: "The main benefit that is obtained by preaching is by impression made upon the mind in the time of it, and not by the effect that arises afterwards by a remembrance of what was delivered. Preaching in other words, must first of all touch the affections."[12]

12. Marsden, *Jonathan Edwards*, 282. (Marsden writes in the note: "I am indebted

I asked Keller about this quotation; he replied: "A major purpose of preaching is to change people *on the spot,* to re-shape their heart with the truth, not merely to give them information on how to live that they can apply later. Preaching does give clear information, but it must not stop at that." In answer to the question, "What is your primary objective in preaching?" Keller replied: "To not only make the truth *clear* but also to make it *real*—compelling, moving, and life-changing."[13] True preaching, as Cas Vos reminds us, "aims to provide music and not a lecture on music."[14] True preaching sounds all the notes of the gospel of grace.

Hearing this music is only possible when the words spoken by the preacher are shaped by the Christ-centered gospel. This has a bearing on one of the most famous definitions of preaching: "Truth through personality." This is helpful as far as it goes; it does remind us that preaching is more than personality—yet John Broadus commenting on this definition contends that Brooks "meant Christian preaching, Christian personality and Christian truth."[15] Allowing the word of Christ into our lives is part of the preacher's experience of the mystery of Christianity: "Christ in you the hope of glory" (Col 1:27, NIV). The preacher and the sermon become gospel because Christ has been invited to be at work in and through the preacher.

We Welcome the Personal Word: Dwell

"Let the word of Christ—the Message—have the run of the house. Give it plenty of room in your lives" (Col 3:16a, *The Message*). If a word has been spoken, and that word represents the most important message that the world has ever heard; we do not want to be in a rush when he hear it. Instead we will want to listen carefully, giving the word space and room in our lives. In this way we seek to carry the biblical text around with us throughout the week.

This means intentionally letting the word do its work, like tea brewing, or coffee percolating in the pot. Some people make tea by means of

---

to Timothy Keller for pointing out this passage to me.")

13. Email correspondence from Tim Keller, March 24, 2011.

14. Vos, "The Sermon as a Work of Art," 372.

15. Broadus, *On the Preparation and Delivery of Sermons,* 58. The full quotation for Brooks is: "Preaching is the communication of truth by man to men. It has in it two essential elements, truth and personality. Truth through personality is our description of real preaching." Brooks, *The Joy of Preaching,* 25.

the briefest introduction of a tea bag to a cup of hot water; other more discerning tea drinkers allow the tea to infuse the water so that the full flavor can be released. In a recent sermon series on Ephesians, Tim Keller describes the process he uses in reflecting on Scripture. He talks about wrestling the truth into his heart, thinking, reflecting, applying and connecting until we feel and sense and see change. In this process he identifies three components: reading, praying, and meditation. When I asked Keller: "If you could leave one piece of advice for preachers what would it be?" His reply was: "More prayer. Much more." It is in this way that preachers can allow Scripture to penetrate their thinking in such a way that it begins to do its work. In this way the word will be given sufficient space to be "an abundant resource as it permeates their lives."[16]

In this way the act of preaching becomes not a message I want to get over to others, but a message that is already actively at work in my life. Allowing the word of Christ to permeate our lives adds a note of authenticity to our preaching. Is this what William Willimon is describing when he talks about his experience in the preaching moment?

I, unlike some of my preacher friends, relish that moment just before I preach. . . . I find my little life swept up into the life of God, subsumed by whatever work of the Holy Spirit intends to do through me that day. In that sacred instant, I become the artist who is totally consumed in the act of creation, subsumed in the art itself. I become the sermon. I have no needs, want nothing else. I am what I'm trying to talk about . . .[17]

We welcome the Permeating Word:
"Within You/Among You"

Barbara Lundblad in her Lyman Beecher Lectures writes: "Our task is not to update the Bible, but to open up a hermeneutical space in which life itself serves to explain the text, a space in which time and text are in lively conversation with each other."[18]

Whether Paul is describing the inner lives of believers or their corporate experience of the word going to work among them, the importance of creating a space for the word to work is crucial. Such a space allows room for a "lively conversation" between our situation and the

16. Lincoln, "Colossians," 648–49.

17. Willimon, *The Collected Sermons of William Willimon*, xiii.

18. Lundblad, *Marking Time*, 74.

text of Scripture. Sermons that are rooted both in divine revelation and human experience are created in this space. Fred Craddock, one of the gurus of the New Homiletic says that he has "a large interior world."[19] My son, Andrew, used to call this his "imagination station." Every preacher needs to cultivate such a space for their creativity to be developed. Rebecca Kruger-Gaudino writes concerning the sermons of the Old Testament scholar Walter Bruggemann: "These sermons take the drama of the text and make it live again,"[20] adding, "In the end, Brueggemann's sermons invite us to enter the free space of imagination . . ."[21] All too few preachers suffer from too much imagination, many preachers, and their congregations, suffer from a woeful lack of imagination. Nancy Lammers Gross likens the relationship of the preacher with the text to the relationship between a husband and a wife; not so much a one night stand with a text that has the single objective of getting a message, but a lifelong commitment to understand the text in an intimate and ongoing way.[22]

We Welcome the Abundant Word: "Richly"

William Willimon the United Methodist Bishop of Birmingham, Alabama, when reflecting on a life time of preaching could testify: "The God who supplies my sermons is extravagantly revealing."[23] In Scripture: "There is a richness . . . which makes it an inexhaustible source of spiritual resource, intellectual stimulus, and personal and corporate challenge."[24]

When preachers begin to preach they wonder how they are going to string enough words together to make it to the end of the designated sermon slot. Novice preachers wonder whether the Scriptures they hold in their hands can sustain a year, let alone a lifetime's ministry. With a mixture of awe and gratitude seasoned preachers realize that they will never do justice to a fraction of the unsearchable riches deposited in Scripture. I recently encountered a line from a sermon by Dorothee Sölle: "'God is love' is a sentence that is several sizes too large for us."[25]

19. Interview with Fred Craddock at Cherry Log Center, October 2005.

20. Kruger-Gaudino, *The Collected Sermons of Walter Brueggemann*, xx.

21. Ibid., xxi.

22. Gross, "A Re-Examination of Recent Homiletical Theories," 220.

23. Willimon, *The Collected Sermons of William Willimon*, 199

24. Dunn, *Colossians and Philemon*, 237.

25. From a sermon reproduced in Hermelink, "The Theological Understanding of Preaching Hope," 57.

Every preacher has had this experience of encountering a text that seems vast, formidable, abundant and brimming with possibilities. In my own preaching I have been helped by meditating on the words of advice given to Timothy:

> But as for you, continue in what you have learned and have become convinced of, because you know those from whom you learned it, and how from infancy you have known the holy Scriptures, which are able to make you wise for salvation through faith in Christ Jesus. All Scripture is God-breathed and is useful for teaching, rebuking, correcting and training in righteousness, so that the man of God may be thoroughly equipped for every good work. In the presence of God and of Christ Jesus, who will judge the living and the dead, and in view of his appearing and his kingdom, I give you this charge: Preach the word; be prepared in season and out of season; correct, rebuke and encourage—with great patience and careful instruction (2 Tim 3:14—4:2, NIV).

Timothy is urged to appreciate the richness of God's word. This word comes via the relationships he has with trusted teachers, it is the product of divine breath prompting human authors, and it is a sufficient word. There is enough here for the formation and complete equipping of God's servants. With this in mind Timothy is encouraged to preach the word; a word rich enough for every situation and every need. This richness does not diminish with changing times, but is adequate "in season and out of season." The richness of God's word is appropriate for every season of human experience: correction, rebuke, encouragement, and instruction.

From time to time preachers lose confidence in the richness of the divine word. They think that Scripture is as threadbare as their own narrow horizons and wafer thin imaginations. This is not so. Long stresses that the Bible has a central role in this preparation process: "The Bible must not be viewed as a senile dinner companion who always has to say something. The goal is to go down so deep into the text . . . to discover something that is worth preaching. Something that is fresh and imaginative." For Long this journey of discovery requires the following two steps:

1. Grasping the claim of the text—we preach not about a text, but preach the text coming with force through to the people.

2. Teasing the text apart to determine focus and function, following our nose so as to discover the destination of the sermon.[26]

26. These comments are from a session at the Marcy Fellowship Preaching Seminar

Such intentionality helps the preacher keep on message by being in tune with the distinctive music of Scripture. If this does not happen the preacher is pitched into the situation that Richard Lischer describes: "When ministers allow the word of God to be marginalized, they continue to speak, of course, and make generally helpful comments on a variety of issues, but they do so from no centre of authority and with no passion."[27]

We Welcome the Word of Wisdom: "With All Wisdom"

All speech acts in the Christian community are to be conducted with all the wisdom we can muster. Foolishness is destructive of community life; wisdom brings us to maturity and stability. If this is true of all speech acts it is particularly true of preaching. As we have noted, these words in chapter 3 echo Paul's words in chapter 1:28, "We proclaim him, admonishing and teaching everyone with all wisdom, so that we may present everyone perfect in Christ."

Preaching Christ is preaching the one "in whom are hidden all the treasures of wisdom and knowledge" (Col 2:3, NIV). Jesus is the one who "grew in wisdom and stature and in favor with God and men" (Luke 2:52, NIV). His life and teaching are a continuation of the wisdom tradition of the Old Testament. David Ford suggests that "Christian wisdom is shaped by and in relation to Jesus Christ."[28] There is a direct correspondence between the dwelling of the word of Christ in the Christian community and the experience of wisdom. He is our wisdom, the pattern of his commitment to the Father's will, the penetrating wisdom of his

---

in Atlanta in October 2006, where I was present as an observer. Focus and Function are two of the key tools that Long uses in moving from a biblical text to a message or sermon. Long defines these terms in his classic textbook *The Witness of Preaching*, 108–9: "A focus statement is a concise description of the central controlling, and unifying theme of the sermon. In short, this is what the whole sermon will be 'about.' A function statement is a description of what the preacher hopes the sermon will create or cause to happen for the hearers. Sermons make demands upon the hearers, which is another way of saying that they provoke change in the hearers (even if the change is a deepening of something already present). The function statement names the hoped for change." For Long, the aims of the focus and function statements are that they provide a roadmap that indicates where a sermon is going. This sense of direction is based on finding the central focus of the text and discovering its intended function.

27. Lischer, *End of Words*, 23.

28. Ford, *Christian Wisdom*, 153.

words, and the nature of his self-offering on the cross are to shape our living and preaching.

Wisdom is all about choosing appropriate words when we speak. Jesus always had the right word for the right person at the right time. This is something that is emphasized in the Book of Proverbs. Wisdom helps us to listen to the voice of God in Scripture; to discern the claim of the timeless word for today. When we get it right it is a beautiful thing: "A word aptly spoken is like apples of gold in settings of silver" (Prov 25:11, NIV). Preaching is all about finding apt, well-turned, well-timed words. Derek Kidner writes: "A truth that makes no impression as a generalization may be indelibly fixed in the mind when it is matched to its occasion and shaped to its task."[29]

If the preacher's mouth is the timely tick of communication, the listener's ear is the timely tock. In preaching it takes two to tango! For an apt word to be spoken, requires a well-timed word finding a listening ear. "Like an ear-ring of gold or an ornament of fine gold is a wise man's rebuke to a listening ear" (Prov 25:12, NIV). Words like an earring fitting nicely on the listening ear; words well said and well received. Eloquent words, even when they are reprimands, are like well-crafted jewels in well matched settings. We would expect a rebuke to be unwelcome and jarring. It is, after all, intended to shake the listener out of complacency. A wise rebuke and a listening ear match each other like two pieces of elegant jewelry. We see this in the penetrating words of Nathan to David: "You are the Man!" (2 Sam 12:7, NIV).

We Welcome the Doxological Word,
"Gratitude . . . in the Name of Jesus, Giving Thanks

Preaching is not the end of worship, it is its catalyst and stimulus. "At its best," writes Peter Lewis, "the Free Church tradition has always believed in preaching as the climax of worship and not merely as an adjunct to it. And at its best preaching is itself an act of *congregational participation* in which the hearts of people rise in adoration or confession or thanksgiving as the words of the preacher become in Calvin's phrase "the voice of God resounding in them."[30]

Preaching should awaken grateful joy in the hearer. This is accomplished as the preacher worships God while preaching. Piper describes

29. Kidner, *Proverbs*.

30. Lewis, *"Free Church" Worship in Britain,* 157

this as "the exulting over the excellency of God in the pulpit," in what he describes as, "Expository exaltation." In John Piper's estimation one of the greatest problems for the church is when a preacher is not worshipping.[31] This exultation is not to be confused with excessive theatrics on the part of the preacher. Piper's role model is Jonathan Edwards who read his sermon manuscripts. The worship happens as the preacher communicates the glory of the God who gives us joy as we trust in him. Paul writes: "God, whom I serve (worship) with my whole heart in the preaching of the gospel of his son . . ." (Rom 1:9, NIV).

Old, commenting on this passage writes: "The preaching and hearing of the word of God is in the last analysis worship, worship in its most profound sense. Preaching is not an auxiliary activity to worship, nor is it the kind of preparation for worship which one hopes to follow."[32]

This view of preaching is made more explicit still in Paul's words in Romans 15:15–16, where he speaks of the relationship between his preaching and his hearers in the following terms: "I have written to you quite boldly on some points, as if to remind you of then again, because of the grace God has given me to be a minister of Christ Jesus to the Gentiles with the priestly duty of proclaiming the gospel of God, so that the Gentiles might become an offering acceptable to God, sanctified by the Holy Spirit."

Again this establishes a very high view of preaching, Paul appears to view the preaching and hearing of God's word to be in correspondence to, and fulfillment of the sacrificial worship of the Old Testament.

At this point the Tidal bore has reversed the flow of the river and has come crashing upon the shoreline. The full impact of the spoken word has filled the life of the preacher with a Christ-centered, personal, permeating, and abundantly rich word. This word is wise, worshipful, and woven with grateful wonder. The preacher is full and ready to preach a message full of Christ, rich in wisdom that leads to grateful praise and community alive to God and one another.

Preaching of course does not always fulfill these high aims. Lincoln complains that many preachers miss the point of preaching and fail in the sermon to: "allow the listeners into their own encounter with the word of Christ, which addresses us through the Scriptures."[33] Maybe this could

31. Comments made at a Proclamation Trust conference: "Preaching as Worship," October 17th 2001.

32. Old, *The Reading and Preaching of the Scriptures,* 187.

33. Lincoln, "Colossians," 665.

be done by taking a cue from John Goldingay, and rather than always beginning our sermons with reading the preaching text, we might try reading it at the end: "Let the word of Christ dwell in you richly . . ."

Afterword Concerning Method

As a result of reading a lot of writing on preaching I have come to the conclusion that Scripture has not always been used as an integral resource for shaping the homiletic practice. John Webster writes:

> Holy Scripture is the centre of theology, not a subdivision within it, and all aspects of theological work are directed towards the reading of Holy Scripture. . . . Reading Scripture is not only that from which theology proceeds, but also that to which theology is directed.[34]

The theological enterprise, states Webster, is a: "summons to attentiveness . . . theology is thus most properly an invitation to read and reread Scripture."[35]

This chapter has been an experiment in reflecting on how Scripture might be used to shape the preacher's method in preparing to preach. It is based on the conviction that within the pages of Scripture there lies an inherent homiletic waiting to be let out. Or in the words of Fred Craddock: "Whoever goes to the Bible in search of *what* to preach but does not linger long enough to learn *how* to preach has left its pages too soon."[36]

34. Webster, *Holy Scripture*, 129.

35. Ibid., 130.

36. Craddock, *Preaching*, 6.

CODA

14

Every Sermon Fights a Battle

"The time is fulfilled, and the kingdom of God has come near; repent, and believe in the good news"
(Mark 1:15, NRSV).

Dave Hansen[1]

THREE THOUSAND PEOPLE HEARD the hellfire preacher. His presumption was our damnation. His sermon drew a line in front of each of us and delivered a summons: Cross it. The line separated death and life. We were on the side of death. We needed to cross the line to life.

This was assault and battery on my integrity. I was an acolyte. I resisted the demand with all my will. I did not flinch before the outrage. He said I was going to hell. He demanded that I accept Jesus Christ as my Lord and Savior. He called me forward. Some migrated to the stage. I sat. Sweat precipitated on my brow: I was boiling. I shook. The line was still there. He insisted: Cross it.

A corn-syrup voice I did not trust interrupted from beside me: "We will wait for you if you go forward." It was my friend's mother. This was a setup. They'd known there was going to be an altar call, and they expected me to go forward. They didn't think I was a Christian. My refusal redoubled. I stared the line down.

---

1. The following is a version of the chapter "Preaching" in my book, *The Art of Pastoring*. Rev. ed. Copyright (c) 2012 David Hansen. Used by permission of InterVarsity Press, P.O. Box 1400, Downers Grove, IL 60515, USA. www.ivpress.com.

At home, in bed, in the dark, in shock, I thought it through. I was proud of myself for not joining the mob that had surged forward. But the line was still there.

It was no longer drawn on the stage; it was scratched in my soul. The demand remained: Cross it. I was afraid. My potent debunking of that gospel-carnival-of the-absurd was impotent when applied to the gospel message.

I sensed God's presence, but how could this be God? Up till now the word "God" meant that everything I did and thought was secure and good. Now God meant that I was lost. My mind clouded and spun in spiritual vertigo. There were no reference points left in my soul—except the line. I refused to cross it. I would not admit that the hellfire preacher was right about anything.

I felt a logical distinction begin to emerge just beneath the surface of my consciousness. I couldn't read it, but I knew that it was there. It suggested reality, so I followed the trail. My will dragged my consciousness into the mental crevasse.

What I saw was that my anger at the gospel sideshow was valid, but my refusal to cross the line and accept Jesus Christ was stubborn pride, maybe even deadly pride. I'd never seen deadly pride in me. It scared me to think that there was something in me that could will my death. I no longer saw the preacher calling me. It was God calling me to cross the line. Still I refused.

Then, accountably, I began to fear my pride more than the humiliation of crossing the line. The superstructure of my will began to collapse. My world was passing away.

The voice summoning me to cross the line softened its tone but increased its urgency. I knew that I was in danger. The call sounded like love. The line became a mercy; a light gathered at the source of the voice on the other side of the line. My mind's eye fixed on the light. "Jesus, I don't know what I'm doing, but I accept you as my Lord and Savior, whatever it means."

Calm came, the light gave way to a peaceful dark, I fell asleep.

The next morning I testified to my friend who had conned me into going to the crusade: "That preacher is a phony. He deliberately turned the air conditioning off so that he could manipulate the crowd."

Now I myself am a preacher. I don't use the methods of the hellfire preacher; I deplore all manipulative methods. But my struggle with Christ on that night, initiated by that man's preaching, is gold to me. It is the treasury out of which I coin my own preaching. It represents the turning point in my life, when Christ fought me and saved me.

The line the preacher drew long ago is engraved in my soul; it is spiritual scar tissue. The deep bruise on Jacob's tendon, brought in mortal conflict with the angel, left him limping; my soul's incision, brought in mortal conflict with Christ, left me preaching. The essence of the line in me is a personal knowledge that pervades my preaching: There is a decision to be made about Christ.

I rarely think about the events of that night. However, the battle between my pride and God's call to salvation is a primary constituent of the hermeneutical cycle of my preaching. Demand and Grace scratched my soul for good.

My first sermon on my first Sunday in Montana was a wicked-cold January day, two days after we slid into Montana in an ice storm. The propane heater in the 1884, white, wood-framed chapel, was out, so we moved the service to the fellowship hall. It had electric base-board heat—reliable, but slow. We worshipped in coats, in hopes that the uninsulated building would warm up by the middle of the service.

I had determined on the drive into Montana that my first sermon series would be from the Gospel according to Mark and that my first sermon I would preach would be from Mark 1:1–20. It didn't take me long to get to Mark's summary of Jesus' preaching. "The time is fulfilled, and the kingdom of God has come near; repent, and believe in the good news" (Mark 1:15, NRSV). In Jesus' preaching and in his parables, there was a line to cross: from repentance of sin to full embrace of the good news. It was getting warmer. I moved directly to Jesus calling fishermen to follow him as he walked along the lake. By that point we didn't need our coats anymore. Then, unexpectedly, a surge of love came over me for the people. I'd preached before in other places. This was my first experience with such a thing. In the Spirit I urged them to turn from the past, to embrace the good news and say yes to the call of Christ. This was now my congregation. I was the new shepherd, and for better or for worse I spoke to my people on behalf of the Good Shepherd; I was his parable in the pulpit.

Whatever else we may imagine a sermon ought to be, it must be the living Christ, doing today what he did then—calling us to follow him. In his masterpiece *Discipleship*, Dietrich Bonhoeffer tells us: "Listen to the preaching and receive the sacrament! Listen to the gospel of the crucified and risen Lord! Here he is, the whole Christ, the very same one who encountered the disciples."[2] Christ present calls us to turn from pride, self-absorption and unbelief to the kingdom reality of grace-driven discipleship. In every offer of grace, there is a line to be crossed. As in the ministry of Jesus then, so is it now, preaching is a dread battle with evil. In his lectures on homiletics Bonhoeffer declares bluntly: "As a witness to Christ, the sermon is a struggle with demons. Every sermon must overcome Satan. Every sermon fights a battle. But this does not occur through the dramatic efforts of the preacher. It happens only through the proclamation of the One who has trodden upon the head of the devil."[3] For Dietrich Bonhoeffer, son of an agnostic psychiatrist, worship was a full-blown, book of Revelation type of apocalyptic event. That's what the hell-fire preacher experience was for me, that's what my dorky first sermon was, and that was the preaching of Jesus. After being tempted by the devil Jesus went out preaching, "The time is fulfilled, and the kingdom of God has come near; repent, and believe in the good news" (Mark 1:15, NRSV).

Preparing the Word

Tuesday, first thing, I open the text. For an hour I want to be alone with the text. I read it over, stop, and stare at it. Stare: "to look fixedly often with wide-open eyes, to fasten an earnest and prolonged gaze on an object."

I put the text on the computer screen. I fiddle with it. With a computer, experimenting with paragraph breaks is easy. Maybe an idea for a sermon presents itself, maybe not. The only rule for Tuesday is "Do not rush."

Greek and Hebrew look like piles of seaweed to me, but I open the text in the original language and try to work through it with the help of the English. I don't think I can make a better English translation. I don't expect to overturn scholarly exegesis with my word studies. Reading the text in its original languages accomplishes two vital things. Looking at the text in its original tongue is another way to fiddle with it. It is a way of spending unhurried, inefficient time with the text. It forces me to slow down and listen more intently. It's a way of chewing on it. This slow work with the text produces the second benefit of original language

---

2. Bonhoeffer, *Discipleship*, 202. This is the new translation of the earlier translation, *The Cost of Discipleship*.

3. Fant, *Worldly Preaching*, 106

study: pictures. Ancient Hebrew and Koine Greek are rich in pictures and metaphors. The pictures underlying the words (especially the theological terms) freshen theology and deliver natural images for preaching.

I own many commentaries, and I use them in my sermon preparation, but I wouldn't trade my Greek and Hebrew Bibles for a thousand commentaries.

I leave my desk and take a walk. I let the text as I can see it— divided into paragraphs, filled with pictures—settle into my mind. I let the text sit in my skull right behind my eyes. I want the text in my subconscious. It takes time to get it there. Walk and pray and leave it alone. When the visual picture of the text disappears from my mind's eye, I return to my desk.

Wednesday and Thursday: I stare at the text more. The word stare is a Latin word related to the Latin word for "strenuous." Staring at the text is strenuous meditation. This strenuous meditation is done inside us, in our hermeneutical chip. Staring at the text puts it in the chip, and that's where the work gets done.

A theologian describing hermeneutics is like a physiologist describing running: both use big words to describe a common experience. We all know how to run, but we can't describe how we do it. It's the same with hermeneutics. We pastors do hermeneutical work all the time, but we can't describe it. Hermeneutics is as primitive to humanity as running.

Our hermeneutics are our ability to understand a story and tell it to someone else in our own words. Hermeneutics happen at the Main Street coffee shop where the good old boys gather to chew tobacco and cuss government. They read the newspaper story about taxes going up, they process it, and they tell it to each other in their own words. They know what the story means: less money for chewing tobacco.

People do pretty well using everyday hermeneutics with the Bible. It's tougher than the newspaper, because its stories happened a long time ago and customs were different. There's no chewing tobacco in the Bible, but there are taxes. Bible farmers didn't have tape decks in their harvesters, but they had to sow, reap and pray for rain just like today. For the most part, normal people understand the Bible pretty well with the same commonsense hermeneutics they use every day.

Preachers need more than just a commonsense hermeneutic when they read the Bible for sermon preparation. They aren't reading the Bible for themselves or to teach a Bible study. A sermon is not thoughts about the Bible. Preachers make war on the human heart. Preaching hermeneutics prepare a pastor to decay sin, to look into the eyes in the pews and say with Nathan the prophet: "Thou art the man!"

Pastors take the message of the text and pass it through the logic of their hermeneutic. A computer chip is a thin silicon wafer with a specific logic etched into it by a laser beam. When information is put into the chip, the chip's logic rearranges the information into a different form, but one that corresponds logically to the input. A computer chip can take the input "2 + 2" and process an answer: 4. The logic of the computer chip processes the input and, in a sense, tells the story in its own words.

Preachers' hermeneutical chip is the line embedded in their soul, etched by the laser beam of the word of God on the day they heard the word and obeyed the summons. This chip processes the word of God in Scripture and transforms it into the word of God that will be preached

Computer chips get hot because processing the input and rearranging it into a new form is a lot of work. Likewise, sermon meditation takes time, and it is hard work. Just sitting there (looking like you're doing nothing), contemplating the Scriptures, is some of the hardest work of the week. Rushing through Scripture meditation causes shallow sermons.

Friday. More than anything, I pray. I pray a simple prayer over and over: "Lord, of all the things I can say about this text, what do your people need to hear this week?"

I add a variable at this point to my meditation on the text. I begin to consider what I've heard from my people all week. I spend much of my pastoral time listening to people, trying to crack the code of their lives. I hear about their progress in Christ and the sin that drags them down.

I want the biblical text to be the primary input to the sermon. However, the input of the congregation is crucial to the process, because I need to know what kinds of decisions they need to make to follow Christ. I need to know where and how the line must be drawn.

The sermon will, if properly prepared and delivered, be able to encourage the people of God in their progress, admonish them to turn from their sin and introduce some to Christ for the first time. I know that it is possible to accomplish all these agendas in every sermon, because the text contains the code that meets the needs of every heart present. This is the presupposition of biblical expository preaching.

The prayer and meditation continue, working with the Scripture, the people's needs and everything in the hermeneutical chip, every aspect of every variable, to create an answer, the sermon, the biblical story in new words—new words that will be the word of God preached. Meditation is hard work.

Slowly the sermon emerges. I think best in outlines, so I try to develop a coherent outline for the sermon, correlating the elements of the sermon to the order of the text.

In any case, the most important aspect of the sermon is the thesis. The thesis contains the indicative and the imperative of the sermon. The indicative is the sinners' condition and God's provision for sin; the imperative is the demand that one redress sin by crossing the line, coming to Christ for renewal and repentance.

Once I have the thesis and a simple outline, Friday's work is done. Saturday: I forget about the sermon and do something with my kids. Sunday: I rise early to read the Bible and pray. I review the outline and touch it up. Sometimes I throw the outline out and construct a new one.

Delivering the Word

> We all know what it is to play warfare in a mock battle that it means to imitate everything just as it is in war. The troops are drawn up, they march into the field, seriousness is evident in every eye, but also the courage and the enthusiasm, the orderlies rush back and forth intrepidly, the commander's voice is heard, the signals, the battle cry, the volley of musketry, the thunder of cannon—everything exactly as in war, lacking only one thing . . . the danger. So also it is with playing Christianity, that is, imitating Christian preaching in such a way that everything, absolutely everything is included in as deceptive a form as possible—only one thing is lacking . . . the danger.[4]

In a Roman Catholic hospital in our town, in the elevator hallway, there stands a life-size statue of Mary. Her face is perfect serenity. Her body is upright but not tense. Under one of her feet writhes a thickly muscled serpent; in its open mouth, fangs drip poison.

That's what preaching is. Preaching is stepping on the snake. Children leave during the hymn that precedes the sermon. I enter the pulpit, read the Scripture and fiddle with my notes as I gather my wits. Nervousness gives way to adrenaline for battle; it swells my awareness. I lift my eyes, open my mouth: the sermon begins.

4. Kierkegaard, *Attack Upon Christendom*, 180.

I've heard of the art of preaching, and I've heard of the art of war. Preparation for preaching and for war requires human creativity. Both activities are acquired crafts. Hand-to-hand combat is not a recital, and neither is preaching. Preaching is an art, but it is not an art show. It isn't a concert, it isn't a speech. Preaching is a form of aggression. As we preach, Yahweh, the God of war, conducts holy war to conquer territory. The field of conflict is the human heart.

I begin slowly, letting the words come as they will, following my outline section by section. I lay the groundwork for the thesis by commenting on the text and introducing the thesis slowly. I methodically scan the eyes in the congregation, reading every reaction.

As the sermon progresses and the thesis is revealed, the congregation divides up, splinters into individuals. Some are comforted, others are in distress. Some are angry or stubborn. I feel the battle engage. A line must be drawn in front of every listener.

One person looks offended I've touched a nerve in a person who is normally self-possessed. What can I say to offend their pride even more?

This is where preaching really begins. The offense is what counts. Stepping on a snake is an offense to the snake. Its pride must be mortally wounded.

It's easy to back off from the offense. The flesh will scream, and the devil will bare his venom-dripping teeth. The human heart is the most fiercely guarded piece of ground in the universe. The fortress is built up through years and years of self-justification and rationalization. The soul in sin feels alive, but it is dead. The sermon must shed light on the soul's dire circumstances so it may turn from sin and live. The people must hear the indicative of the sermon—"Thou art the man!"—if they are to hear the imperative of the sermon, "Repent and be baptized, every one of you, in the name of Jesus Christ for the forgiveness of your sins. And you will receive the gift of the Holy Spirit."

I feel the offense of the words as they pierce hearts. I cannot stop until the whole truth is known: they are lost. Damnation must be preached. As Forsyth says, "There are not nearly enough preachers who preach, nor people who take home, the reality of damnation, or the connection of liberty with it."[5]

I am a well-educated, mainline denomination preacher, quite shy by nature. I don't give altar calls. But when the battle for the human

---

5. Forsyth, *The Justification of God*, 87.

heart is pitched, the line scratched in my soul by that hellfire preacher leads me unfailingly where the sermon must go. The sermon needs to go to Christ. The line needs to be drawn. The demand needs to be made. Christ crucified must be placarded before every listener. There is a light, a calling, a demand, a raised voice, a pounded fist, the stamp of a foot. The snake is crushed.

Now the gospel. At the right moment, with the end in sight, the gentle voice. The Savior who would never snuff the smoking flax or break the bruised reed must also speak and make the plea for the soul to cross the line to life. Grace comes unexpectedly. The Way presents itself. The law raged, the gospel gently beckons. The law has condemned, the Savior pleads for mercy and peace. The corridor opens for the listener, the opportunity presents itself receive the Savior; cross the line; enter life.

Recovering the Word

Monday must be free of work and, if at all possible, fun. With word, Spirit, and soul the preacher preaches from a rock, but the rock is gone by Sunday afternoon. Monday I can't remember a word I said. I feel vague embarrassment. The scar in my soul is sore. I'd best go fishing.

My system needs Sabbath. If Tuesday's work with the text is to be joy and anticipation, Monday must be restful.

Preaching wanes even when you take good care of yourself. Theology grows stale. Sermons get predictable. Instead of a joy, preaching becomes a burden. Compliments from parishioners help. Continuing education opportunities for preaching exist. But what helps most is to hear good preaching and read good theology, because the thing that goes haywire in us is our hermeneutic.

A computer chip is etched silicon. Chips don't wear out but they quickly become outdated. The downside of that is that computer chips get outdated rather quickly. They can't be rewritten, so they get thrown out.

The logical instructions in our hermeneutical chip can wear out. Conductivity goes down, which slows down our meditation process, making it more laborious. The instructions can become rutted. We can end up preaching the same thing over and over. The instructions can become overwritten or infected with bad code (such as when the virus of universalism gets into our hermeneutics). The upside to this is that the medium of our hermeneutical chip is malleable. It can be rewritten very easily. We can renew our hermeneutics, and we must. The way we renew the instructions in our hermeneutical chip is to hear good preaching and read good theology.

A pastor friend, now retired from pastoral ministry, used to read a sermon of Alexander Whyte every Sunday morning before he preached. He did this throughout his ministry. He figured that he needed to hear good preaching himself before he could preach. This was an excellent practice.

Reading Christian literature is enormous help in restoring our preaching. Different pastors prefer different types of literature. But in all cases the point of reading Christian literature isn't to find sermon illustrations or ideas for sermons; it is to renew our hermeneutic.

It works so well that good hard theological reading makes my sermon preparation go faster. I've noticed this for years: authors like Karl Barth, Jonathon Edwards, Dietrich Bonhoeffer, or P. T. Forsyth, saves me hours of sermon preparation and will produce a deeper, more searching thesis. These teach me to think Christocentrically. Thinking Christocentrically helps me sort through the side issues and leads me straight to the heart of every biblical text and the subject of all sermons: Jesus Christ.

The more searching my understanding of Christ, the better my sermon preparation. Given my antipathy to time management schemes, it's a little hard to admit, but reading difficult theology is one the best time-savers I know.

Jonathan Edwards, St. John of the Cross, Dietrich Bonhoeffer—the range of literature is wide. I find that the theologians worth reading all write about Christ. They all know how to handle a biblical text. More than that, they all know where the danger is in the text, and they are unafraid to expose it. They have a deep innate sense for where the text drastically contradicts our lives and where we are in serious trouble. From their expositions of the text we feel our danger. They step on the snake in us and present Christ to us. They call us to repentance. They summon us from death to life.

Having heard, we believe—then we can preach. This is what renews our hermeneutic: hearing Christ preached and taught by authors and preachers who are unafraid to tell us the truth. And that is the whole point of preaching: to tell the truth boldly and unashamedly.

Hearing the Word

A Christian heavy metal band and a hellfire preacher came to town to put on a show. The youth group wanted to go, so we took them, with some reluctance. I went in silent protest; I felt this was beneath me; I had passed this kind of thing up long ago. (Thinking back, I'm surprised I didn't scrape my nose on the door header as I entered the arena: my schnoz was in the stratosphere.)

Three thousand kids were there—including my son, sitting beside me, as old as I was when I heard the hellfire preacher who first drew the line for me.

The show began with blinding lights, belching smoke and blasting music that made the Wizard of Oz seem like St. Francis. Since I love rock music (and these guys were good), I had to admit that I enjoyed the first half of the show.

The hellfire preacher came on. He talked about sex, real frank, honest talk about sexually transmitted disease. No show, just the truth. Then he preached the gospel. He was hot, and I was drawn into it. I knew that I needed to cross the line.

I was tempted to debunk the show just as I had twenty-five years earlier. I could see the showmanship. I could also see that all my hotsy-totsy theologizing wasn't reaching three thousand kids with the gospel of Jesus Christ. I listened.

I was glad my son was there, and I know that I needed to be there. I didn't lean over to him and say, "We'll wait for you if you go forward." He didn't go forward; I didn't go forward, but I crossed the line that night. I think he did too.

Bibliography

Foreword

Wardlaw, Don M., editor. *Learning Preaching: Understanding and Participating in the Practice*. Lincoln, IL: Lincoln College and Seminary Press and the Academy of Homiletics, 1989

Wharton, James A. "Protagonist Corner: Her Name Was 'Fifi.'" *Journal for Preachers* 6.2 (1983) 28–29.

Introduction

Dodd, C. H. *Apostolic Preaching and Its Developments*. New York: Harper & Row, 1964.

Ellul, J. *The Humiliation of the Word*. Grand Rapids: Eerdmans, 1985.

Fant, Clyde. *Worldly Preaching*. New York: Thomas Nelson, 1975.

Lee, P. J. *Against the Protestant Gnostics*. Oxford: Oxford University Press, 1987.

Lischer, R. *The End of Words: The Language of Reconciliation in a Culture of Violence*. Grand Rapids: Eerdmans, 2005.

Norrington, D. C. *To Preach or Not to Preach*? Carlisle, UK: Paternoster, 1996.

Pearse, M., and Matthews, C. *We Must Stop Meeting Like This*. Eastbourne, UK: Kingsway, 1999.

Stackhouse, Ian. "Charismatic Utterance: Preaching as Prophecy." In *The Future of Preaching*, edited by G. Stevenson, 42–46. London: SCM, 2010.

Chapter 1

Achtemeier, Elizabeth. "The Canon as the Voice of the Living God." In *Reclaiming the Bible for the Church*, edited by Carl E. Braaten and Robert W. Jenson, 119–30. Edinburgh: T. & T. Clark, 1995.

Attridge, Harold. "God in Hebrews." In *The Forgotten God: Perspectives in Biblical Theology*, edited by Andrew Das and Frank Matera, 197–209. Louisville: Westminster John Knox, 2002.

————— "God in Hebrews." In *The Epistle to the Hebrews and Christian Theology*, edited by Richard Bauckham, Daniel Trier, Trevor Hart, and Nathan MacDonald, 103–8. Grand Rapids, Eerdmans, 2009.

Barth, Karl. *The Word of God and The Word of Man*. London: Hodder and Stoughton, 1928.

Beasley-Murray, George. *Preaching the Gospels from the Gospels*. London: Lutterworth Press, 1957.

Campbell, Charles L. *Preaching Jesus: New Directions for Homiletics in Hans Frei's Postliberal Theology*. Grand Rapids: Eerdmans, 1997.

————— "Introduction." In *The Threat of Life* by Walter Brueggemann, vii–xii. Minneapolis: Fortress, 1996.

Dawson, Gerrit Scott. *Jesus Ascended: The Meaning of Christ's Continuing Incarnation*. Phillipsburg, NJ: Presbyterian & Reformed, 2004.

Eliot, T. S. "East Cocker." In *Four Quartets*, 21–30. London: The Foilio Society, 1968.

Fant, Clyde. *Bonhoeffer: Worldly Preaching*. New York: Thomas Nelson, 1975.

Farrow, Douglas. *Ascension Theology*. London: T. & T. Clark, 2011.

Firet, Jacob. *Dynamic Pastoring*. Grand Rapids: Eerdmans, 1986.

Forde, Gerhard. *The Preached God: Proclamation in Word and Sacrament*. Grand Rapids: Eerdmans, 2007.

Forsyth, P. T. *Positive Preaching and the Modern Mind*. New York: Armstrong, 1907.

France, R. T. "The Writer of Hebrews as a Biblical Expositor." *Tyndale Bulletin* 47.2 (1996) 245–76.

Greenslade, Philip. *Ministering Angles: How to Minister When "How to" Books Fail*. Farnham, UK: CWR, 2009.

————— *Worship in the Best of Both Worlds: An Exploration of the Polarities of Truthful Worship*. Milton Keynes, UK: Paternoster, 2009.

Greib, Katherine. "Time Would Fail Me to Tell. . . . The Identity of Jesus Christ in Hebrews." In *Seeking the Identity of Jesus; A Pilgrimage*, edited by Beverley Roberts Gaventa and Richard Hays, 200–214. Grand Rapids: Eerdmans, 2008.

Guthrie, George. *Hebrews*. NIV Application Commentary. Grand Rapids: Zondervan, 1998.

Hall, Douglas John. *Bound and Free: A Theologian's Journey*. Minneapolis: Fortress, 2005.

Hahn, Scott. *The Kingdom of God as Liturgical Empire: A Theological Commentary on 1–2 Chronicles*. Grand Rapids: Baker, 2012.

————— "Liturgy and Empire." *Letter & Spirit* 5 (2009) 13–50.

Hays, Richard. *The Conversion of the Imagination*. Grand Rapids: Eerdmans, 2005.

————— *Echoes of Scripture in the Letters of Paul*. New Haven: Yale University Press, 1989.

Horton, Michael. *Covenant and Salvation: Union with Christ*. Louisville: Westminster John Knox, 2007.

Johnson. *The Glory of Preaching: Participating in God's Transformation of the World*. Downers Grove, IL: InterVarsity, 2009.

Lischer, Richard. "Resurrection and Rhetoric." In *Marks of the Body of Christ*, edited by Carl Braaten and Robert Jenson, 13–24. Grand Rapids: Eerdmans, 1999.

Lane, William. *Hebrews: A Call to Commitment*. Peabody, MA: Hendrickson, 1985.

————— *Hebrews 1–8*. Word Biblical Commentary. Dallas: Word, 1991.

————— *Hebrews 9–13*. Word Biblical Commentary. Dallas: Word, 1991.

Long, Tom. *Hebrews: Interpretation Commentary*. Louisville: John Knox, 1997.

Lincoln, Andrew. *Hebrews: A Guide*. London: T. & T. Clark, 2006.

Lischer, Richard. *The End of Words*. Grand Rapids: Eerdmans, 2005.

———. *The Theology of Preaching*. Eugene, OR: Wipf & Stock, 2001.

Koester, Craig. *Hebrews*. The Anchor Yale Bible. New Haven: Yale University Press, 2001.

Manning, Bernard Lord. *A Layman in the Ministry*. London: Independent, 1953.

Moltmann, Jürgen. *The Way of Jesus Christ: Christology in Messianic Dimensions*. London: SCM, 1990.

Mosser, Carl. "Rahab outside the Camp." In *The Epistle to the Hebrews and Christian Theology*, edited by Richard Bauckham, Daniel Trier, Trevor Hart, and Nathan MacDonald, 383–408. Minneapolis: Fortress, 2009.

Moule, C. F. D. *The Birth of the New Testament*. London: A. & C. Black, 1966.

Scherer, Paul. *The Word God Sent*. London: Hodder, 1965.

Schreiner, Thomas. "Warning and Assurance: Run the Race to the End." In *The Perfect Saviour: Key Themes in Hebrews*, edited by Jonathan Griffiths, 89–106. Nottingham, UK: InterVarsity, 2012.

Smith, D. Moody. "Gospels." In *Concise Encyclopedia of Preaching*, edited by William H. Willimon and Richard Lischer, 165–67. Louisville: Westminster John Knox, 1995.

Taylor, John Randolf. *God Loves Like That! The Theology of James Denney*. London: SCM, 1962.

Vanhoozer, Kevin. *First Theology: God, Scripture, and Hermeneutics*. Downers Grove, IL: InterVarsity, 2002.

Walker, Peter. "A Place for Hebrews: Contexts for a First-Century Sermon." In *The New Testament in its First-Century Setting: Essays in Honour of B. W. Winter on his 65th Birthday*, edited by P. J. Williams, Andrew Clarke, and David Instone-Brewer, 231–49. Grand Rapids: Eerdmans, 2004.

Webb, Stephen H. *The Divine Voice: Christian Proclamation and the Theology of Sound*. Grand Rapids: Brazos, 2004.

Willimon, William H. *Shaped by the Bible*. Nashville: Abingdon, 1999.

Wills L. "The Form of the Sermon in Hellenistic Judaism and Early Christianity." *Harvard Theological Review 77* (1984) 277–99.

Witherington III, Ben. *Letters and Homilies for Jewish Christians: Socio-Rhetorical Commentary on Hebrews, James and Jude*. Downers Grove, IL: InterVarsity, 2007.

Wright, John W. *Telling God's Story: Narrative Preaching for Christian Formation*. Downers Grove, IL: InterVarsity, 2007.

Chapter 2

Barnes, C. *The Pastor as Minor Poet: Texts and Subtexts in the Ministerial Life*. Grand Rapids: Eerdmans, 2009.

Capon, R. Farrar. *The Foolishness of Preaching: Proclaiming the Gospel against the Wisdom of the World*. Grand Rapids: Eerdmans, 1998.

Carson, D. A. *Exegetical Fallacies*. Grand Rapids: Baker, 1984.

Fant, C. E. *Bonhoeffer: Worldly Preaching*. New York: Thomas Nelson, 1975.

Forsyth, P. T. *Positive Preaching and the Modern Mind*, London: Independent, 1907.

Huntemann, G. *The Other Bonhoeffer: An Evangelical Reassessment of Dietrich Bonhoeffer*. Grand Rapids: Baker, 1993.

Lischer, R. *The End of Words: The Language of Reconciliation in a Culture of Violence*, Grand Rapids: Eerdmans, 2005.

Long, T. G. *The Witness of Preaching*. Louisville: Westminster/John Knox, 1989.

Miller, C. *Letters to a Young Pastor*. Colorado Springs: David. C. Cook, 2011.

Resner Jr, A. *Preacher and Cross: Person and Message in Theology and Rhetoric*. Grand Rapids: Eerdmans, 1999.

Chapter 3

Alter, Robert. *The Art of Biblical Narrative*. New York: Basic, 1981.

Attridge, Harrold W. *The Epistle to the Hebrews*, edited by Helmut Koester. Philadelphia: Fortress, 1989.

Bar-Efrat, Shimon. *Narrative Art in the Bible*. Sheffield, UK: Almond, 1989.

Beale, G. K. *The Temple and the Church's Mission: A Biblical Theology of the Dwelling Place of God*. Downers Grove, IL: InterVarsity, 2004.

Block, Daniel I. *The New American Commentary: Judges, Ruth*. Nashville: Broadman & Holman, 1999.

———. "Tell Me the Old, Old Story: Preaching the Message of Old Testament Narrative." In *Giving the Sense: Understanding and Using Old Testament Historical Texts*, edited by David M. Howard Jr. and Michael A. Grisanti, 409–38. Grand Rapids: Kregel, 2003.

Brueggemann, Walter. *First and Second Samuel*. Interpretation: A Bible Commentary for Teaching and Preaching. Louisville: John Knox, 1990.

Chapell, Bryan. *Christ-Centered Preaching: Redeeming the Expository Sermon*. 2nd ed. Grand Rapids: Baker, 2005.

Greidanus, Sidney. *The Modern Preacher and the Ancient Text: Interpreting and Preaching Biblical Literature*. Grand Rapids: Eerdmans, 1988.

———. *Preaching Christ from the Old Testament: A Contemporary Hermeneutical Method*. Grand Rapids: Eerdmans, 1999.

———. *Sola Scriptura: Problems and Principles in Preaching Historical Texts*. 1970. Reprint. Eugene, OR: Wipf and Stock, 2001.

Dempster, Stephen G. *Dominion and Dynasty: A Theology of the Hebrew Bible*. Downers Grove, IL: InterVarsity, 2003.

Calvin, John. *The Epistle of Paul the Apostle to the Hebrews and The First and Second Epistles of St. Peter*. Translated William B. Johnston. Grand Rapids: Eerdmans, 1963.

Fokkelman, J. P. *Reading Biblical Narrative: An Introductory Guide*. Louisville: Westminster John Knox, 1999.

Hupping, Carol et al. *JPS Guide: The Jewish Bible*. Philadelphia: Jewish Publication Society, 2008.

Inrig, Gary. *Hearts of Iron, Feet of Clay*. Chicago: Moody, 1979.

Janzen, David. "Why the Deuteronomist Told about the Sacrifice of Jephthah's Daughter." *Journal for the Study of the Old Testament* 29.3 (2005) 339–57.

Keller, Timothy. *Counterfeit Gods: The Empty Promises of Money, Sex, and Power and the Only Hope That Matters*. New York: Dutton, 2009.

———. *The Prodigal God: Recovering the Heart of the Christian Faith*. New York: Dutton, 2008.

Klein, Lillian R. *The Triumph of Irony in the Book of Judges*. Sheffield, UK: Almond, 1988.

Krakauer, Jon. *Into Thin Air*. New York: Villard, 1997.

Lane, William L. *Hebrews 9–13*. Word Biblical Commentary 47B. Dallas: Word, 1991.

Mathewson, Steven D. *The Art of Preaching Old Testament Narrative*. Grand Rapids: Baker Academic, 2002.

———. "An Exercise in Theology and Ethics: Preaching the Story of Jephthah's Vow." Paper delivered to the Old Testament Narrative Literature Section of the Evangelical Theological Society at its annual meeting in New Orleans, Louisiana, on November 19, 2009.

———. *Joshua and Judges*. The People's Bible Commentary. Oxford: The Bible Reading Fellowship, 2003.

O'Connell, Robert H. *The Rhetoric of the Book of Judges*. Vetus Testamentum Sup 63. Leiden: Brill, 1996.

Packer, J. I. *Knowing God*. Downers Grove, IL: InterVarsity, 1973.

Robinson, Haddon W. *Biblical Preaching: The Development and Delivery of Expository Messages*. 2nd ed. Grand Rapids: Baker, 2001.

———. "The Danger of a Strong Faith and a Weak Theology." Online: PreachingToday. com.

Sailhamer, John H. *NIV Compact Bible Commentary*. Grand Rapids: Zondervan, 1994.

Ska, Jean Louis. *"Our Fathers Have Told Us:" Introduction to the Analysis of Hebrew Narrative*. Rome: Editrice Pontificio Instituto Biblico, 1997.

Van der Merwe, Christo H. J. Jackie A. Naude, and Jan H. Kroeze. *A Biblical Hebrew Reference Grammar*. Sheffield, UK: Sheffield Academic Press, 1999.

Webb, Barry G. *The Book of the Judges: An Integrated Reading*. JSOTSup 46. Sheffield, UK: Sheffield Academic Press, 1987.

Wenham, Gordon J. *Story as Torah: Reading Old Testament Narrative Ethically*. Grand Rapids: Baker Academic, 2000.

Wolf, Herbert M. "Implications of Form Criticism for Old Testament Studies." *Bibliotheca Sacra* 127.508 (1970) 303–6.

Wright, Christopher J. H. *Old Testament Ethics For the People of God*. Downers Grove, IL: InterVarsity, 2004.

Younger Jr., K. Lawson. *Judges, Ruth*. The NIV Application Commentary. Grand Rapids: Zondervan, 2002.

Chapter 4

Brueggemann, Walter. "Psalms and the Life of Faith: A Suggested Typology of Function." *Journal for the Study of the Old Testament* 17.1 (1980) 3–32.

———. *Spirituality of the Psalms*. Minneapolis: Augsburg Fortress, 2002.

Carney, Sheila. "God Damn God: A Reflection on Expressing Anger in Prayer." *Biblical Theology Bulletin* 13.4 (1983) 116–20.

Gerstenberger, Erhard S. *Psalms, Part 1: With an Introduction to Cultic Poetry* and *Psalms* and *Part 2 and Lamentations*. Forms of the Old Testament Literature XIV and XV. Grand Rapids: Eerdmans, 1988, 2001.

Gunkel, Hermann. *Einleitung in Die Psalmen.* 2nd ed. Edited by J. Begrich. Göttingen: Vandenhoeck und Rupprecht, 1933; English translation: *Introduction to the Psalms: The Genres of the Religious Lyric of Israel,* translated by J. D. Nogalski. Macon, GA: Mercer University Press, 1998.

———. *The Psalms: A Form-Critical Introduction,* translated by T. M. Horner. Philadelphia: Fortress, 1967.

Howard, Jr. David M. "Psalm 88 and the Rhetoric of Lament." In *"My Words Are Lovely": Studies in the Rhetoric of the Psalms,* edited by R. Foster and D. Howard, 132–46. Library of Hebrew Bible/Old Testament Studies 467. London: T. & T. Clark, 2008.

Osbeck, Kenneth W. *101 Hymn Stories.* Grand Rapids: Kregel, 1982.

Taylor, Justin. http://thegospelcoalition.org/blogs/justintaylor/2011/11/01/the-true-story-behind-the-hymn-it-is-well-with-my-soul/ (accessed January 16, 2012).

Westermann, Claus. *Praise and Lament in the Psalms.* Translated by K. R. Crim and R. N. Soulen. Atlanta: John Knox, 1981.

Chapter 5

Beach, N. *Gifted to Lead: The Art of Leading as a Woman in the Church.* Grand Rapids: Zondervan, 2008.

Capel, Anderson J., and S. D. Moore. *Mark and Method: New Approaches in Biblical Studies.* 2nd ed. Minneapolis: Fortress, 2008.

Childers, J., editor. *Birthing the Sermon: Women Preachers on the Creative Process.* St. Louis: Chalice, 2001.

Durber, S. *Preaching Like a Woman.* London: SPCK, 2001.

Durber, S., and Heather Walton, editors. *Silence in Heaven: A Book of Women's Preaching.* London: Trinity, 1994.

Durso, P. R. editor. *This is What a Preacher Looks Like: Sermons by Baptist Women in Ministry.* Macon, GA: Smyth and Helwys, 2010.

Foskett, M. F. *Interpreting the Bible: Approaching the Text in Preparation for Preaching.* Minneapolis: Fortress, 2009.

Graham, E. *Transforming Practice: Pastoral Theology in an Age of Uncertainty.* Eugene, OR: Wipf and Stock, 2002.

Matthews, A. *Preaching that Speaks to Women.* Downers Grove, IL: InterVarsity, 2003.

Ostriker, A. Suskin. *Feminist Revision and the Bible.* Oxford: Wiley-Blackwell, 1992.

Purvis-Smith, V. "Gender and the Aesthetic of Preaching." In *A Reader on Preaching: Making Connections,* edited by D. Day, J. Astley, and L. J. Francis, ?–?. Ashgate, 2005.

Radford Reuther, R. *Sexism and God-Talk.* London, SCM Press, 1983.

Sanders, C. J. "The Woman as Preacher." In *A Reader on Preaching: Making Connections,* edited by D. Day, J. Astley, and L. J. Francis, 211–23. Farnham, UK: Ashgate, 2005.

Schussler Fiorenza, E. *Bread Not Stone: The Challenge of Feminist Biblical Interpretation.* Boston: Beacon, 1995.

———. *In Memory of Her: A Feminist Theological Construction of Christian Origins.* London, SCM, 1983.

Smith, C. *Weaving the Sermon: Preaching in a Feminist Perspective.* Louisville: Westminster/John Knox, 1999.

Stephens, J. and Zades, S. *Mad Dogs, Dreamers and Sages: Growth in the Age of Ideas.* New York: Elounda, 2003.

Trible P. *Literary Feminist Readings of Biblical Narratives.* Minneapolis: Augsburg Fortress, 1984.

Volf, M. *Captive to the Word of God: Engaging the Scriptures for Contemporary Theological Reflection.* Grand Rapids: Eerdmans, 2010.

Walton, H. "Breaking Open the Bible." In *Life Cycles: Women and Pastoral Care*, edited by E. Graham and M. Halsey, 192–99. London: SPCK, 1993.

Chapter 6

Baym, Nina, Wayne Franklin, Philip F. Gura, Arnold Krupat, and Robert S. Levine, editors. *The Norton Anthology of American Literature, Shorter Seventh Edition.* New York: Norton, 2007.

Dallimore, Arnold. *George Whitefield.* 2 vols. Edinburgh: Banner of Truth, 1970 and 1980.

Dwight, Sereno E. *Life of President Edwards.* New York: Carvill, 1830.

Edwards. "A Divine and Supernatural Light." In *Sermons and Discourses 1734–1738, The Works of Jonathan Edwards Vol. 19*, edited by M. X. Lesser, 405–26. New Haven: Yale University Press, 2001.

———. *The "Miscellanies," Nos. a-z, aa-zz, 1–500.* In *The Works of Jonathan Edwards Vol. 13*, edited by Thomas Schafer. New Haven: Yale University Press, 1994.

———. *Religious Affection.* In *The Works of Jonathan Edwards, Vol. 2*, edited by John E. Smith. New Haven: Yale University Press, 1959.

———. *Scientific and Philosophical Writings.* In *The Works of Jonathan Edwards, Vol. 6*, edited by Wallace E. Anderson. New Haven: Yale University Press, 1980.

———. *The Sermons of Jonathan Edwards: A Reader*, edited by Wilson Kimnach, Kenneth P. Minkema, and Douglas A. Sweeney. New Haven: Yale University Press, 1999.

———. *Some Thoughts Concerning the Present Revival of Religion.* In *The Great Awakening: The Works of Jonathan Edwards, Vol. 4*, edited C. C. Goen, 386–88. New Haven: Yale University Press, 1972.

———. *Typological Writings.* In *The Works of Jonathan Edwards Vol. 11*, edited by Wallace E. Anderson and David Watters. New Haven: Yale University Press, 1993.

Hopkins, Samuel. *The Life and Character of the Late Learned Mr. Jonathan Edwards, President of the College of New Jersey, Together with Extracts from His Private Writings and Diary, And Also Seventeen Select Sermons On Various Important Subjects.* Northampton, MA: Andrew Wright, 1804.

Kimnach, Wilson H. "Jonathan Edwards's Pursuit of Reality." In *Jonathan Edwards and the American Experience*, edited by Nathan Hatch and Harry S. Stout, 102–17. New York: Oxford University Press, 1988.

———. "The Sermons: Concept and Execution." In *The Princeton Companion to Jonathan Edwards*, edited by Sang Lee, 243–57. Princeton: Princeton University Press, 2005.

Lambert, Frank. *"Peddler in Divinity": George Whitefield and the Transatlantic Revivals, 1737–1770.* Princeton: Princeton University Press, 2002.

Locke, John. *An Essay Concerning Human Understanding* (1690). Edited by Peter Nidditch. Oxford: Oxford University Press, 1979.

Miller, Perry. *Errand into the Wilderness.* Cambridge: Harvard University Press, 1956.

Smith, John E. *Jonathan Edwards: Puritan, Preacher, Philosopher.* London: Chapman, 1992.

Stout, Harry S. *The Divine Dramatist: George Whitefield and the Rise of Modern Evangelicalism.* Grand Rapids: Eerdmans, 1991.

Stowe, Harriet Beecher. *The Minister's Wooing.* New York: Derby and Jackson, 1859.

Chapter 7

Arnold, Matthew. *Culture and Anarchy* (1869). Cambridge: Cambridge University Press, 1935.

Bacon, Ernest W. *Spurgeon: Heir of the Puritans.* London: Allen and Unwin, 1967.

Bebbington, David W. *Holiness in Nineteenth-Century England.* Carlisle, UK: Paternoster, 2002.

———. "Spurgeon and the Common Man." *Baptist Review of Theology* 5.1 (1995) 63–75.

Colwell, John E. "The Church as Ethical Community." In *The Bible in Pastoral Practice: Readings in Place and Function of Scripture in the Church*, edited by Paul Ballard and Stephen R. Holmes, 212–24. London: Darton, Longman, and Todd, 2005.

Cox, Thomas. "Notes on C. H. Spurgeon." Spurgeon Archive, Spurgeon's College (B1.17).

Fullerton, William Y. *C. H. Spurgeon: A Biography.* London: Williams and Norgate, 1920.

———. "C. H. Spurgeon's Pulpit Notes." Spurgeon Archive, Spurgeon's College, London (L2.1).

Hedley, Douglas. "Theology and the Revolt against the Enlightenment." In *World Christianities, c.1815–c.1914*, edited by Sheridan Gilley and Brian Stanley, 30–52. Cambridge: Cambridge University Press, 2006.

Hopkins, Mark. *Nonconformity's Romantic Generation: Evangelical and Liberal Theologies in Victorian England.* Studies in Evangelical History and Thought. Carlisle, UK: Paternoster, 2004.

North American Review. Boston: Crosby and Nicholls, 1858.

Kruppa, Patricia S. *Charles Haddon Spurgeon: A Preacher's Progress.* New York: Garland, 1982.

Longfellow, Henry W. *Favourite Poems.* London: Routledge, 1878.

Magoon, Elms Lyman, editor. *"The Modern Whitefield:" Sermons of the Rev. C. H. Spurgeon, of London, With an Introduction and Sketch of his Life.* New York: Sheldon, Blakeman, and Co., 1857.

Morden, Peter J. *C. H. Spurgeon: The People's Preacher.* Farnham, UK: CWR, 2009.

———. *"Communion with Christ and His People": The Spirituality of C. H. Spurgeon.* 2010. Reprint. Eugene, OR: Pickwick, 2014.

———. "Spurgeon and Humour." *The Bible in TransMission*, Spring, 2011, 20–22.

Munson, James. *The Nonconformists: In Search of a Lost Culture.* London: SPCK, 1991.

Peterson, Eugene H. *Christ Plays in Ten Thousand Places: A Conversation in Spiritual Theology.* London: Hodder and Stoughton, 2005.

————. *Subversive Spirituality*. Vancouver, BC: Regent College, 1997.

Ruskin, John. "John Ruskin to C. H. Spurgeon, 25 November 1862." Spurgeon Archive, Spurgeon's College.

Smiles, Samuel. *Self Help: With Illustrations of Character, Conduct, and Perseverance* (1859). Oxford: Oxford University Press, 2002.

Spurgeon, C. H. *Autobiography: Compiled from his Diary, Letters, and Records by his Wife and His Private Secretary*. 4 vols. London: Passmore and Alabaster, 1897–99.

————. "Bankrupt Debtors Discharged." *MTP*, Vol. 29, S. No. 1739-40, Luke 7.42, delivered 16 September 1883.

————. "The Bible", *NPSP*, Vol. 1, S. No. 15, Hosea 8.12, delivered 18 March 1855.

————. *Commenting and Commentaries* (1876). London: Banner of Truth, 1969.

————. "The Common Salvation." *MTP*, Vol. 27, S. No. 1592, Jude 3, delivered 10 April 1881.

————. "General and Yet Particular." *MTP*, Vol. 10, John 17.2, delivered 24 April 1864.

————. *The Gospel of the Kingdom: A Popular Exposition of the Gospel according to Matthew*. London: Passmore and Alabaster, 1893.

————. "High Doctrine and Broad Doctrine." *MTP*, Vol. 30, S. No. 1762, John 6.37, n.d.

————. "The Holy Road." *MTP*, Vol. 32, S. No. 1912, Isaiah 35.8, delivered 1 August 1886.

————. "How To Read The Bible." *MTP*, Vol. 25, S. No. 1503, Matthew 12.3-7, n.d.,

————. "The Infallibility Of Scripture." *MTP*, Vol. 34, S. No. 2013, Isaiah 1.20, delivered 11 March 1888.

————. *John Ploughman's Talk; Or, Plain Advice for Plain People*. London: Passmore and Alabaster, n.d.

————. "Messrs. Moody And Sankey Defended; Or, A Vindication of the Doctrine of Justification by Faith." *MTP*, Vol. 21, S. No. 1239, Galatians 5.24, n.d.

————. "The Pitifulness of the Lord and the Comfort of the Afflicted." *New Park Street Pulpit (NPSP)/ Metropolitan Tabernacle Pulpit*. London: Passmore and Alabaster, 1856–1917, *MTP*, Vol. 31, Sermon Number (S. No.) 1845, James 5.11, delivered 14 June 1885.

————. "Plain Directions to Those Who Would Be Saved from Sin." *MTP*, Vol. 34, S. No. 2033, Psalm 4.4,5, delivered 15 July 1888.

————. "The Present Position of Calvinism in England." In *The Sword and The Trowel: A Record of Combat with Sin and Labour for The Lord*, edited by C. H. Spurgeon, 49–53. London: Passmore and Alabaster, 1865–92.

————. "Redemption By Price." *MTP*, Vol. 26, S. No. 1554, 1 Corinthians 6.19-20, 22 August 1880.

————. "The Sacred Love-Token." *MTP*, Vol. 21, S. No. 1251, Exodus 12.13, 22 August 1875.

————. "The Saint of The Smithy." In *The Spare Half Hour*. London: Passmore and Alabaster, n.d.

————. "The Sin Bearer," 1 Peter 2.24-25, "A Communion Meditation At Mentone." In *Till He Come: Communion Meditations and Addresses*. London: Passmore and Alabaster, 1896.

————. "The Talking Book." *MTP*, Vol. 17, S. No. 1017, Proverbs 6.22, delivered 22 October 1871.

————. "The Singing Pilgrim." *MTP*, Vol. 28, S. No. 1652, Psalm 119.54, n.d.

————. *The Treasury Of David: Containing an Original Exposition of the Book of Psalms*, 7 vols. London: Marshall Brothers, n.d. [1869–85]).

————. "The Word a Sword." *MTP*, Vol. 34, S. No. 2010, Hebrews 4.12, delivered 17 May 1887.

————. "Understandest Thou What Thou Readest?" *MTP*, Vol. 30, S. No. 1792, Acts 8.30–33, delivered 11 May 1884.

Thielicke, Helmut. *Encounter with Spurgeon*. London: James Clark, 1964.

Tidball, Derek J., David Hilborn, and Justin Thacker editors. *The Atonement Debate: Papers from the London Symposium on the Theology of Atonement*. Grand Rapids: Zondervan, 2008.

Chapter 8

Augustine. *De Doctrina Christiana*. Translated by D. W. Robertson. Indianapolis: Bobbs-Merrill, 1984.

Battenson, H. *Later Christian Fathers: A Selection from the Writings of the Fathers from St Cyril of Jerusalem to St Leo the Great*. Oxford: Oxford University Press, 1972.

Behr, John. "On the 1600th Anniversary of St. John Chrysostom's Death." Delivered at the Orthodox Church of America, parish of St John Chrysostom, Home Springs, MO, September 29th 2007.

Bugeon, J. W. *Byzantine Texts, Revision Revised*. Edited by M. L. Chadwick & V. A. Chadwick. London: John Murray, 1883.

John Chrysostom. *Adversus Judaeos: Homily V*. The Fathers of the Church vol. 68. Translated by P. W. Hartings. Washington, DC: Catholic University Academic Press, 1979.

Kerr, H. *Preaching in the Early Church*. New York: Revell, 1942.

Lewis, C. S. "Preface." In *The Pilgrim's Regress*. 3rd ed. London: Dent, 1943.

Lloyd Jones, Martyn. *Romans: An Exposition of Chap 7:1—8:4. "The Law. Its Function & Limits."* Edinburgh: Banner of Truth, 1974.

————. *Romans: An Exposition of Chap 8:5-7. "The Sons of God."* Edinburgh: Banner of Truth, 1974.

Nowak, K. et al., editors. *Adolf Harnack: Christentum, Wissenschaft und Gesellschaft*, Göttingen: Vandenhoeck & Ruprecht, 2003.

Pelikan, J. *Christianity and Classical Culture*. New Haven: Yale University Press 1993.

Pirsig, R. *Zen and the Art of Motor Cycle Maintenance*. New York: Morrow 1974.

Rapp, Christoff. "Aristotle's Rhetoric." In *Stanford Encyclopaedia of Philosophy*, edited by E. N. Zalsa. 2010. Online: http://plato.stanford.edu/entries/aristotle-rhetoric/.

Schememann, A. *Church World Mission*. NY: St. Vladimir's Seminary Press, 1979.

Troparion of the Feast of the Annunciation, Orthodox liturgy.

Trubetskoi, Prince. *Icons: Theology in Colour*. NY: St Valdimir's Seminary Press, 1973.

Walker, A. "Scripture, Revelation, and Platonism in C. S. Lewis." *Scottish Journal of Theology* 55.1 (2002) 19–35.

Walker, Andrew, and Luke Bretherton, editors. *Remembering Our Future: Explorations in Deep Church*. Milton Keynes, UK: Paternoster, 2007.

Williams, D. H. *Evangelicals and Tradition*. Grand Rapids: Baker Academic, 2005.

Chapter 9

Bailey, K. E. *Poet and Peasant and Through Peasant Eyes: A Literary Cultural Approach to the Parables in Luke, Combined Edition, Two Volumes in One*. Grand Rapids: Eerdmans, 1983.

Barnes, C. *The Pastor as Minor Poet: Texts and Subtexts in the Ministerial Life*. Grand Rapids: Eerdmans, 2009.

Bonhoeffer, Dietrich. *Worldly Preaching*. Edited by C. E. Fant. Nashville: Thomas Nelson, 1985.

Brueggemann, W. *Finally Comes the Poet: Daring Speech for Proclamation*. Minneapolis: Fortress, 1989.

Capon, R. *The Foolishness of Preaching: Proclaiming the Gospel against the Wisdom of the World*. Grand Rapids: Eerdmans, 1998.

Eliot, T. S. *Collected Poems: 1909–1962*. London: Faber and Faber, 1974.

Ellsworth, W. *The Power of Speaking God's Word: How to Preach Memorable Sermons*. Fearn, UK: Christian Focus, 2000.

Ellul, J. *The Humiliation of the Word*. Translated by J. M. Hanks. Grand Rapids: Eerdmans, 1985.

Galli, M. *Jesus Mean and Wild: The Unexpected Love of an Untameable God*. Grand Rapids: Baker, 2006.

Johnson, D. *The Glory of Preaching: Participating in God's Transformation of the World*. Downers Grove, IL: InterVarsity, 2009,

Lindbeck, G. A. *The Nature of Doctrine: Religion and Doctrine in a Post-Liberal Age*. Philadelphia: Westminster, 1985.

Lischer, R. *A Theology of Preaching: The Dynamics of the Gospel*. Nashville: Abingdon, 1986.

Lischer, R. *The End of Words: The Language of Reconciliation in a Culture of Violence*. Grand Rapids: Eerdmans, 2005.

Long, T. *The Witness of Preaching*. Louisville: Westminster/John Knox, 1989.

Newbigin, L. *The Light Has Come: An Exposition of the Fourth Gospel*. Grand Rapids: Eerdmans, 1982.

Peterson, E. H. *Leap Over a Wall: Earthy Spirituality for Everyday Christians*. San Francisco: Harper, 2008.

———. *Under the Unpredictable Plant: An Exploration in Vocational Holiness*. Grand Rapids: Gracewing/Eerdmans, 1992.

Radcliffe, T. *Why Go to Church? The Drama of the Eucharist*. London: Continuum, 2009.

Robinson, M. *Gilead*. London: Virago, 2004.

Willimon, W. H. *Conversations with Barth on Preaching*. Nashville: Abingdon, 2006.

———. *Shaped by the Bible*, Nashville: Abingdon, 1990.

Wright, N. T. *Fresh Perspectives on Paul*. London: SPCK, 2005.

Chapter 10

Aesop. "The Fox and the Lion." *An Aesop's Fable*. Online: http://www.aesops-fables.org.uk/aesop-fable-the-fox-and-the-lion.htm.

Alter, R. *The Art of Biblical Poetry*. New York: Perseus, 2011.

———. *The Book of Psalms*. New York: Norton, 2007.

American Beauty. Directed by Sam Mendes, 1999; DVD, Los Angeles and Sacramento, and Burbank: Dreamworks SKG, 2000.

Balthasar, H. U. von. *Herrlichkeit: Eine theologische Ästhetik* Band I: *Schau der Gestalt*. 1961. English translation by Erasmo Leiva-Merikakis. *The Glory of the Lord: A Theological Aesthetics*, Vol. 1. Edinburgh: T. & T. Clark, 1982.

Barnes, M. *The Pastor as Minor Poet: Texts and Subtexts in the Ministerial Life*. Grand Rapids: Eerdmans, 2009.

Bell, R. *Trees*. 003, DVD. Grand Rapids: Zondervan, 2005.

Berman, A. *L'épreuve de l'étranger: Culture et traduction dans l'Allemagne romantique, Les Essais*. Paris: Gallimard, 1984.

Bonhoeffer, D. "The Causality and Finality of Preaching." In *Bonhoeffer: Wordly Preaching*, edited by C. E. Fant, 137–42. New York: Thomas Nelson, 1975.

Bretherton, L. "Beyond the Emerging Church." In *Remembering Our Future: Explorations in Deep Church*, edited by A. Walker and L. Bretherton, 30–58. Milton Keynes, MK: Paternoster, 2007.

Brueggemann, W. *Finally Comes the Poet*. Minneapolis: Augsburg Fortress, 1989.

Calvin, John. *Institutes of Christian Religion*. Translated by Henry Beveridge, Esq. London: Bonham Norton, 1599. Online: http://www.ccel.org/c/calvin/institutes/institutes.html.

Chaucer, G. "Tale of Melibee." From *The Canterbury Tales* in *The Riverside Chaucer*. Oxford: Oxford University Press, 1987.

Chesterton, G. K. *Orthodoxy*. New York: Image, 1959.

Clarke, E. "Sacred Singer/Profane Poet." In *George Herbert: Sacred and Profane*. Amsterdam: VU University Press, 1995.

The Concise Oxford Dictionary. Oxford: Oxford University Press, 1990.

Crouch, A. "The Emergent Mystique." *Christianity Today,* September 21, 2004. Online: www.christianitytoday.com/ct/2004/november/12.36.html.

Dickinson, E. *The Collected Poems of Emily Dickinson*. Edited by R. Wetzsteon. New York: Barnes and Noble, 2004.

Elliot, T. S. "Burnt Norton." *The Four Quartets*. London: Faber and Faber, 1944.

Fuller, T. *Comment on Ruth*. Online: http://www.highbeam.com/doc/1090.

Gibbs, E., and R. Bolger. *Emerging Churches: Creating Christian Community in Postmodern Cultures*. Grand Rapids: Baker Academic, 2005.

Hart, T. "A Suspicion Observed: Christian Responses to the Imagination." Paper given at The Billy Graham Center and Marion E. Wade Center Evangelism Roundtable V: *Imagination and the Gospel*, April 23–26, 2008. Online: http://www.wheaton.edu/BGC/Ministries/ISE/Specialty-Programs/~/media/Files/Centers-and-Institutes/BGC/Roundtable/2008/2008-Session- 2-Hart.pdf

Hodges, P. "Cultural Approach to Translation Theory." Online: http://www.translationdirectory.com/articles.

Keats, J. "Lamia." In *John Keats: Selected Poetry*, 175–95. London: Penguin, 1988.

Lewis, C. S. *The Horse and His Boy*. London: Harper Collins, 2001.

———. *Mere Christianity*. New York: Macmillan, 1952.

———. *On Stories: And Other Essays on Literature*. Edited by Walter Hooper. New York: Harcourt Brace, 1982.

———. *Surprised by Joy*. London: Fontana, 1955.

Lischer, R. "Stick with the Story." In *The Christian Century*, July 26, 2005, as cited by T. Brock and W. Brock in Religion-online.org. http://www.religiononline.org/showarticle.asp?title=3236.

Martz, L. *George Herbert and Henry Vaughan*. Oxford: Oxford University Press, 1986.

McIntyre, J. *Faith, Theology and Imagination*. Edinburgh: Handsel, 1987.

Michaels, A. *Fugitive Pieces*. London: Bloomsbury, 2009.

Robinson, E. *The Language of Mystery*. London: SCM, 1987.

Radcliffe, T. *Sing a New Song: The Christian Vocation*. Dublin: Dominican, 1999.

Ryken, L. *The ESV and the English Bible Legacy*. Wheaton, IL: Crossway, 2011.

Shklovsky, V. "Art as Technique." In *Debating Texts*, edited by R. Rylance, 48–56. Oxford: Oxford University Press, 1987.

Taylor, B. *The Preaching Life*. Lanham, MD: Cowley, 1993.

Taylor, J. V. *The Go-Between God: The Spirit and the Christian Mission*. London: SCM, 1972.

Thomas, E. "Words." In *The Collected Poems of Edward Thomas*, edited by R. Thomas, 71–73. Oxford: Oxford University Press, 1978.

Tobin, J. *George Herbert: The Complete English Poems*. London: Penguin, 1991.

Veith, G. *The Soul of Prince Caspian: Exploring Spiritual Truth in the Land of Narnia*. Colorado Springs: David C. Cook, 2008.

Young, R. "Herbert and Analogy." In *George Herbert: Sacred and Profane*, edited by H. Wilcox and R. Todd, 92–103. Amsterdam: VU University Press, 1995.

Chapter 11

Augustine, Saint. *On Christian Teaching*. Translated by R. P. H. Green. Oxford: Oxford University Press, 1997.

Booth, John N. *The Quest for Preaching Power*. New York: Macmillan, 1943.

Broadus, John. *On the Preparation and Delivery of Sermons*. 1870. 4th ed. Revised by Vernon L. Stanfield. New York: HarperOne, 1979.

Brueggemann, Walter. "That the World may be Redescribed." *Interpretation* 56.4 (2002) 359–67.

Childers, Jana. *Performing the Word: Preaching as Theatre*. Nashville: Abingdon, 1998.

Collins, Colonel Tim. "Colonel Tim Collin's Speech." Online: http://journal.dajobe.org/journal/2003/03/collins/. Accessed 12 December 2013.

Craddock, Fred B. *Preaching*. Nashville: Abingdon, 1985.

Edwards Jr., O. C. *A History of Preaching*. Nashville: Abingdon, 2004.

Fant, Clyde E. *Preaching for Today*. New York: Harper and Row, 1975.

Forsyth, James. "The No Notes Speech Does the Trick for Cameron Again." Online: http://blogs.spectator.co.uk/coffeehouse/2010/02/the-no-notes-speech-does-the-trick-for-cameron-again/. Accessed 12 December 2013.

Graves, Mike. *The Fully Alive Preacher: Recovering from Homiletical Burnout*. Louisville: Westminster John Knox, 2006.

Koller, Charles W. *Expository Preaching without Notes*. 1962. Reprint. Grand Rapids: Baker, 1982.

Leith, Sam. *You Talkin' to Me: Rhetoric from Aristotle to Obama*. London: Profile, 2011.

Long, Thomas G. *Preaching the Literary Forms of the Bible*. Philadelphia: Augsburg Fortress, 1988.

———. *The Witness of Preaching.* Louisville: Westminster/John Knox, 1989.

Lybrand, Fred R. *Preaching on Your Feet: Connecting God and the Audience in the Preachable Moment.* Nashville: Broadman & Holman, 2008.

Quicke, Michael. *360 Degree Preaching.* Grand Rapids: Baker Academic, 2003.

———. "History of Preaching (3)." Online: http://michaelquicke.blogspot.com/2011/07/history-of-preaching-3.html.

———. *Preaching as Worship: An Integrative Approach to Formation in Your Church.* Grand Rapids: Baker, 2011.

Stone, Dave. *Refining Your Style: Learning from Respected Communicators.* Loveland, CO: Group, 2004.

Webb, Joseph M. *Preaching Without Notes.* Nashville: Abingdon, 2001.

———. "Without Notes." In *The New Interpreter's Handbook of Preaching,* edited by Paul Scott Wilson, 429–31. Nashville: Abingdon, 2008.

Chapter 12

Adam, Peter. *Speaking God's Words: A Practical Theology of Expository Preaching.* Downer's Grove, IL: InterVarsity, 1996.

Broadus, John A. *On the Preparation and Delivery of Sermons,* 4th ed. San Francisco: Harper and Row, 1986.

Cox, James W. *A Guide to Biblical Preaching.* Nashville: Abingdon, 1976.

Craddock, Fred. *Preaching.* Nashville: Abingdon, 1985.

Earle, Ralph. *1, 2 Timothy.* In *The Expositor's Bible Commentary,* vol. 11, edited by Frank E. Gaebelein. Grand Rapids: Zondervan, 1978.

Freeman, Harold. *Variety in Biblical Preaching: Innovative Techniques and Fresh Forms.* Waco, TX: Word, 1986.

Griedanus, Sidney. *The Modern Preacher and the Ancient Text: Interpreting and Preaching Biblical Literature.* Grand Rapids: Eerdmans, 1988.

Guthrie, Donald. *The Pastoral Epistles.* Grand Rapids: Eerdmans, 1978.

Hamilton, Donald. *Homiletical Handbook.* Nashville: Broadman and Holman, 1992.

Hendricksen, William. *Thessalonians, Timothy, and Titus.* Grand Rapids: Baker, 1983.

Liefeld, Walter L. *New Testament Exposition: From Text to Sermon.* Grand Rapids: Zondervan, 1984.

Lewis, Ralph L., and Gregg Lewis. *Inductive Preaching: Helping People Listen.* Westchester, IL: Crossway, 1983.

Long, Thomas. *Preaching and the Literary Forms of the Bible.* Philadelphia: Fortress, 1989.

Olford, Stephen G., and David L. Olford. *Annointed Expository Preaching.* Nashville: Broadman and Holman, 1998.

Robinson, Haddon W. *Biblical Preaching.* Grand Rapids: Baker, 1980.

Stott, John R. W. *Between Two Worlds: The Art of Preaching in the Twentieth Century.* Grand Rapids: Eerdmans. 1982.

Chapter 13

Barth, Karl. *Church Dogmatics, Volume I, Part 2*. Edited by G. W. Bromiley and T. F. Torrance. Edinburgh: T. & T. Clark, 1956.

Broadus, J. A. *On the Preparation and Delivery of Sermons*. Rev. ed. by Jesse Burton Weatherspoon. London: Hodder and Stoughton, 1944.

Brooks, Phillips. *The Joy of Preaching*. Grand Rapids: Kregel, 1989.

Craddock, Fred B. *Preaching*. Louisville: John Knox, 1985.

Davis, Ellen F. *Getting Involved with Go: Rediscovering the Old Testament*. Cambridge, MA: Cowley, 2001.

Dunn, James D. G. *Colossians and Philemon*. New International Greek Text Commentary. Carlisle, UK: Paternoster, 1996.

Ford, David F. *Christian Wisdom: Desiring and Learning in Love*. Cambridge: Cambridge University Press, 2007.

Forsyth, P. T. *Positive Preaching and the Modern Mind*. Hodder and Stoughton, 1907.

Goldingay, John. "The Pastor's Opportunities." *The Expository Times* 98.7 (1997) 197–203.

Gross, Nancy Lammers. *The Collected Sermons of William Willimon*. Louisville: Westminster/John Knox, 2010.

———. "A Re-Examination of Recent Homiletical Theories in the Light of the Hermeneutical Theory of Paul Ricoeur." Ph.D. diss, Princeton Theological Seminary, 1992.

Hermelink, Jan. "The Theological Understanding of Preaching Hope." In *Preaching as the Language of Hope: Studia Homiletica 6*, edited by Cas J. A Vos, Lucy L. Hogan, Johan H. Cilliers, 29–57. Pretoria: Pretoria Book House, 2007.

Kruger-Gaudino, Rebecca J. *The Collected Sermons of Walter Brueggemann*. Louisville: Westminster/ John Knox, 2011.

———. "Foreword." In *The Collected Sermons of Walter Brueggemann*, xi–xv. Louisville: Westminster/John Knox, 2011.

Lewis, Peter. "'Free Church' Worship in Britain." In *Worship: Adoration and Action*, edited by D. A. Carson, 147–57. Carlisle, UK: Paternoster, 1993.

Lincoln, Andrew T. "Colossians." In *The New Interpreter's Bible* XI, 553–669. Abingdon: Nashville: Abingdon, 2000.

Lischer, Richard. *End of Words: The Language of Reconciliation in a Culture of Violence*. Grand Rapids: Eerdmans, 2005.

———. *The Senses of Preaching*. Atlanta: John Knox, 1988.

Long, Thomas G. *The Witness of Preaching*. 2nd ed. Louisville: Westminster/John Knox, 2005.

Lundblad Barbara K. *Marking Time: Preaching Biblical Stories in the Present Tense* Nashville: Abingdon, 2007.

Marsden, George M. *Jonathan Edwards: A Life*. New Haven: Yale University Press, 2003.

McKenzie, Alyce M. "Homiletical Proverbs." In *Best Advice*, edited by William J. Carl, 114–20. Louisville: Westminster/John Knox, 2009.

O'Brien, Peter. *Colossians and Philemon*. Word Biblical Commentary. Waco, TX: Word, 1982.

Old, Hughes Oliphant. *The Reading and Preaching of the Scriptures in the Worship of the Christian Church Volume 1–The Biblical Period*. Grand Rapids: Eerdmans, 1998.

Peterson, Eugene. *Eat this Book*. Grand Rapids: Eerdmans, 2006.

Vos, Cas. "The Sermon as a Work of Art." *The Expository Times* 116.11 (2005) 371–73.

Webster, *Holy Scripture: A Dogmatic Sketch*. Cambridge: Cambridge University Press 2003.

Willimon, William. "Preface." In *The Collected Sermons of William Willimon*, ix–xiv. Louisville: Westminster/John Knox, 2010.

———. *The Collected Sermons of William Willimon*. Louisville: Westminster/John Knox, 2010.

Woods, J. D. *Bearing Witness: The Homiletic Theory and Practice of Thomas G. Long*. D.Min thesis, University of Wales, 2008.

Chapter 14

Bonhoeffer, Dietrich. *Discipleship*. Translated by Barbara Green and Reinhardt Krauss, edited by Geoffrey B. Kelly and John Godsey. Minneapolis: Fortress, 2001.

Fant, Clyde. *Worldly Preaching*. New York: Thomas Nelson, 1975.

Forsyth, P. T. *The Justification of God*. London: Independent, 1917.

Hansen, David. *The Art of Pastoring: Ministry Without All the Answers*. Rev ed. Downers Grove, IL: InterVarsity, 2012.

Kierkegaard, Søren. *Attack upon Christendom*. Translated by Walter Lowrie. Boston: Beacon, 1963.

28379764R00148

Made in the USA
San Bernardino, CA
27 December 2015